HUMAN-COMPUTER INTERACTION SERIES

Human-Computer Interaction is a multidisciplinary field focused on human aspects of the development of computer technology. As computer-based technology becomes increasingly pervasive – not just in developed countries, but worldwide – the need to take a human-centered approach in the design and development of this technology becomes ever more important. For roughly 30 years now, researchers and practitioners in computational and behavioral sciences have worked to identify theory and practice that influences the direction of these technologies, and this diverse work makes up the field of human-computer interaction. Broadly speaking it includes the study of what technology might be able to do for people and how people might interact with the technology.

In this series we present work which advances the science and technology of developing systems which are both effective and satisfying for people in a wide variety of contexts. The human-computer interaction series will focus on theoretical perspectives (such as formal approaches drawn from a variety of behavioral sciences), practical approaches (such as the techniques for effectively integrating user needs in system development), and social issues (such as the determinants of utility, usability and acceptability).

Author guidelines: springer.com > Authors > Author Guidelines

For other titles published in this series, go to http://www.springer.com/

EDITORS:
THOMAS BINDER, JONAS LÖWGREN, LONE MALMBORG

(RE)SEARCHING THE DIGITAL BAUHAUS

Springer

Thomas Binder, ph.d.
Danish Center for
Design Research

Jonas Löwgren, ph.d.
Malmö University
Sweden

Lone Malmborg, ph.d.
IT University of Copenhagen
Denmark

Graphic design and illustrations: Tove Svensson and Jonas Löwgren
Typesetting: Jonas Löwgren

Human-Computer Interaction Series ISSN 1571-5035
ISBN 978-1-4471-5821-9 ISBN 978-1-84800-350-7 (eBook)
DOI 10.1007/978-1-84800-350-7

British Library Cataloguing in Publication Data
A catalogue record for this book is available from the British Library

Printed on acid-free paper

Springer Science+Business Media
springer.com

AUTHORS

thomas binder, jonas löwgren, lone malmborg

yngve sundblad

kari kuutti

liam bannon

kim halskov

margot brereton

jeanette blomberg

giorgio de michelis

bill gaver

eric zimmerman

johan redström

CHAPTERS

sara ilstedt hjelm

joan greenbaum

brenda laurel

erik stolterman

peter ullmark

frieder nake

ylva gislén, åsa harvard, maria hellström reimer

INTRODUCTION

THOMAS BINDER, JONAS LÖWGREN, LONE MALMBORG

INTRODUCTION

– (RE-)PROGRAMMING INTERACTION DESIGN

introduction – (re-)programming interaction design

Interaction design emerged in the early 1990s as a new design field, combining the fields of computer science and informatics with creative input from the traditional design disciplines and their increasing orientation towards the digital design materials (see Moggridge, 2007, for one view of the roots of the field and its practice).

Researchers and educators embraced the notion of design to re-position the shaping of technologies from the domains of instrumental reasoning and indisputable rationalization to the realms of ethical and aesthetical concern. With possible parallels to the old Weimar Bauhaus motto *Art and technology – A new unit*, they envisioned a new designer capable and willing to work responsibly with interaction as technology-in-use.

Today design, digital media and emergent technologies combine freely in discussions on innovation and change. Even issues of co-design and participation are widely adhered to in search of strategic renewal in industry under headings like user-driven innovation, design to improve quality of life, or design for long-term sustainability (Mau and Leonard 2004). In professional education we see B-(usiness) schools turning into D-(esign) schools, engineering programs re-inventing themselves into product design programs and even media studies and humanities embracing social constructivism in new inter-disciplinarity around centers of virtuality, performance and the experience economy. Long forgotten are the debates on taylorism, automation and de-skilling as are the high hopes for deliberating aesthetics, frictionless technological progress and artificial intelligence.

Something new has happened over the last few decades, but unlike the big moves of the twentieth century it is less a turn of the tide pioneered by a recognizable avant-garde but more of a proliferation of multiplicity itself emerging out of a sprawl of globalized cultures. Has the time passed for programmatic efforts? Or has programming just become such a mundane everyday practice that we fail to recognize it in the flow of events? Is what we experience the unfolding of tacit structural dynamics? Or have we just not adjusted to a post-modern condition where all that is solid melts into air?

This book is an open and collective exploration of these issues. We start from the standpoint that it must be possible to understand where we are, from both a genealogy of past efforts and from a prospective envisionment of possible routes to take.

MANIFESTO FOR A DIGITAL BAUHAUS

We dedicate this book to Pelle Ehn, taking the occasion that he turns 60 in August 2008 as a good opportunity to re-visit, reflect upon and perhaps even re-think the ideas of a third culture bringing art and science together in a committed digital Bauhaus for the twenty-first century.

Pelle and many fellow researchers of his generation turned computation into interaction design. In his 1998 article *Manifesto for a digital Bauhaus*, Pelle linked to the old Bauhaus school of design by suggesting that what he called »nerds« and »digerati« come together to combine the forces of design and technology to shape visions of pleasure and progress (Ehn 1998). The manifesto was less one of autocratic certainty than the programs of the Weimar Bauhaus. Even in the heyday of digital media, the position advocated by the generation of computer scientists and other researchers who have been dedicated to understanding human action in the context of information technologies was not one of futurism but one of participation. In his manifesto, Pelle wrote that:

> what is needed is not the modern praise of new technology but a critical and creative aesthetic-technical production orientation that unites modern information and communication technology with design, art, culture and society and at the same time places the development of the new mediating technologies in their real everyday context of changes in lifestyle, work and leisure. [...] What is needed is a humanistic and user-oriented education and research that will develop both a critical stance to information and communication technology and at the same time competence to design, compose and tell stories using the new mediating technologies.

Today, in many ways, we live in a third-culture universe, and in the last decade we have seen industry and educational institutions explore this new condition of productive blurriness. It is still exciting but also an overwhelming new realm of possibilities. In this book, we bring together a stellar collection of authors – scholars, designers and artists from interaction design, digital media and related fields – who have all put something at stake in establishing a critical and creative stance towards the new third-culture condition.

As stepping stones for an introduction of the steps the authors take on the path of (re)-searching the digital Bauhaus, we have chosen a selection of Pelle's titles to connect past and present efforts. Different genealogies could have been chosen, but in our view Pelle's work – involving many colleagues over the years – traces one of the important trajectories leading up to where interaction design is today.

SCANDINAVIAN DESIGN – ON SKILL AND PARTICIPATION

There is a certain Scandinavian current in interaction design that goes back to the pioneering collaboration between Norwegian computer scientist Kristen Nygaard (and his colleagues) and the Norwegian Metal Workers union on ideologically and socially acceptable use of computer technology in the workplace. This collaboration opened up and vitalized the issue of participation and co-determination in the shaping of future technology. A collection of this work is presented by Ehn, Bjerknes and Kyng (1987) in the book *Computers and democracy*. It has had a lasting impact in two directions. First, it made it clear that the issue of technology is one of politics and negotiation and, second, it showed in very practical terms that the people affected have something to say that can be productively fed back into the work of technologists.

Picking up on the second point, concepts such as »cardboard computers« (Ehn and Kyng 1991) became emblematic for prototyping that made participatory design, or co-design, an important part of what some called the Scandinavian approach to systems design. As a reaction against automation the call for design for democracy at work was supplemented by a call for designing for skill. Workers' participation in the design of, for example, computer technology for pre-print is not only a negotiation of goals but a mutual learning process in which typographers have as equally important contributions to make as the computer scientists.

Skill and participation continue to be important themes in a conceptualization of interaction design and are also troubling challenges to more conventional design fields. What is different today from when these themes were first taken up is the loss of stability both in terms of who is skilled and in terms of what participation is.

Yngve Sundblad (SE) and *Kari Kuutti* (FI) lay out the historical backdrop of the book in their opening chapters. Sundblad sketches how the Scandinavian tradition of IT design for workplaces has developed in terms of design and use contexts over more than 30 years, bringing social as well as technical and economical aspects to bear. Kuutti provides a closer look at the relationships between human-computer interaction (HCI) and design by analyzing the intellectual developments of the two fields. *Liam Bannon* (IE) adds to the foundation by pointing out that Scandinavian design has always walked »the path less trodden« to provide new ways of seeing human-technology relationships.

FROM SYSTEMS DESCRIPTIONS TO SCRIPTS FOR ACTION

One of the amazing features of the early work on participatory or cooperative design in Scandinavia was the willingness to combine a utopian horizon with a serious engagement with the here-and-now of the everyday, whether this was the everyday of shopfloor workers or the everyday of computer programmers. A good example is the work of Ehn and Sjögren (1991) on games and enactment, where carpenters and graphical workers play with present challenges and future possibilities in board games and enacted scenarios. These are not merely techniques to capture system specifications but a genuine design approach to embodied interaction which resonates well with other influential currents of empathic design and skillful interaction, including the ability to sketch as most recently advocated by Buxton (2007).

The issue has never been one of methods. In line with the work of Winograd and Flores (1986), Ehn and others in the Scandinavian tradition were active in suggesting new foundations for the design of computer artifacts. Drawing on Heidegger, the computer was conceived as a tool to be apprehended in use, and design as a process could be understood in Wittgensteinian terms as a »meeting of language games« (Ehn 1988).

The foundational work temporarily gave way to a turn towards practical design action, as illustrated most clearly in *Bringing design to software* (Winograd et al. 1996), but as the design portfolios of interaction designers are growing, discussions on foundations are attracting a renewed interest. An influential example is the work of Paul Dourish (2001) on embodied interaction.

The next set of chapters in this volume carries on the discussion of interaction design, its foundations and where it is headed. *Kim Halskov* (DK) draws on Pelle Ehn's widely cited concepts of tradition and transcendence to discuss recently opened design vistas of digital experience outside the workplace. *Margot Brereton* (AU) explores a view of design that emphasizes the multiplicity of relationships between the designer, the community for whom the design is intended and the development of the design over time. *Jeanette Blomberg* (US) examines how participatory design can inform the emerging field of service design. *Giorgio De Michelis* (IT) attempts to grasp the increasing complexity of contemporary design and multidisciplinary design collaboration by searching for an essential understanding of design in phenomenological philosophy.

PLAYING IN REALITY

Playfulness has not come easily to the design of computational technologies. Computation more than any other technology of the twentieth century incarnated Cartesian rationality. It held promises of substituting man with machine. This was serious business that demanded devotion and careful guarding of both conception and implementation. However, as the computer became personal, something changed in a significant way. Industrial designers and artists started to look into the possibilities of making computation playful, pleasurable and even desirable. Designers like Brenda Laurel and her colleagues started mapping out the possibilities in »designerly« ways (Laurel 1990) whereas graphic designers and visual artists like John Maeda started to play literally with design by numbers (Maeda 2000).

Even though play and playfulness have made their way into the interaction design only relatively recently, it can be noted that they have transformed into a particular flavour which goes somewhat beyond the traditional lightness and humoristic creativity of industrial design. From the early days of role playing and «mocking it up« in participatory design (Ehn and Sjögren 1991) and up until today there has been a thread of playful participation that cuts across the distinction between design and use.

As a strong protagonist of this thread *Bill Gaver* (UK) introduces Homo Ludens – playing man – and illustrates through a range of examples the new design challenges and use contexts that follow from such a notion of »the user«. The idea of play is followed up by *Eric Zimmerman* (US) who looks at gaming not as a market or an application domain but as a more profound issue of gaming literacy: How playing, understanding and designing games embody important ways of looking at and being in the world.

PARTICIPATION IN INTERACTION DESIGN – ACTORS AND ARTIFACTS IN INTERACTION

The issue of participation in design has been contested many times since its conception at the 1971 conference on design participation, organized by the Design Research Society (Cross 1971). The potentials of putting design at the service of political aspirations, whether at the workplace, community or society level, have been alternating with the urge for a well-defined professionalism of design offering recognized translations in the difficult borderland between people and things. Interaction technologies and digital media seemed, for a long time, to be an ideal material of bodiless mediation. But computation became ubiquitous (Weiser 1991) and it proliferated into a plethora of things that began to participate in the everyday. Bruno Latour talks about a parliament of things (Latour and Weibel 2005) and with examples ranging from hotel keys to mobile phones he and others in the sociology of science and technology have shown that things have a voice that can be heard.

Artifacts are not only outcomes of negotiation. They are arguments in their own right, posing claims and creating realities that must be taken seriously in design as well as in use (Ehn 2006). The implications of this point are still difficult to grasp, as we have been long used to separating people from things, process from product, communication from materiality; one as the realm of participation, the other as the realm of uncontestable reality. However, the pervasiveness of the artificial is creating a role for interaction design taken up for example in critical design (Dunne 1999) also to critically explore what kind of tales are told and can be told with digital design materials.

Johan Redström (SE) notes how the disruptions inherent in interaction with digital products are often glossed over, and asks the question of what an aesthetic for interaction design would be like that revealed disruptions and made them essential design elements. *Sara Ilstedt Hjelm* (SE) provides a close look at the most humble of artifacts – electrical appliances and infrastructures – and points to the Bauhaus relations in terms of an aesthetics of function. *Joan Greenbaum* (US) addresses hybrid environments where physical and digital materials blend, and how they are appropriated in everyday life (where »use« is a much too narrow construct). *Brenda Laurel* (US) explores the new forms of narrative and experience that such hybrid environments afford, in a way sketching a poetics of ubiquitous computing.

THE ART AND SCIENCE OF DESIGNING COMPUTER ARTIFACTS

Paradoxically, design is still a contested term, despite more than three decades of debate. Computation and the status of the artificial played a key role when Simon in the 1960s proposed a science of design to be the new backbone in the education of professionals from lawyers to city planners (Simon 1981). The provocative, but also highly influential, definition of design as »a change in man-made things that alter existing situations into preferred ones« indicates that the knowledge produced by designers cannot be separated from an intentional engagement with a particular world of opportunities. For Simon, this engagement should be one of operational analysis and logical deduction. However, this turned out to be a very poor match with the actual practice of designing. Schön showed that design is rather a reflective conversation with the materials of the design situation; and Schön's work has continued to be an inspiration for those who want to understand design as knowledge production (Schön 1983).

Designing computer artifacts is both art and science (Ehn 1991), and interaction design can be informed by criticism in the tradition of cultural studies (Johnson 1997) as well as by theories of knowledge (Krippendorff 2006). The challenge to designers and design researchers is to find a way to connect the knowledge production for design with the knowledge production inherent in the practice of designing.

Erik Stolterman (SE) discusses how the two seemingly incommensurable positions of closeness and distance need to be synthesized in design thinking and design practice, and sketches a critical stance in which closeness and distance form a synergistic whole. *Peter Ullmark* (SE) takes a hard look at design research in terms of the epistemological problems of dealing with possible realities. *Frieder Nake* (DE) reflects on the computer in the most general terms as a malleable semiotic machine, and on our Homo Faber ways of approaching it – be it as researchers, designers or artists, we do what we do because we couldn't otherwise stand the world.

NEITHER NERD NOR BAUHÄUSLER – EDUCATING THE INTERACTION DESIGNER

There are profound differences between the traditional education in the sciences and the many new educational programs in interaction design. The traditional science or engineering student has to piece together a knowledge base whereas design students, in the words of Donald Schön, are educated in a reflective practicum – a setting for learning where the student from the first day is confronted with the full complexity of a design task (Schön 1987).

The studio model of design education has been picked up by many interaction design programs, but the venerable Bauhaus model of studio education where apprentices work under the guidance of knowledgeable masters is not without its problems in a landscape of global communication and a globalized fluctuation of knowledge.

What seems promising today is to create educational settings where the exchange and flow of ideas and people are open and ongoing, oriented towards professional environments as well as research (Ehn 2002). These studios of the future are probably not isolated places of study but more likely open landscapes in which design takes place spatially as well as conceptually.

The book closes by taking the broad spectrum of ideas back to the School of Arts and Communication (K3), Malmö, Sweden. This is done in the final chapter by *Ylva Gislén*, *Åsa Harvard* and *Maria Hellström* who provide a psychogeography, tracing the parallel intellectual and spatial development of the environment in the form of a collage of associations and recollections forming a spatial narrative of the place. Hence, it also takes us back where we started in a most literal way: The school that Pelle Ehn and his colleagues have founded and maintained for the last ten years in an attempt to build a digital Bauhaus for the twenty-first century.

REFERENCES

Buxton, B. (2007). *Sketching user experiences: Getting the design right and the right design.* San Francisco: Morgan Kaufmann.

Cross, N. (1971). Design participation. Proceedings of the design research society's conference 1971. London: Academy editions.

Dourish, P. (2001). *Where the action is: The foundations of embodied interaction.* Cambridge, MA: MIT Press.

Dunne, A. (1999). *Hertzian tales: Electronic products, aesthetic experience and critical design.* London: Royal College of Art.

Ehn, P. (1988). *Work-oriented design of computer artifacts.* Swedish Center for Working Life and Lawrence Erlbaum.

Ehn, P. (1991). The art and science of designing computer artifacts, in Scandinavian. In Dunlop C., Kling, R. (Eds.) *Computerization and controversy.* Academic Press.

Ehn, P. (2002) Neither Nerd nor Bauhäusler: Educating the interaction designer. Proc. Symp. Designing Interactive Systems (DIS '02). London: ACM Press.

Ehn, P., Sjögren, D., Möllerud, B. (1992). Playing in reality. *European Journal of Information Systems*, 5.

Ehn, P. (1998). Manifesto for a Digital Bauhaus. *Digital Creativity*, 9(4):207–216.

Ehn, P. (2006). Participation in interaction design: Actors and artifacts in interaction. In Bagnara, S., Smith, G.C. (Eds.) *Theories and practice in interaction design*. London: Routledge.

Ehn, P., Bjerknes, G., Kyng, M. (eds.,1987). *Computers and democracy*. Aldershot: Avebury.

Ehn, P., Kyng, M. (1991). Cardboard computers. In Greenbaum, J., Kyng, M. (Eds.) *Design at work*. Hillsdale, NJ: Lawrence Erlbaum.

Ehn, P., Sjögren, D. (1991). From system descriptions to scripts for action. In Greenbaum, J., Kyng, M. (eds.) *Design at work*. Hillsdale, NJ: Lawrence Erlbaum.

Johnson, S. (1997). *Interface culture: How new technology transforms the way we create and communicate*. New York: Basic Books.

Krippendorff, K. (2006). *The semantic turn: A new foundation for design*. Boca Raton, FL: CRC Press.

Latour, B., Weibel, P (eds., 2005). *Making things public: Atmospheres of democracy.* Cambridge, MA: MIT Press and Karlsruhe: ZKM.

Laurel, B. (ed., 1990). *The art of human-computer interface design*. New York: Addison-Wesley.

Maeda, J. (2000). *Maeda @ media*. London: Thames & Hudson.

Mau, B., Leonard, J. (2004). *Massive change*. London: Phaidon.

Moggridge, B. (2007). *Designing interactions*. Cambridge, MA: MIT Press.

Schön, D. (1983). *The reflective practitioner: How professionals think in action.* New York: Basic Books.

Schön, D. (1987). *Educating the reflective practitioner: Toward a new design for teaching and learning in the professions*. New York: Basic Books.

Simon, H. (1981). *The sciences of the artificial*. Cambridge, MA: MIT Press.

11

Weiser, M. (1991). The computer for the 21st century. *Scientific American*, 265(3), 94–104.

Winograd, T., Flores, F. (1986). *Understanding computers and cognition: A new foundation for design.* Reading, MA: Addison-Wesley.

Winograd, T. et al. (eds., 1996). *Bringing design to software.* Reading, MA: Addison-Wesley.

12

YNGVE SUNDBLAD

FROM UTOPIA 1981 TO UTOPIA 2008

YNGVE SUNDBLAD
FROM UTOPIA 1981 TO UTOPIA 2008

Studies and design of Information Technology (IT) support for workplaces, especially workshop floors and offices, have a strong tradition in Scandinavia, involving workplace users and trade unions as well as other stakeholders.

The projects emphasize the active co-operation between researchers, developers and the workers of the organizations in order to help improve their work situation. While researchers got their results, the people that they worked with were equally entitled to get knowledge, experience and improvements out of the projects.

Since then the obvious idea to involve the users as early as possible in systems and interface design, using low and high tech prototypes, has become a standard to which most developers pay at least lip service. That it is not necessarily followed in practice is usually because of time constraints and lack of insight rather than reluctance, but there are also inherent difficulties.

This tradition is here put into perspective, starting with the roots in Norway in the early 1970s, highlighting the seminal UTOPIA project, led by Pelle Ehn 1981–86, and its off-springs all the way up to the UsersAward and KLIV workplace projects of today. Changes in design and use context, from social and technical aspects, over three decades, are anlysed.

In the early 1970s computer technology and use in Scandinavia was dominated by mainframes in »computer centres«, guarded by technicians in white coats, with text input and output, and rudimentary communication between the installations. Few were aware of the future, broad and powerful use of computers being formed in laboratories, especially in California.

Today computer use and interaction possibilities are changing quickly, while use contexts and application types are radically broadening. Technology no longer consists of static tools belonging only to the workplace, but permeates work on the move, in homes and everyday lives.

Pervasive technologies, augmented reality, small interfaces, tangible interfaces, etc. are dramatically changing the nature of HCI (human-computer interac-

Kristen Nygaard, 1926–2002

tion) and its possibilities for workplace settings. We witness the creation of ad-hoc configurations of large and small user interfaces. The new interfaces are moveable and used in changing locations and contexts; different tasks are done through a combination of specialized technologies. A wider repertoire of physical devices is available than just the keyboard, the screen and the mouse.

The Scandinavian tradition of user involvement in development is facing up to the challenges of new contexts. In this chapter, I will concentrate on work contexts.

HISTORICAL ROOTS

We all owe to Kristen Nygaard immense gratitude, as the father of worker involvement in workplace computer development and use. His project with the Norwegian Iron and Metal Workers Union (NJMF) in 1972 took the first move from traditional research and development of computer systems into working with people, directly changing and making more active the role of the local unions. This project has had a great influence on all subsequent research and development of user participation in systems development, leading into cooperative (or participatory) design. In general, the tradition has developed strategies and techniques for workers to influence the design and use of computer applications at the workplace. Not only did Kristen give my generation of academic computer scientists in Scandinavia their mother tongue, the programming language Simula which is the root of all main object oriented concepts, he also gave us the workplace user involvement tradition.

He soon inspired a group of Danish, Norwegian and Swedish young computer and information science researchers and students. One of these was Pelle Ehn, who in 1975 initiated the DEMOS project (Demokratisk planering och styrning i arbetslivet, i.e., Democratic planning and control in working life), involving workers and their local unions at a repair workshop, a daily newspaper, a metal industry and a department store, studying conditions for participation in planning and use of new technology. A similar project was DUE (Demokratisk udvikling og EDB, i.e., Democratic development and computer processing) with researchers from Aarhus, e.g. Morten Kyng. The projects emphasized the active co-operation between researchers and workers of the organization to help improve their work situation. One strong goal was to »give the end users a voice« in design and development of computer support in work places, thus enhancing the quality of the resulting system. These projects were part of the start of the »Scandinavian tradition« in system design.

UTOPIA 1981–1986

Based on the DEMOS and DUE experience, and shortcomings when having to use and adapt the technical systems at hand, Pelle Ehn and Morten Kyng decided to try a more offensive (»utopist«) strategy for worker involvement, direct participation in all phases of design and development of the computerised tools and systems on the workplace. They found a good partner through their contacts with newspaper graphic workers, NGU, the Nordic Graphic Union, which became so interested that it financed half-time participation of six graphic workers, from Stockholm and Aarhus, and formed a reference group, led by the Norwegian NGU board member Gunnar Kokaas. The natural choice of project leader was Pelle Ehn, then researcher at ALC, the Centre for Working Life in Stockholm, from which an interdisciplinary group with social and information

UTOPIA

Gunnar Kokaas
graphic worker, chairman of the reference group

Pelle Ehn
project leader, Swedish Center for Working Life

Angelika Dilschmann
researcher, Swedish Center for Working Life

Martin Eriksson
graphic worker, Svenska Dagbladet, Sweden

Malte Eriksson
graphic worker, the Swedish Graphic Workers' Trade Union

Ewa Gunnarsson
researcher, Swedish Center for Working Life

Gunnar Rasmussen
graphic worker, Jyllands-Posten, Denmark

Kerstin Severinson-Eklundh researcher, Royal Institute of Technology, Sweden

Bernt Eriksson
graphic worker, Svenska Dagbladet, Sweden

Björn Burell
graphic worker, the Swedish Graphic Workers' Trade Union

Yngve Sundblad
researcher, Royal Institute of Technology, Sweden

Staffan Romberger
researcher, Royal Institute of Technology, Sweden

Dan Sjögren
researcher, Swedish Center for Working Life

John Kammersgaard
researcher, Aarhus University, Denmark

Susanne Bødker
researcher, Aarhus University, Denmark

Morten Kyng
researcher, Aarhus University, Denmark

Kerstin Frenckner
researcher, Royal Institute of Technology, Sweden

Åke Sandberg
researcher, Swedish Center for Working

Image from an edition of Thomas More's Utopia from 1516.

sciences background became involved.

I only have second-hand information about the developments that led to UTOPIA and hope that this account is reasonably correct. My, and NADA's (the KTH Computer Science department), involvement came when Pelle, whom I knew from other contexts, asked me to contribute with »technical imagination«. As head of department I could get us, including about five other young researchers, involved in this, for NADA, somewhat unorthodox project.

In the picture on the previous page, taken from the UTOPIA dissemination booklet *Graffiti*, we see most of the participants, including the graphic workers, and the researchers from DAIMI at Aarhus University.

UTOPIA is a somewhat far-fetched acronym: Utbildning, Teknik Och Produkt i Arbetskvalitetsperspektiv (working in Scandinavian languages), i.e. Training, Technology and Product in Work Quality Perspective.

UTOPIA became a seminal project on methods for involving end users in all phases of design and development of IT support for their activities. Graphic workers were involved in building new technology and the project invented methods such as low-tech prototyping, workflow wallpapers, and work organisation toolboxes (Bødker et al. 1987).

From a research perspective the UTOPIA project may be seen as an ambitious continuation and follow-up of the DEMOS, DUE and other projects in Norway, Sweden, and Denmark in the 1970s, in which researchers followed and supported the attempts of local trade unions to influence the use of technology at work.

OBJECTIVE. The overall objective of UTOPIA was to contribute to the development of powerful skill enhancing tools for graphic workers, in the light of the emerging graphic workstation technology. Quality of work and product was very important. Both technical and social prerequisites, as well as obstacles and limitations, were examined. The labour processes of page make-up and image processing in integrated computer based newspaper production were in focus.

ACTIVITIES. Main activities during UTOPIA (1981–86) were:

- Mutual learning between the active participants: graphic workers, computer scientists and social researchers.
- Common study tours to graphic industry exhibitions and to important laboratories in the US, including Xerox PARC and Stanford University, where Terry Winograd (see below) was an important contact and supporter.
- Requirement specification for a system for newspaper text and image prepress production, under development by a Swedish manufacturer.
- Studying a pilot installation of the image system in real production at the Swedish newspaper Aftonbladet.

Mock-up situation.

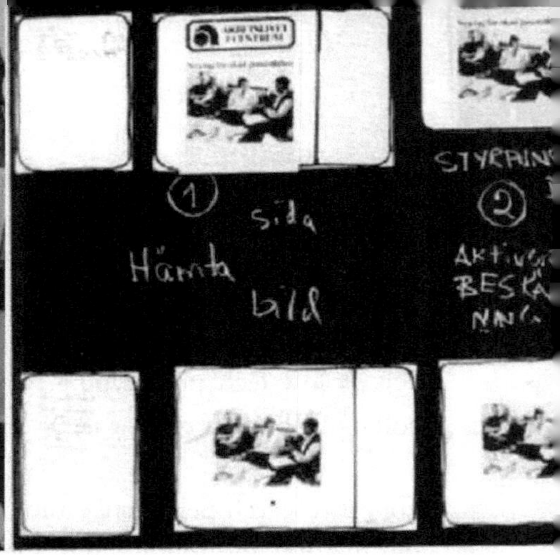

Blackboard image sequence for cropping.

- Dissemination, especially to the graphic workers and to the scientific community (see below). 20 UTOPIA reports in Swedish or Danish on different aspects of technology, work organisation and work environment were produced. All members of NGU (approx. 50 000) got the final, 48-page, edition no.7 of the project newsletter, *Graffiti.*

TOOLS AND METHODS. In order to accomplish this we established a »technology laboratory« with development tools to simulate different kinds of page make-up, image processing and the surrounding organisation. Thus we made it possible for the graphic workers in the project to develop requirements and wishes on a concrete level by actually carrying out the page make-up and image processing on simulation equipment.

The tools and methods in the laboratory were innovations:

- Colour slide mock-ups with picture sequences that were also pasted on the walls, for simulation of work processes.
- Low tech mock-ups of equipment (wooden mouse, cardboard laser writer, etc.), material and menus (paper).
- A graphic workstation for illustrating prototypes of computer based tools.
- A tool kit (box with waxed cards) for modelling and experimenting with work organisation.

Graphic workstation with A4 screen (Perq,1983, first commercially available in Scandinavia).

RESULTS. The main results from UTOPIA were not so much the pilot computer tool built and used at Aftonbladet as the experience and methods:

- For the *Nordic Graphic Union members*, who from Utopia knew, at least as well as their employers, the pros and cons of the emerging technology and what to require from it, for a functionally and socially acceptable introduction in their work.
- For the *researchers* the challenging insight that the human interface is very important for how useful a computer based tool will be, inspiration for establishing IPLAB at NADA and similar efforts in Aarhus.
- For the *researchers and the design community in general* a methodology, Cooperative Design (also called Participatory Design), for involvement of end users together with interface designers and program developers on equal footing in computer application projects.

UTOPIA EXPERIENCE

In retrospect we can see the following four main features of qualities in and experience from UTOPIA.

WHERE WORKERS CRAFT TECHNOLOGY. This characterisation comes from MIT Technical Review (Howard 1985) with the observation that UTOPIA showed that it is possible to design information technology based on use requirements such as work organisation, work environment, forms of co-oper-

Work organisation and flow toolkit.

ation and working skills. This idea was almost blasphemy in some management circles then, which is hardly the case today.

SETTING THE STAGE FOR DESIGN IN ACTION. UTOPIA was precursor to current practices in interaction design in staging active design exercises, such as the organisational tool-box and use of mock-ups and prototypes, as a way to involve end users in design. The means to create meaningful design objects for all participants (different groups of users and designers) are crucial.

PLAYING THE LANGUAGE GAME OF DESIGN AND USE. UTOPIA gave a lasting contribution to the theoretical understanding of design with users, through contributions such as Pelle Ehn's and Susanne Bødker's dissertations (Ehn 1988, Bødker 1991, Bødker 1999) and several other papers. Today a »Communities of Practice« perspective is mainstream for understanding design and learning.

BRINGING DESIGN TO SOFTWARE. By this title, borrowed from Terry Winograd (Winograd et al. 1996), I want to point out that UTOPIA can be seen as a »paradigmatic example« of how design thinking and practise can be brought into software development.

48 pages distributed to all Nordic graphic workers.

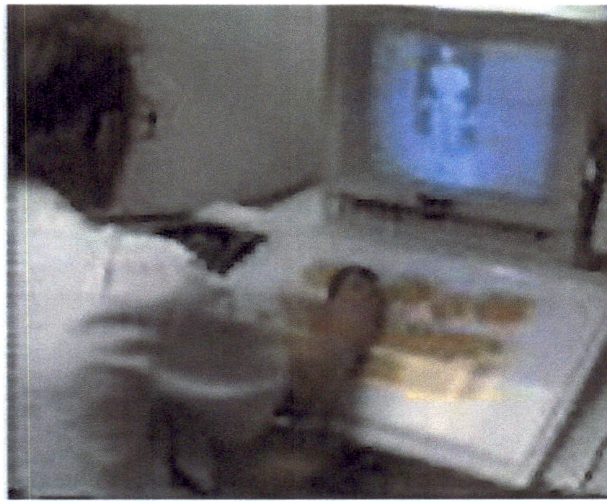

Pilot installation at Aftonbladet.

INTERNATIONAL RECOGNITION

The experience formed a main theme of the 1985 *Computers and Democracy* conference in Aarhus, with Pelle Ehn as a main organiser, e.g. with the paper (Bødker et al.1987).

At the 1988 CSCW (Computer Supported Cooperative Work) conference in Portland, Oregon, Pelle Ehn and others presented the UTOPIA results in an invited paper (Bødker et al. 1988). There were several more contributions by UTOPIA members and others from Scandinavia on cooperative design and collaboration.

Many scientists from the US and Europe have been involved in and greatly contributed to the further development and spread of these ideas. From a long list I mention one inspirational supporter, Terry Winograd, with whom we have had contacts and discussed UTOPIA and design since the early 1980s. In 1982 and 1983 we made study tours to the US, and were invited by Terry to give presentations of UTOPIA at Stanford University. He has continued to be an important contributor to the user oriented software design field, with the landmark text book *Bringing Design to Software* (Winograd et al 1996) as inspiration to many researchers and students around the world. One chapter, by Sarah Kuhn

Terry Winograd.

with an introduction by Terry, is devoted to »Design for People At Work«, with Participatory Design and UTOPIA as example.

The term »Scandinavian model of IT design« is frequently used today, in many contexts, all over the world, to characterise the methodology and practice emanating from these experiences.

IMPACT ON IT DESIGN IN PRACTICE

The »secondary result« of Utopia, the methodology, with ingredients such as low-tech prototyping, early design sessions with users etc., has had great impact on IT design in general. This is the case not only where the methods are a main ingredient as in Cooperative Design/Participatory Design, but also as part of now common practices in HCI and in CSCW in general and in later methodologies such as Consensus Participation, Contextual Design and Cooperative Inquiry.

Since then the methodology has developed, see (Bødker et al. 2000), and been complemented with a battery of other methods into strategies for involving users for better suited IT support. Some examples, many from Scandinavia, are use scenarios (Kyng 1995), cooperative inquiry (Druin 1999), technical probes (Hutchinson et al. 2003), video prototyping (Mackay et al. 2000), vision games (Hornecker and Buur 2006), close cooperation with joint user experience between ethnographer, industrial designer and programmer (Westerlund et al. 2003) and overall process design, e.g. Cooperative Experimental Systems Development (Grønbæk et al. 1997) and MUST (Kensing et al. 1998), which provides an industrial method for the early phases of design.

The methodology has, in my practice, been used successfully for design, study and evaluation of IT support for, e.g., graphic workers, office workers, programmers, teachers, elementary school children, family members for intergenerational communication, call centre workers, and artists (see Bødker and Sundblad 2008). Other researchers and developers in the cooperative design tradition can most certainly extend this list of user categories considerably.

FROM EXCLUSIVE TO BROAD MASSIVE USE – CHALLENGES

In our 25 years of practical experience with many co-operative design and development projects there has been tremendous growth in the spread of IT use, based on technical and organisational developments. At the present time, computer use and interaction possibilities are expanding quickly. At the same time, use contexts and application types are broadening. Technology no longer consists of static tools belonging only to the workplace. It presents users with the possibilities of working 24 hours a day, 7 days a week, while on the move, at home and in public space.

At the same time as work technologies permeate the boundaries between the workplace and human life in general, other technologies expand from home life and leisure into the workplace. Text messaging is a classic example and blogs a more recent one. We witness the creation of ad-hoc configurations of large and small user interfaces. The new interfaces are moveable and used in changing locations and contexts; different tasks are done through a combination of specialised technologies. A wider repertoire of physical devices is available than the keyboard, screen and mouse. These recent trends of pervasive computing place the user in dynamic configurations of technology, where human activity is not necessarily performed through a single computer application but supported by a range of technologies and physical artefacts that are often dynamically changing through mobility. This kind of multiplicity is well-known from everyday artefacts in general: When a pilot is controlling an aircraft, the captain a cargo ship, or the mason is building a house, there is not necessarily one single unified interface between the user and whatever is the object of the activity, be this the safe journey of the aircraft, the optimal route of the cargo ship, or the brick walls of the house.

In this way, pervasive technologies, augmented reality, small interfaces, tangible interfaces, etc. are dramatically changing the nature of IT applications as regards their conceptual basis, their design possibilities and their everyday analysis and design methods, issues often connected to usability.

As IT applications expand from the workplace into everyday life in general, cooperative design in the Scandinavian tradition is now also used for home and leisure IT applications and for everyday communication situations. This, together with the new, more decentralised and portable forms of, and interaction with, the technology leads to new challenges. These challenges include methods for observational and in-situ studies in people's homes and similarly intimate situations; concern for learning and skill-development outside well-defined work situations; and ways of moving the fundamental focus of human-computer interaction away from efficiency and effectiveness towards experience. They are not isolated to the cooperative design tradition but stands as challenges to the entire field of interaction design (the current »Digital Bauhaus«).

This is further discussed in Bødker and Sundblad (2008). Here we now concentrate on current workplace projects in the Scandinavian tradition, »UTOPIA 2008«.

UTOPIA 2008 - TRADITIONAL WORKPLACES, WITH UNTRADITIONAL USER/WORKER INVOLVEMENT

One strong goal of the UTOPIA project was to »give the end-users a voice« in design and development of computer support in workplaces, thus enhancing the quality of the resulting system. The »secondary result«, the methodology, with ingredients such as low-tech prototyping and early design sessions with users, has had great impact on IT design in general. A third outcome, which was highlighted as possibly the main result for the trade union participants, was that the union members' active engagement in the research gave them an understanding and a know-how that turned out to be an important resource in the ensuing negotiations about work organisation and systems deployment.

Even with the fast IT developments, basic human needs are the same, and »traditional workplaces« still dominate. Still the possibilities of the technology, for human communication, control over own work and explorative development of skill, for work floor users, or as a lever for a more democratic working life, is often not used to its full extent in those workplaces.

Let us look at three current activities that show the possibilities of being inspired by the three kinds of results from UTOPIA in current workplaces, for communication and control over the work and using and developing common skill, in production, education and health care work.

UTOPIA 2008: USERSAWARD – USER QUALITY ASSURANCE OF IT IN WORKPLACES

It is specifically in relation to the result of workers and their organisations gaining understanding and know-how, that the UsersAward activities can be seen as inspired by the UTOPIA project.

In spite of more than a decade with the »Scandinavian model« it was clear in the late 1990s that the practice of IT use in the workplace was still poor and, in most cases, did not use all the possibilities of IT support for creating »the good work«, satisfying the workers' abilities and skill for communication, production and taking initiatives.

Based on this insight LO (Swedish Trade Union Confederation), in cooperation with the TCO (Swedish Confederation for Professional Employees) launched the UsersAward network of user oriented activities in 1998. The goal was to *develop and maintain a strategy for better workplace software through user influence*, where union and consumer organisations cooperate with researchers, user companies and software providers in *a powerful combination of user movement and research*. This strategy for user influence has, over the last decade, been manifested in a combination of user surveys, user conferences, pilot projects, a yearly IT Prize contest and, last but not least, a users' certification process for workplace software packages.

The ITQ project, which constituted a research part of the network, brought together a multidisciplinary team of researchers from four universities in Sweden: KTH in Stockholm (coordinator), Uppsala University, University College of Gävle, and Luleå Technical University.

The activities thus were inspired by the »Scandinavian model« of involving users in IT development for use in workplaces. Other sources of inspiration were the TCO certification of personal computers, (Boivie 2007, Sundblad et al. 2002), an extremely successful union driven activity – literally hundreds of millions of users around the world use TCO certified personal computers – and also the consumer movements and the »User certification index«, developed by Claes Fornell, Director of the National Quality Research Center (NQRC) at the University of Michigan, and widely used as consumer product quality indicator (Fornell 2007).

A challenge for UsersAward was to develop a quality assurance framework for workplace software that would support an active and ongoing trade union engagement with the software tools of their members.

USER SURVEYS – STILL POOR IT TOOLS AND USE IN THE WORKPLACE. As mentioned above there was insight that IT support was, in general, far from as good in workplaces as it could be. One of the first activities of UsersAward was a broad survey – »IT map« – about worker satisfaction with the IT tools for production planning at their workplace. The opinions of 1124 industrial workplace users, most in direct production, were appalling and showed the need of UsersAward:

Simulation of daily flow of material and work in Arvika Foundry.

- About 50% regarded the IT system to be useful in their own work situation.
- Less than half of all users found that the IT systems gave them a satisfactory overview of the workflow. Only 14% felt that they could influence how the systems were deployed.
- Three out of ten agreed that the systems had helped develop the work organisation.
- Only one out of ten stated that they had obtained appropriate training.
- Out of the personnel working in direct production, just over 10% found that the IT systems supported learning and experimentation.

PILOT PROJECTS - SIMULATION PILOT AT FOUNDRY. In order to find good examples of IT support and develop and underpin quality criteria, several pilot projects were performed in 2000 by UsersAward/ITQ 1999–2002

(Walldius et al. 2008, Sundblad et al. 2002). One example, from the shop floor at a foundry, illustrates that modern computer technology makes it feasible for workers to be involved in simulations for better understanding of how to plan the daily production (see picture on previous page). Traditionally in the production industry simulation is used for dimensioning machine and workflow capacities. This example, on continuous use in daily production, is a clear innovation, giving the workers the possibility to use their experience and skill in planning and pursuing the production more efficiently.

IT PRIZE – BASED ON USER NOMINATIONS. The yearly IT Prize, based on nominations by workplace users of good IT support at their workplace, has been handed out in an »Oscar-like« ceremony since 2000. Five finalists present, one gets the first prize, one gets a runner-up prize, all get diplomas. The intention is to present these good examples broadly, as inspiration for IT support development at other work places. The relevance of the more than 30 criteria used, in questionnaires and interviews of users and management, made by the project members and the jury for selecting the five finalists, has been evaluated and updated where necessary from the experience, but have been quite stable, as seen in the next section.

The nominated IT systems have come from various sectors, such as: production industry, health care, education, banks, agencies within government and municipalities.

WORKPLACE USERS INVOLVEMENT IN CERTIFICATION. Through iterative development of quality criteria – in several pilot studies, in yearly evaluations of a total of more than 100 nominees to the IT Prize, and in several user certifications – six groups of criteria have emerged. The groups have been almost identical over nearly ten years, but the criteria have developed in number and formulation based on the experience. In UsersAward 2006 there are 38 criteria:

1. Overall benefits (5: quality, efficiency, competence development, for customers, total).

IT Prize winners from an old-people care agency in a rural municipality, using specially developed software for Communicators in their daily practice and communication, saving time and effort and increasing security.

2. Deployment method (4: idea, participation in deployment and work routines, education).
3. Technical features (13: overview, easy to learn and navigate, integrity for customer and employed, help function, undo, adapted to other IT, adapting interface, functionality, robustness, up-time, response time).
4. Work task support (8: overview, facilitating, engaging, flexibility, error prevention, less stress, follow-up, learning).
5. Communication support (5: independence, cooperation with colleagues, customers and providers).
6. Follow-up (3: follow-up of satisfaction, other assessment, IT support).

This set of criteria provides the basis for a workplace software certification procedure, in which interviews and questionnaires at three reference workplaces, chosen by the software supplier in his self-declaration, constitute the basis for the evaluation. For the software to pass the certification at least two of the workplaces must have users that are satisfied enough to having given at least 4 (on the scale 1–6, best) to at least 67% of the criteria. These conditions might seem random, but are well motivated through the use and refinement of the criteria used over many years in hundreds of interviews and thousands of questionnaires. How well the figures capture different qualities has been subject for several investigations by the researchers in UsersAward.

The diagrams on the opposite page show some of the evaluation protocols from a successful certification of an ERP (Enterprise Resource Planning) software, used in medium-sized production companies for planning and follow-up.

UTOPIA 2008: COPLAND – IT IN ISOLATED WORK SITUATIONS

As current examples of UTOPIA:s »second outcome«, cooperative design methods used at work places I take a recent project using IT for breaking isolation in work situations in the rural archipelago of Stockholm, consisting of 20 000 islands in a 200 x 80 km area.

SCHOOL TEACHERS, ISOLATED WITH A CLASS ON AN ISLAND. In the project COPLand, on Communities of Practice, we identified an interesting community: a »school«, consisting of five classes, each with 5–12 children, situated on five different islands several tens of kilometres apart in Stockholm archipelago. The teachers, one or two on each island, met once a week, often with the principal, who had the office on a large island, closely connected to the mainland.

In a cooperative design process with the teachers, breaking the isolation by allowing daily communication with the other teachers was defined as the most urgent need. A low-tech prototype and scenario of a communication device, with digital exchange of drawn notes, was agreed on as well as a good place for having it alerted, together with other notices, on the whiteboard. It was some-

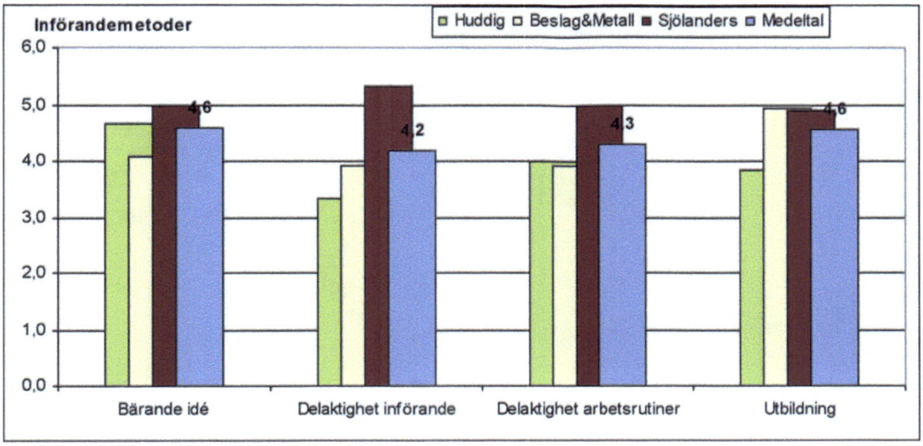

Above: User evaluation of deployment method criteria for an ERP software at three workplaces (green, yellow, red), mean value in blue.

Below: Summary protocol for the ERP software certification, for the six types of criteria (Benefits, Deployment, Technology, Work task support, Communication, Follow-up). Green is approved, red is not approved, blue is not relevant. Well over 67% approved criteria!

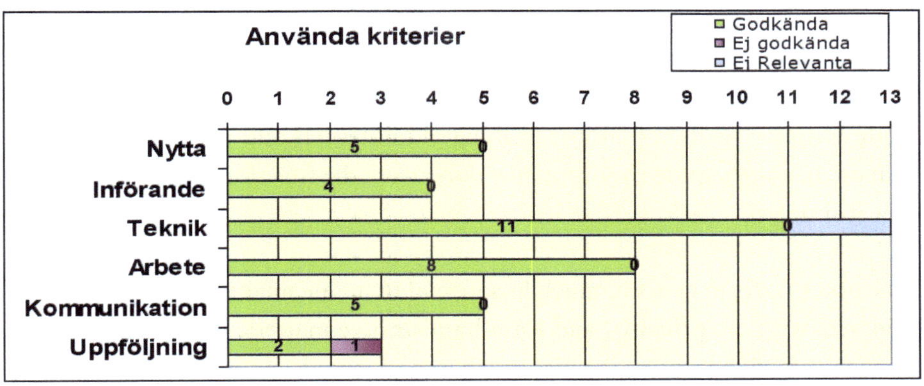

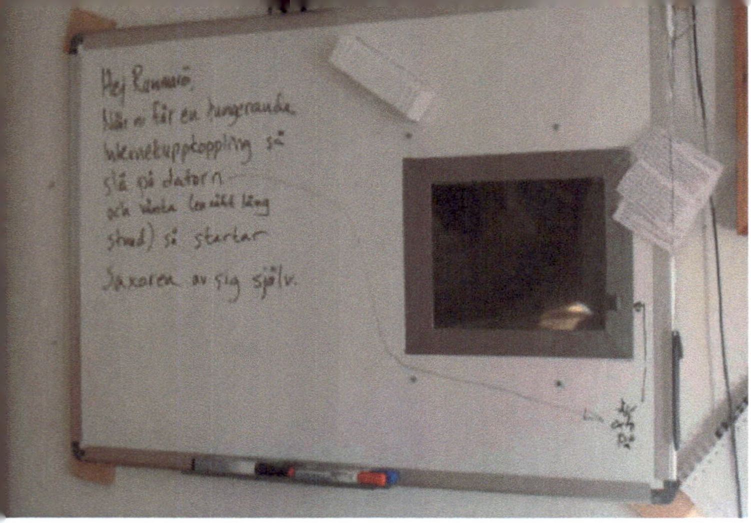

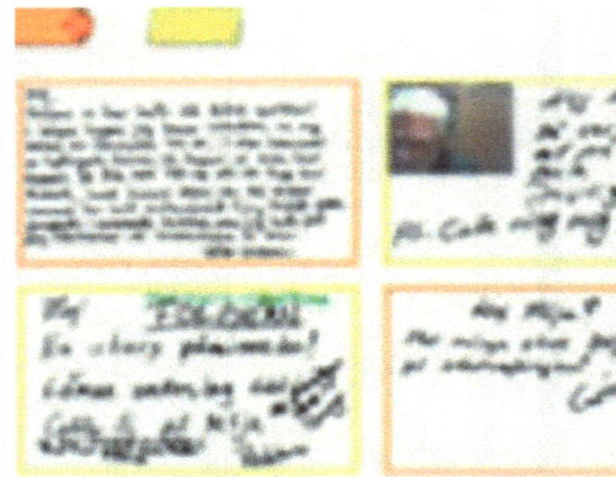

what inspired by a presentation of a similar device in another of our projects, interLiving (Lindquist et al. 2007).

The device, named Saxaren, was implemented on a Tablet PC, iteratively, with four new versions from the first in November 2004, to the last in May 2005. The first version had just the main drawing and inspection tools, the last also a connected web camera.

A main design result was the importance of simplicity. Buttons and tools for arranging the notes, starting and stopping the drawing, etc, were done away with when we realised that just pushing old notes left and up, and putting the pen on an empty space to start a new note, were the functions needed and were much simpler.

The notes were, in general, much less formal than one might expect, even in the contacts with the principal and for administrative matters, like meeting times, agendas etc. Playfulness was also used, and accepted, for socialising messages like Merry Christmas, Happy birthday and for drawing eyeglasses on people's photos. In general it was very successful, daily messages were exchanged from its introduction, and it is still used.

Installation, note organisation, and a note.

Thus, by installing a simple to use device (on the whiteboard) for drawing and sending notes to each other, the single-working teachers on islands in the Stockholm archipelago could form a community, for work and leisure (Groth et al. 2006).

UTOPIA 2008: KLIV – LEARNING AND USE OF COMMON SKILL

My last example of UTOPIA 2008 comes from Malmö, where research students at K3 at Malmö Högskola have worked, under the guidance of Pelle Ehn and Thomas Binder, together with nurses and doctors at the academic hospital, MAS (Malmö Allmänna Sjukhus), on developing KLIV (Kontinuerligt Lärande inom Vården, i.e. Continuous Learning within Healthcare).

In a cooperative process the personnel at the intensive care unit at MAS, together with research students Erling Björgvinsson and Per-Anders Hillgren, developed the recording and use of film sequences on handling the equipment in intensive care. The film recordings were made in close discussion on how to present the handling of the equipment in a situation of use for proper understanding. The films were available for the care situations on handheld computers. Thus the less experienced could learn from the more experienced and use their expertise even when not present. Bar codes on the equipment and a bar code reader on

Discussion of KLIV film.

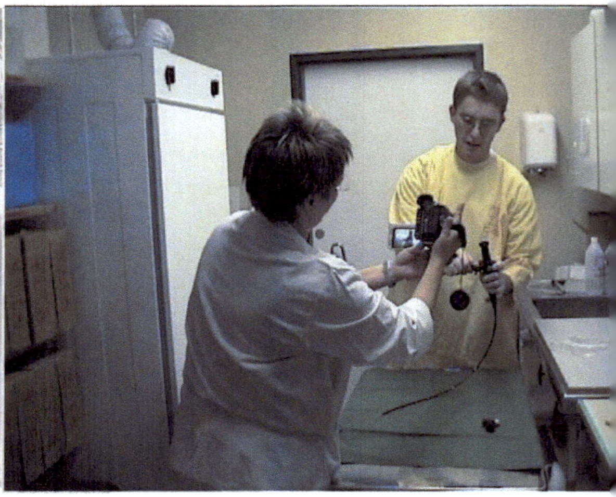

Recording.

the computer was an extra help, allowing the computer to find the appropriate instruction film fast.

This clever use of IT was nominated by the personnel at MAS to the UsersAward IT Prize and KLIV was the Prize winner in 2004. This connects this example with my first example of UTOPIA 2008: UsersAward.

Thorough discussions of this experience, from many aspects including learning, knowing, action, media, cooperation, etc. can be found in the two dissertations by Hillgren (2006) and Björgvinsson (2007). Here I give some photographical illustrations from Björgvinsson and Hillgren (2004).

CONCLUSIONS

It is clear from the »2008 examples« that the »Scandinavian model« for IT system development and use, as it was conceived in the 1970s and 1980s, notably through the UTOPIA project, is at least as important for forming the practice of today. This is true for giving the users a voice and understanding and know-how as well as for the cooperative design methodology.

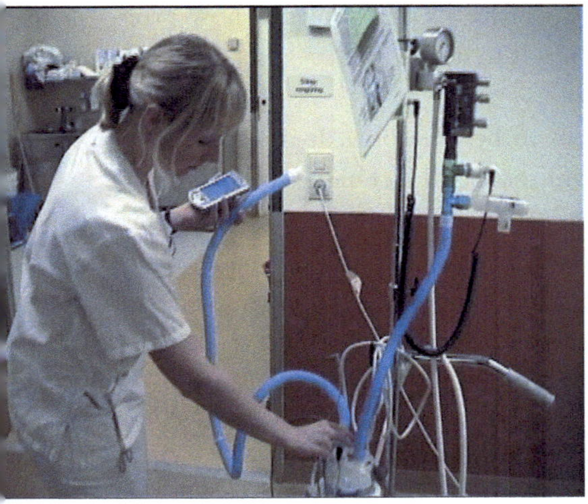

Using as instruction.

Handheld display.

We observe a clear facilitation in IT use, in work places and in education and leisure, for mixing activities, devices and collaborators, for pursuing them wherever we are and whenever we need and want, for keeping closer contact.

When neither applications nor users are islands (but maybe on islands geographically) they can form contact networks and communities for mutual benefit. Even at the early stages, where the purpose of the design is not yet known, it is important to focus on multiple users and uses and on the experience of use. Post-design evaluation is not enough.

For exploring the many innovative new forms of interaction and their use in mixing old and new technologies, multiplicity and ad-hoc configuration, everywhere and anytime, for tailorability, adaptation and awareness in networks and communities, the »Scandinavian« Cooperative Design with users is needed as much as before.

Often the problems of user participation are discussed from the point of view of researchers getting access to the users. Yet, user participation should also be seen from the point of view of the conditions of the participation process, i.e. how the conditions are set for the users to participate together with designers (and managers). Experiences from Co-operative Design projects show problems that Co-operative Design research needs to deal with.

There are indeed a number of difficulties to be overcome. It is important to find the right set of participants, the right tools and techniques as well as the right location and physical space for the Co-operative Design. It is not least as important to create a setting where all involved groups can make active contributions that are meaningful to themselves as well as to other groups of participants. In our experience, this, in some cases, requires a serious change in attitude from some members of the groups involved.

The role personal computers and other IT now play in everyday life makes participation possible but also, in some cases, a burden. When the boundaries between work-life and other parts of life become fuzzier it is natural that the differences in IT support and user influence become fuzzier, while drawing upon each others' strengths. It is often seen that influence in non-work use of technology goes through consumerism and »voting with the users/›buyers‹ feet«, which can also be a lever for workplace democracy when it comes to IT support. Hence, the ideal that everyone could have full participation and control, and *make use of head, hand and heart*, in their whole life, including work, can move closer as a result of cooperative IT design and use. The workplace democracy ideas from the 1970s, to some extent manifested in co-determination laws, can be revived and more fully pursued, with the kind of worker participation exemplified in UsersAward.

Here, »common« workplaces are at least as challenging and inspiring as the more »fancy« new mobile workplaces for media design etc. We need to work with all, old and new, workplaces in the spirit of »Digital Bauhaus«.

ACKNOWLEDGEMENTS

The Cooperative Design tradition owes its development to a large number of practitioners and researchers. I recognise the importance of discussions with many of them for our understanding of possibilities and limitations.

Specifically I want to thank the researchers and users in the projects described. The UTOPIA group should be named for a great experience of fruitful cooperation of lifelong importance:

- Gunnar Kokaas, chairman of Nordic Graphic Union reference group.
- Gunnar Rasmussen, graphic worker in Aarhus.
- Björn Burell, Bernt Eriksson, Bo Eric Ericsson, Malte Eriksson, Martin Eriksson and Björn Sporsén, graphic workers in Stockholm.
- Pelle Ehn, Angelika Dilschmann, Ewa Gunnarsson, Åke Sandberg and Dan Sjögren, Centre for Working Life Research, Stockholm.
- Merete Bartholdy, Susanne Bødker, Kurt Jensen, John Kammersgaard and Morten Kyng, DAIMI, Aarhus University.
- Björn Eiderbäck, Kerstin Frenckner, Caroline Nordquist, Staffan Romberger and Kerstin Severinson Eklundh, NADA, KTH.

REFERENCES

Björgvinsson, E. (2007). Socio-material mediations: Learning, knowing, and self-produced media within healthcare. Dissertation, Blekinge Institute of Technology, Doctoral Dissertation Series No. 2007:03.

Björgvinsson, E., Hillgren, P.-A. (2004). Vardagligt lärande på en. intensivvårdsenhet. med stöd av egenproducerad video. Intensivvårdsenheten, Universitetssjukhuset MAS (in Swedish).

Boivie, P. E. (2007). *Global standard: How computer displays worldwide got the TCO label.* Stockholm, Sweden: Premiss förlag.

Bødker, S., Ehn, P., Kammersgaard, J., Kyng, M., Sundblad, Y. (1987). A Utopian experience. In G. Bjerknes, P. Ehn, M. Kyng (Eds.), *Computers and democracy: A Scandinavian challenge*, pp. 251–278. Aldershot, UK: Avebury.

Bødker, S., Ehn, P., Lindskov Knudsen, J., Kyng, M., Halskov Madsen, K. (1988). Computer support for cooperative design. In Proc. Conf. Computer Supported Cooperative Work (CSCW '88), pp. 377–394. New York: ACM.

Bødker, S. (1991). *Through the interface: A human activity approach to user interface design*. Hillsdale, NJ: Lawrence Erlbaum.

Bødker, S. (1999). Computer applications as mediators of design and use: A developmental perspective. Doctoral dissertation, Department of Computer Science, University of Aarhus.

Bødker, S., Ehn, P., Sjögren, D., Sundblad, Y. (2000). Co-operative design: Perspectives on 20 years with »the Scandinavian IT Design Model«. Invited paper, Proc. NordiCHI 2000, pp. 1–11. KTH, Stockholm.

Bødker, S., Sundblad, Y. (2008). Usability and interaction design: New challenges for the Scandinavian tradition. *Behaviour and Information Technology*. Vol.27, in press.

Druin, A. (1999). Co-operative inquiry: Developing new technology for children with children. Proc. CHI 99, pp. 223–230. New York: ACM Press.

Ehn, P. (1988). *Work-oriented design of computer artifacts*. Falköping: Arbetslivscentrum/Almqvist & Wiksell International, Hillsdale, NJ: Lawrence Erlbaum.

Fornell, C. (2007). *The satisfied customer: Winners and losers in the battle for buyer preference*. New York, NY: Palgrave Macmillan.

Groth, K., Lindquist, S., Bogdan, C., Lidskog, T., Sundblad, Y., Sandor, O. (2006). Saxaren: Strengthening informal collaboration among geographically distributed teachers. Proc. OzCHI.

Grønbæk, K., Kyng, M., Mogensen, P. (1997). Toward a cooperative experimental system development approach. In Kyng, M., Mathiassen, L. (Eds.) *Computers and design in context*, pp. 201–238. Cambridge, MA: MIT Press.

Hillgren, P.A. (2006). Ready-made-media-actions. Dissertation, Blekinge Institute of Technology, Doctoral Dissertation Series No. 2006:07.

Hornecker, E., Buur, J. (2006). Getting a grip on tangible interaction: a framework on physical space and social interaction. Proc. CHI 06, pp. 437–446. New York: ACM Press.

Howard, R. (1985). Utopia: Where workers craft new technology. *Technological Review*, 88(3):43–49. Massachusetts Institute of Technology.

Kensing, F., Simonsen, J., Bødker, K. (1998). MUST: A method for participatory Design. *Human-Computer Interaction*, 13(2):167–198.

Kyng M. (1995). Creating contexts for design. In Carroll, J. M. (Ed.), *Scenario-based design: Envisioning work and technology in system development*, pp. 85–108. New York: Wiley.

Lind, T. (2002). IT-kartan, användare och IT-system i svenskt näringsliv. Stockholm: Landsorganisationen (in Swedish).

Lindquist, S., Westerlund, B., Sundblad, Y., Tobiasson, H., Beaudouin-Lafon, M., Mackay, W. (2007). Co-designing communication technology with and for families: Methods, experience, results and impacts. In Streitz, N., Kameas, A., Mavrommati, I. (Eds.) *The disappearing computer*, pp. 99–120. Berlin: Springer-Verlag.

Mackay, W.E., Ratzer, A.V., Janecek, P. (2000). Video artefact for design: Bridging the gap between abstraction and detail. Proc. DIS 2000, pp. 72–82. New York: ACM Press.

Räsänen, M. (2006). Islands of togetherness: Rewriting context analysis. Doctoral thesis, TRITA-CSC-A 2006: 29, Royal Institute of Technology, Dec. 2006.

Sundblad, Y., Lind, T., Rudling, J. (2002). IT product requirements and certification from the users' perspective, Proc. WWDU '2002, pp.203–205.

Walldius, Å., Sundblad, Y., Sandblad, B., Bengtsson, L., Gulliksen, J. (2008). User certification of workplace software: Assessing both artefact and usage. *Behaviour and Information Technology*. Vol.27, in press.

Westerlund, B., Lindqvist, K., Mackay, W., Sundblad, Y. (2003). Co-designing methods for designing with and for families. Proc. 5th European Academy of Design.

Winograd, T., Bennett, J., De Young, L., Hartfield, B. (1996). *Bringing design to software*. Addison-Wesley.

42

KARI KUUTTI

HCI AND DESIGN – UNCOMFORTABLE BEDFELLOWS?

KARI KUUTTI
HCI AND DESIGN
– UNCOMFORTABLE BEDFELLOWS?

It would be rather natural to think that human-computer interaction and design (industrial design, graphic design) would, as professions and as disciplines, easily form an alliance. After all, there is so much that HCI design as a newcomer could have learnt from long-established design professions, on the other hand, the penetration of information technology in everyday life has greatly increased public awareness and prestige of good design. In reality, the relationship between these two areas has been far from straightforward, but strained and complex. It took 15 years before an industrial designer was able to give a talk in the major HCI conference as a designer, and the relationship in other direction has not been much more embracing. Although some development has taken place, the contact points between the areas are still sparse after a quarter of a century of overlapping existence.

Why is this so? This chapter will explore the issue by tracing the intellectual development of HCI during the last 25 years and comparing that with the design world. The point of interest will be the HCI »turn to design« in the 1990s. There was a lively theoretical discussion within IT in the 1980s about the philosophical foundations of information technology design, resulting, for example, in such classics as Winograd and Flores' *Understanding Computers and Cognition* in 1986 and Ehn's *Work-Oriented Design of Computer Artifacts* in 1988. This discussion did not, however, continue into the 1990s but it was replaced ten years later with a novel direction, the »turn to design.« Why did this turn take place, and did it succeed?

MAIN ORIENTATIONS IN DESIGN THINKING

Let us start with a short look at design thinking. Along the industrial needs to design consumer products for mass markets, different ideologies of design evolved. As a rough caricature, we can identify two influential traditions in industrial design; the legacy of both is still very much alive. One of them is, naturally, functionalism or »modernistic« thinking in design, and the emergence of it is usually connected with the Bauhaus school of design in Germany (1919–1933). The basic idea behind Bauhaus thinking was that there was a possibility to develop a new aesthetics for industrial products, that by skillfully taking into account the functionality of products, the nature of materials used and industrial production processes available, it was possible to develop aesthetically pleasant new forms for those products. The new products would not only function well and be economical to produce, but they would also improve the aesthetical quality of life of their users. These ideas have been very influential and they are still part of most design education, and »postmodernist« design approaches are still often defined as the opposition of Bauhaus functionalism. The functionalistic tradition has been criticized, in particular by the postmodernists, as having an elitist and patronizing view on the users of the products of design: the elite designer knows what is needed and is capable to raise the cultural level of the masses by means of design.

Another influential tradition in industrial design emerged in the 1930s in the USA. Its beginnings cannot be pinpointed with the same accuracy as the Bauhaus ideology, but it is often connected with »The Big Four« designers of the 1930s (Loewy, Teague, Bel Geddes, Dreyfus). This tradition of »styling« or »consumer appeal« was, and is, unashamedly commercial: the purpose of this form of design is to help sell, and sell more. While Bauhaus built its aesthetics on functionality, the consumer appeal designers were much more liberal in this sense: they realised, that the decisions to purchase a product were often heavily influenced by the different meanings that buyers connect with products, and that – with a help from marketing – it was possible to design positive immaterial meanings related with a product even when they were not directly connected with the functionality of the thing itself – meanings such as social status, youth or sexual attractiveness. The consumer appeal tradition has also been subjected to scathing criticism within the design community (e.g. Papanek 1971), as selling all moral principles for money and exploiting the lowest features of human nature. Despite that, if Bauhaus' legacy has lasted in design education, the consumer appeal has perhaps had a stronger influence in actual design practices.

A FRAMEWORK FOR ANALYSIS

Let me construct a simple model to compare the worlds of HCI and design. It is based on the idea that the essence of different artefacts is to mediate between humans and the world, and that this mediation takes place in a variety of ways. The original idea that artefacts mediate only as tools, as expenders of human capabilities, has long been found to be too narrow. In this discussion a hypothesis is made that there is a triple mediation between humans and the world through artefacts – as if artefacts would at the same time belong in three different spheres which are connected but which cannot be reduced to each other. The hypothesis is based on cultural-historical activity theory (Kuutti 1996), but it cannot be elaborated here further. The mediations are:

FUNCTIONALITY. The immediate usefulness of an artefact is based on how it functions. The materiality and making of an artefact are connected to this relation.

MEANINGFULNESS. As discussed in the previous section, an artefact can be a bearer of culturally founded meanings, which are sometimes crucial aspects of the artefact. A person buying a Mercedes or a BMW does not buy only moulded and painted sheets of steel, a motor and wheels, but also a lot of such meanings. A recent book by Krippendorff (2006) is a good example of conceptualising and theorising on this mediation.

ECONOMY. A rather small portion of all artefacts is crafted and used by persons themselves, but they are produced in a very organised way and distributed within the social division of labour. They are subjects of exchange – selling and buying – at the market, where they obtain an exchange value besides their use value.

Figure 1 shows a simple graphical description of the model.

There is quite a lot of variance within each relation: we have artefacts where the functionality is restricted to be a material bearer of meanings (objects of art); artefacts to which it is almost impossible to hang any additional meaning besides functionality (computer utility programs); and artefacts which are created and distributed outside the market mechanism (video clips on YouTube). All these can, however, be considered within the model, so it is covering a broad area and may serve as our sounding board when we look at the differences between HCI and the design professions.

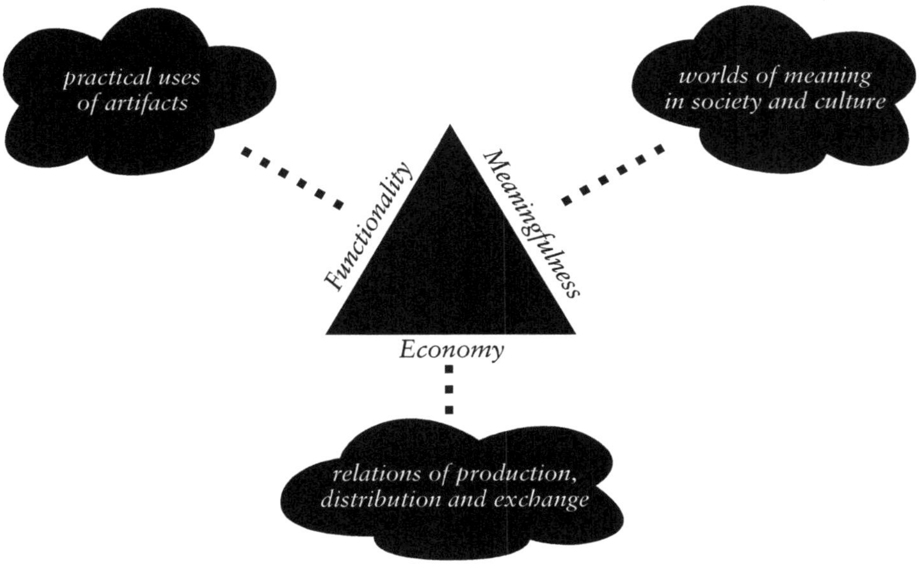

Figure 1. The triple mediated-ness of artefacts.

The task of a »traditional« designer is (within the confines of this model) to solve the problem arising from a design brief: how the needed functionality can be produced smartly by using the available materials and production technologies. At the same time he or she has to shape this functionality into a form which references the world of meanings in culture and society in such a way that the buyer and user will gain some added value from that, for example aesthetic pleasure. And all the time this must happen within the limits given by potential production volumes and costs of production, distribution and marketing.

Thus all three mediations have been taken into account in design education. Although the artistic component of dealing with meanings – creating forms that make a unique reference to cultural sphere – has, without doubt, been the leading motive, the functional/material and production/distribution economics relations have also been kept in mind. Design education has not been heavily interested in training students in detailed methods of how to do design, but more in educating such personalities who can filter and crystallize cultural influences into effective and meaning-laden forms. So development of personal judgement of what is good design and what is not has always been one of the goals in design education. This also means certain individualism; it is assumed that a design brief interpreted by two designers will lead to two different designs.

The sketch on the design world presented above is crude indeed, but perhaps enough to help the discussion about the tensions between it and the HCI world later in the chapter. Let us now turn to HCI.

A SHORT HISTORY OF CURRENT HCI

First it must be noted, that during the last quarter of a century technology and our ways of using it have developed enormously. From an HCI point of view, the major steps could perhaps be identified as follows:

- The emergence of the desktop PC and the stabilisation of the graphical user interface (GUI), which was initially a great step forward as it enabled computer use to spread beyond professional users, but the legacy of which has started to hinder the development further;
- The emergence of the World Wide Web, which, from a technical and interaction point of view, was a definite step backward from desktop GUI, but which enormously enlarged both the user population and the number of people capable to develop interfaces for new systems;
- The emergence of mobile devices, of which mobile phones are certainly the most numerous, and besides them personal digital assistants, MP3 music players, digital cameras and so on. This has brought forward many challenges to design, but also revitalized the interest in the physical aspects of design;
- Finally, the communication networks and penetration of information technology into everyday objects and environments, which is currently changing the technology design landscape.

Given this change in the technology landscape it is clear that the following sketch attempt is not to give an accurate history of the development of the field, but only to outline some significant features related to the development of the »mainstream« ideas during the period.

BACKGROUND. To keep the story of the development of HCI over last 25 years short and coherent it must be distorted into an one-dimensional caricature. The story tells about the baseline, »mainstream« HCI, but there were important parallel side currents as well. Perhaps most important of them were Participatory Design movement discussed elsewhere in this book, and anthropologically and microsociologically inspired Computer-Supported Cooperative Work. The ideas and methods developed within these communities started eventually, towards the end of 1990s, filter into the mainstream HCI, and so the current landscape is more rich and varied than the rather bleak one presented in the story. For the purpose of this paper the caricature is useful, however. The story of HCI is, however, naturally not the whole story: there have been other studies on the relationship between humans and computers from the 1960s onwards, than the information-processing cognitive psychology dominating the earlier phase of HCI, and discussed a bit later (one such was the psychology of programming, where very interesting work was done in the 1970s). And there was, and still is, a strong and rather separate tradition of research in ergonomics, in particular in areas such as production automation and cockpit design, from which HCI could have learnt a lot, and perhaps still could – but that is a story for another book. In any case, to follow the development a starting point is needed: the research landscape on humans and computers in late 1970s and early 1980s.

For the purposes of this chapter we can limit ourselves to two dominating traditions of research: management information systems (MIS) direction in information systems (IS), and AI/information processing psychology in HCI. There is a certain symmetry with these traditions, and they fit well enough together in the same textbooks. In the late 1970s and early 1980s, IS was a very important area. The methods for, and research on, it were dominated by MIS ideology, which saw organisation as a rational machine, which can be better and better controlled by management with information technology. The standard mode of software development was a contract-based one, where a software vendor developed a unique system for a particular customer. The last phase of such a project was called implementation, where the system was installed for use, and users were trained and software tweaked until the combination finally became, at least minimally, fit for the purpose.

After the »cognitive turn« in psychology in the 1950s, the information processing variant of cognitive psychology had won the day and become a standard. The central idea of it was (and is) that human thinking is, in principle, similar to the functioning of a computer (and thinking is what matters). Artificial intelligence (AI) was the extremist branch of this tradition. The central research paradigm was careful modelling and factorization of use situations based on theories of information processing psychology, and the testing of these models in controlled laboratory experiments, according to the best traditions of experimental psychology.

Thus in late 1970s and early 1980s the landscape of human- and organisation-oriented IT research looked rather different to the present. The PC revolution had not yet happened, and, correspondingly, HCI was far from the industry-academy mass movement we know now – it was a small, rather esoteric and purely academic area. Theoretically the artificial intelligence/information processing cognitive psychology had dominated the field for some 20 years, and was still going strong, although its impact in the practical design of systems had always remained minimal. Perhaps the most »progressive« area was information systems design, where the penetration of large systems further and further within the organisations had led to larger and larger and more and more diversified groups of people to become end-users of the systems; continuously causing situations where the prevailing marriage of system-theoretical (cog in the organisational machinery) and information processing psychology (humans as rational information processors) was feeling less and less adequate.

HISTORY OF CURRENT HCI. This changed during the 1980s because of what happened in the market – the PC emerged and brought with it a mass market for usable software. Two significant issues can be highlighted here: one interface invention, another commercial innovation. The interface invention was the development of spreadsheet software, the first of which was called VisiCalc, developed by Dan Bricklin and Bob Frankston for Apple II in 1979, and probably the most influential single program in the history of the PC. Suddenly there was an interface that was easy to understand and manipulate, so that many kinds of tedious calculations could be automated without learning computer programming. This made the personal computer demonstrably useful for a variety of purposes and many people bought Apple II just to use VisiCalc. The commercial innovation was of course IBM's decision to go into the PC business, only after that did organisational decision-makers start to believe that a PC is not a toy or passing fad but something serious that can be really useful, and that enabled the PC to become a real mass phenomenon.

The commercial success of PC machines also developed a potential mass market for additional software for them. There was one serious problem, however: such mass-marketed software should be easy enough to learn and use »off-the-shelf« so that no extra training would be needed, because with training the business could hardly be made commercially viable. But nobody – neither industry nor academy – knew how to develop such quality in software, and this gap between what was needed and the available knowledge was the start of the HCI research and community, as we now know it. Wisely enough, both academic and industrial resources were pooled together to solve the problem, the first CHI conference was organised in 1983, and since then the community and research area have been expanding and diversifying to become an important, visible and respected part of the IT research field – and one where cooperation between academy and industry has been, and still is, particularly close.

This development has had its own turns and twists. In the beginning, the »old« HCI research tradition rose eagerly to face the challenge of helping commercial software development. During the 1980s, however, it started to become more and more apparent that there was no success in sight: that academic research was not able to deliver any results that would be useful in industry. Broadly taken, two reasons can be identified. Firstly, to make laboratory experiments controllable enough, the information processing psychology-based modelling had to abstract away from use situations so many practically relevant issues, that the results had very little meaning with respect to real-life development. Secondly, the time needed for a proper series of laboratory experiments did not fit in at all with the hectic pace of development. Towards the end of the 1980s this was evoking two different responses. In academia, there was an increasing call for new theoretical foundations for HCI research, foundations that would be better in grasping what is happening in real-life situations. Researchers such as Liam Bannon, Philip Barnard and John M. Carroll tried to open such foundational discussions. On the industry side there was a growing disappointment in academic research and distrust in the usefulness of any theoretical accounts.

By the end of 1980s an innovation emerged from industry research laboratories (IBM and Digital were both very active at that time), one which shaped the HCI research landscape far into the future: usability testing. Interestingly enough it was based on the psychological laboratory experiments and maintained the appearance of such (IBM's usability laboratory people are dressed in long white laboratory coats in a widely distributed PR photo – e.g. in Preece et al. 1994), although the scientific content of the experiments (including theory, modelling, factors, control and statistics) was totally discarded. What was left was just observation of actual users in simulated tasks to identify potential problematic moments encountered in the process. Very simple, but also very efficient in practice; the emergence of such working methods directed the whole course of HCI for at least the next decade. Usability became the central concept in HCI and better methods to evaluate and design for it were the major research topic. Unfortunately this also meant a certain intellectual impoverishment: calls to discuss HCI theoretical foundations lost their audience, when the somewhat a-theoretical (and originally, sometimes even anti-theoretical) usability movement took over.

It is good to remember that although personal computers were originally built by hobbyists (and that was also the core customer base of the first commercially successful generation of PCs in the end of 1970s), it was within workplace desktop computing that the need for HCI emerged. Thus HCI was mainly work-oriented during the whole 1980s and long into 1990s, and issues like emerging computer gaming did not receive much attention. Only in the latter part of 1990s did the PC start to evolve towards the consumer appliance it is now, in parallel with the emergence of other computer-based consumer-oriented technology, like digital mobile phones, game consoles, etc.

During the 1990s, and until the early years of the 2000s, usability remained by far the dominating topic in HCI. Better and better methods were developed, evaluation of usability was pushed earlier and earlier in the design process, and even attempts to gain more strategic weight in decision-making within product development organisations were launched. The longevity of usability as a research topic is somewhat surprising, given that it is a rather narrow area, for which no theories have been developed. But the need for more and more usability research has been fuelled by the rapid development of technology during the same period: first stabilisation of GUI interface, then the emergence of WWW and explosion of WWW sites, then the emergence of mobile devices as mass consumer phenomenon and finally the emergence of wireless networks, ubicomp environments and convergence of computers, networks, services and consumer devices. Every technical development has meant a need to rethink how usability can be evaluated and designed, and that has kept the issue alive. Only in the 2000s has some challenge to the usability domination in the field been felt, in particular from new emerging area of »user experience«, of which more will come later in the chapter.

THE RELATION BETWEEN »USABILITY« HCI AND DESIGN

How has the relationship between HCI and design evolved? Or perhaps we could also ask why, despite a clear overlap of interest areas, it has evolved so slowly. Only in the last years of the 25 year history outlined above have ideas developed in design started to have broader influence in the HCI field.

It is rather natural that HCI did not have much contact with the design community in the beginning. It can be speculated that the usability movement could have learnt something from the very practically oriented ergonomics tradition, which was, and still is, in contact with the design community, but ergonomics and HCI were not academically close, the former often within mechanical engineering, the latter in computer science or in another information technology department. The previous academic HCI had practically nothing to do with the design tradition, and when the usability movement broke off, it was left in a vacuum in this respect.

It is also rather easy to see why HCI people did not initially feel a need to contact designers. During the desktop computer era, and in particular after the stabilisation of GUI interface, there was not much else than computer screens or program windows to be »designed«, and because designers seldom had enough understanding of the »material« to be used, they were reduced to changing the appearances. Even this was frustrating, because at that time programs were almost solely for utilitarian purposes. A piece of software made for a particular utility purpose is a quite peculiar object, and it must be one of the most utilitarian things in existence. It is indeed very difficult to load any extra meanings upon a piece of software, although not totally impossible: for example an aspiring sound engineer may attempt to create a feeling of professionalism – for oneself or for others – by using a professional sequencing software, and the diehard users of legacy software, say, the old Macintosh OS9 operating system, are certainly making a symbolic gesture that is also meaningful for them. But in general, it is only the functionality and how it is put in the hands of a user that matters. Thus the strongest area of a designer's competence could hardly be used with respect to HCI at that time.

On the other hand, using the triangle model presented earlier, it is also easy to understand why people belonging to design professions did not joyfully embrace this new group of people who were also calling themselves designers. From the three mediations HCI has been covering only the functionality side, and usability is an even narrower slice of that. During the usability development, interest in costs and benefits of usability work emerged, but interest in meanings, for example in the aesthetic aspects of HCI, have remained always thin. Thus from the viewpoint of a designer HCI people were not designers but »barbarians«, uneducated technicians lacking any understanding of the aesthetics and complexity of the cultural filtration involved in a design. This suspicion was strengthened by the HCI obsession on methods instead of a personal judgement. (It is, by the way, a bit alarming to note that while the eye of a designer is indeed trained with good examples of design and there is almost a whole book industry devoted to the topic, nothing similar exist in HCI: the closest thing available are websites full of bad examples.)

TURN TO DESIGN IN THE MID-1990S

In the mid-1990s a very interesting »turn-to-design« happened. It is hardly an accident that this was also the time when mobile devices, in particular mobile phones, started to become popular. The emergence of mobile devices and the continuing convergence between computers and other specialised devices meant a break in the desktop-dominated HCI. The small size of handheld devices created totally new HCI problems, but it also revived the interest in physical design, that had almost disappeared from HCI during the desktop era. Interest in physical design naturally brought interest in people who are capable to shape physical forms, designers. So the first designer finally got the floor in CHI '98 – in the role of a designer of small computer-based devices: Jose Ferrante from Fluke Corp. in a panel on small interfaces (Marcus et al. 1998).

Prominent authors like Terry Winograd and Pelle Ehn, who ten years earlier had written polemical philosophical books against the overly narrow rationalist-cartesian view on humans dominant in IS design (Winograd 1987, Ehn 1988), had changed their orientation and instead of searching for help from philosophy were turning towards the design profession; Winograd in the book *Bringing Design to Software* (Winograd 1996), and Ehn with his *Manifesto for a Digital Bauhaus* (Ehn 1998). The motivation of both of these is very similar: both regret that the connections between software design and other, older design professions have been lacking, and think that the design tradition can make valuable contributions to the design of software. The question is to find the areas and ways in which these contributions can best be assimilated.

The book edited by Winograd is a collection of 14 rather diverse texts from a number of authors. Its general tenet is that there is a lot to improve in software quality and that a design perspective might be a good one to address these quality aspects. The opening chapter of the book is Mitchell Kapor's famous »A Software Design Manifesto«, where he criticised the lack of quality, in particular use quality, of most existing computer software and suggested that the reason for this was the paucity of design thinking in software development. The definition of what actually is software design remains quite elusive, despite several attempts to clarify it. Of the 20 authors, 17 have an information technology background and only three come from proper design professions, so in the opening of a dialogue between the IT and design professions the book only takes a modest step forward. Ehn's paper has two goals: it is a discussion on the importance of Bauhaus tradition to all design and an exploration of digital technologies as a novel material for design, and, at the same time, it outlines a program for a new curriculum he had been planning for Malmö University, where the idea of a »digital bauhaus« was to be put into practice.

DEVELOPMENT IN THE 2000'S

The book edited by Winograd was an indicator of a broader interest and in the mid-1990s two new forums were opened, both of which still continue. One of them was the launching of a new ACM journal called *interactions*, a professional magazine on HCI and design. The authorship consists of academic and industrial HCI people, but also people coming from design professions. Another opening was a series of biannual conferences called Designing Interactive Systems (DIS), the first of which was organised in 1994. The organisers were members of the HCI community, interested in bringing in more influence from a design tradition and having a forum for a dialogue between HCI and traditional design professions, and it was mostly the Bauhaus inspired tradition the organisers wanted to communicate with. The DIS series has continued, and the 8th DIS was held in 2008, so the interest in design issues has been quite persistent. The conference has not, however, been really able to serve as a forum for a dialogue between HCI and design professions: although there are some contributions in each conference coming from the design side, the majority has always been HCI oriented.

After ten years of usability research and development, in the beginning of the 2000s, it had become clear that usability alone will hardly be a major selling factor for any IT product, but something else is needed. This led to the development of an interesting new concept called »user experience«. As far as I know, it was brought in the design field from HCI side: I encountered it for the first time as a member of the workshop program committee for CHI '98. Among the proposals sent to the committee was one entitled »Emotions and user experience«, and I remember being the only member in the committee suggesting that it should be accepted. My e-mail archive does not reach that far back, but I believe that there was an agreement within the rest of the committee that the topic was »not serious enough for CHI« ... so times have changed a bit since then. After some initial confusion the new concept started to gain a foothold and it has rapidly become a major new feature in the evolution of the HCI design field, almost challenging »usability« as the most popular term used. The interest in the concept has also led to a new series of conferences called Designing User Experience (DUX), of which three have been organised so far (2003, 2005, 2007). If DIS is hanging on the Bauhaus ideals, DUX is clearly leaning towards the Customer Appeal orientation, and design for commercial success. This has led to a certain tension between DIS and DUX communities.

CONCLUSION

This chapter has made a short review of the relation between design and HCI. Although they may superficially seem to have strong similarities, a closer look has found a gap between them, a gap initially wide enough to hinder communication. The origins of the current HCI were in a specific historical situation, which has directed the development of the field and thinking perhaps more than the members of the community are aware of. The usability movement has been a great success that has made the HCI research community grow and flourish. But the success has masked an intellectual void: usability and utility alone are too narrow a perspective to understand the relation between humans and technology from a design point of view. And this void may be the reason why HCI researchers and developers have so eagerly embraced »user experience« during the last few years.

Meanwhile, design has always had a broader and richer view encompassing all sides of our framework – although the articulation of that view has been far from straightforward, but that is another story. Thus the »turn to design« in HCI ten years ago, advocated by sensitive researchers such as Ehn and Winograd, has not remained as an empty gesture, but it indicated a fermenting need within the HCI community. Over ten years design, in several forms, has become a part of the HCI landscape, and there is a possibility that it will lead to a certain reorientation of the whole field. The concept of user experience is still very diffuse, and many people are not happy with the doubtful Customer Appeal overtones in it. It can, however, also be seen in a more positive light: despite the lack of any explicit programme to do so, it is the most serious attempt so far to develop a new foundation for the next stage of HCI research and development. It is also one of the few concepts whose origin is in HCI but which has also become popular within other design professions, and thus might serve as a bridge between different communities. According to the user experience community the concept is holistic and encompasses the issues of functionality and usability, complementing these with the meanings the user gives to interaction. It remains to be seen, if it can be developed further in the future to really serve such an integrative purpose.

Finally, in this context it is interesting to notice, that although Pelle Ehn founded his original manifesto firmly on the Bauhaus ideals, he also raised the need for »production of useful, beautiful and amusing everyday things and experiences for ordinary people« – a visionary touch, we can say now for sure.

REFERENCES

Ehn, P. (1988). *Work-oriented design of computer artifacts*. Stockholm: Arbetslivscentrum.

Ehn, P. (1998). Manifesto for a Digital Bauhaus. *Digital Creativity*, 9(4):207–216.

Krippendorff, K. (2006). *The semantic turn: A new foundation for design*. Boca Raton: Taylor & Francis.

Kuutti, K., (1996). Activity theory as a potential framework for human-computer interaction research. In Nardi, B. (Ed.) *Context and consciousness: Activity theory and human computer interaction*. pp. 17–44. Cambridge, MA: MIT Press.

Marcus, A., Ferrante, J., Kinnunen, T., Kuutti, K., Sparre, E. (1998). Baby faces: user-interface design for small displays. In CHI 98 conference summary on Human factors in computing systems, pp. 96–97. New York: ACM Press.

Papanek, V. (1971). *Design for the real world: Human ecology and social change*. New York: Pantheon Books.

Preece, J., Rogers, Y., Sharp, H., Benyon, D. , Holland, S., Carey, T. (1994). *Human-computer interaction*. Boston: Addison-Wesley.

Winograd, T., Flores, F. (1986). *Understanding computers and cognition*. Norwood, New Jersey: Ablex Publishing.

Winograd, T. et al. (Eds., 1996). *Bringing design to software*. Boston: Addison-Wesley.

60

LIAM BANNON

CONSTRUCTING UTOPIA(S) IN SITU – DARING TO BE DIFFERENT

LIAM BANNON
CONSTRUCTING UTOPIA(S) IN SITU
– DARING TO BE DIFFERENT

Without the Utopias of our times, man would still live in caves, naked and miserable. It was Utopians who first traced the lines of the first city ... Out of generous dreams come beneficial realities. Utopia is the principle of all progress. And the essay into a better future.

Anatole France

A map of the world that does not include Utopia is not worth even glancing at, for it leaves out the one country at which Humanity is always landing. And when Humanity lands there, it looks out, and seeing a better country, sets sail. Progress is the realisation of Utopias.

Oscar Wilde

Not in Utopia, subterranean fields,
Or on some secret island, Heaven knows where!
But in this very world, which is the world
Of all of us, the place where, in the end,
We find our happiness, or not at all!

William Wordsworth

INTRODUCTION

The intent of this chapter is to outline a distinctive way of thinking about issues of technology and society that has characterized many Nordic approaches to the topic. One of the characteristics of this approach has been the recognition of the worth of human labour. Technology is not seen as an alien force, but something which is itself a product of human labour, and it can be designed and utilized in ways which augment human skills and expertise, rather than degrading them. What is particularly striking, at least to this author, in this approach is that we are presented not simply with a vision of how things could be better in our society, but with concrete exemplars of how we can build such a better world. It is in recognition of this fact that I have chosen the title of this chapter, as it emphasizes that, while the tradition of Utopian literature is the delineation of a supposedly idea world which exists no-place (*u-topos*, in Greek), these visions can be an inspiration for quite practical activities on the ground, as steps towards their realization. As Wilde notes (in the quote above) this is a never-ending quest, as with each achievement, we recognize that there are further bridges to cross and places to be visited. It is this combination of some vision of an alternative, and hopefully better, world on the one hand, and the demonstration of a set of practical methods in an attempt to realize this vision, that is so distinctive of the research projects discussed herein.

In what follows, I will not attempt to provide a substantive history of these attempts, as a number of accounts already exist, but rather to highlight certain key concerns and illuminate them, based partly on my own encounters with these projects and the people involved in these activities. My main aim is to highlight how an explicit approach to the design and use of technology that is grounded in a respect for human ingenuity and skill can lead us to an innovative set of practices and inspiring results. My secondary aim is captured in the subtitle to this chapter – Daring to be Different – and relates to the increasing pressure in academic research to adopt a single paradigm of success, using a, to my mind, limited set of metrics. It is my belief that this is a very restricted approach, which will lead to a reduction in real innovations. Part of the reason that the so-called Scandinavian model exists at all is due to the fact that there has, in the past, been some space at a local and national level in these countries to pursue a research agenda that was distinctive, and has resulted in a number of major contributions to our understanding of technology design which are now recognized world-wide. Just as we are having debates about the need to respect and nurture biodiversity and heterogeneity in our animal and plant world, there is a need to allow for, if not encourage, diversity and heterogeneity in our research approaches. We need to Act Up, to develop a rainbow coalition against the forces pushing for a monochrome world!

EARLY DAYS – CARVING OUT A DISTINCTIVE NICHE

As noted above, this is not a history of Scandinavian approaches to the role of information systems in everyday life, as there now exist a number of excellent reports from both inside and outside the community that document developments (e.g. Bansler 1989) but it is worth mentioning that from the very outset of the computer age, there have been a number of quite distinct approaches developed in the Nordic countries. The work of Börje Langefors in Sweden in the 1960s is noted by many, especially his approach to thinking about computer systems not as abstract machines, but as practical tools to support human work and organization. (cf. Dahlbom 1995). In Denmark, Peter Naur was developing a distinctive approach to the field he termed *datalogi* (or »datalogy« in English), where there was a strong focus on practical issues and a respect for human skill and intuition in developing software and building information systems. In Norway, Kristen Nygaard was making waves with his collaborator, Ole Johan Dahl, in developing the SIMULA language to support the construction of models of the world based on objects, originating the powerful paradigm of »object-oriented programming« that was to become universally adopted in subsequent years. As well as making fundamental contributions to programming and specification, Nygaard was instrumental in evolving a research collaboration with the trade union movement with a view to its having an influence on the development and use of computer systems in the workplace. The original project within this framework was the project with the Norwegian Iron and Metal Workers Union in the early 1970s. Nygaard's work influenced many young Scandinavian computing and information systems researchers, and related projects – working with the unions in understanding computer systems and democracy – soon developed, such as DEMOS (Democratic Planning and Control in Working Life – on Computers, Industrial Democracy and Trade Unions) in Sweden in 1975, and DUE (Democracy, development and EDP) in Denmark around the same time. While these projects were seen as useful, it became clear to the researchers that their approach needed to go beyond awareness of technology and negotiation of technology agreements in the workplace, and needed to move into the domain of alternative design of the software and hardware itself.

The UTOPIA project (1981–85), involving partners from Sweden and Denmark, was thus founded with an explicit aim of developing »a type of technology that improves the quality of work and the products, a type of technology that is not inflexible but dynamically changeable at individual workplaces and the employees develop their skills.« (Bødker et al. 1987). What was also significant with UTOPIA was that the approach, while grounded in the specifics of the political, social and economic conditions in Scandinavia, was also outward-looking, in terms of paying attention to the latest developments in new technologies and wishing to make links with the latest thinking in new kinds of software and hardware tools.

> The project should enable this by the development of technology and training programs combined with sociological analysis of the prerequisities of alternatives, and an understanding of the forces acting on technological development nationally and internationally. (*ibid*, p. 257)

The project wished to develop a demonstration example, and it was hoped would serve as a »source of inspiration« for trade unions everywhere. The UTOPIA project has justifiably received a lot of international attention over the years. It was a massive step to move from developing an understanding of the changing conditions of capital and technology to attempt to actually create new kinds of technology, new tools, to allow workers to build on their craft skills. Indeed, one outcome of the project was a more in-depth understanding of how to think about information technology from a tool perspective (Ehn and Kyng 1984). The project also produced material on the project not only in Danish and Swedish, but also in English, which made its work available to a larger audience. They also engaged in conferences and study tours abroad, both in terms of fact-finding on the latest technologies, and in disseminating their ideas. The project was a major part of the Aarhus conference in 1985 on *Development and use of computer-based systems and tools – in the context of democratization at work* (selected papers from this conference with its rather unwieldy title were published in Bjerknes et al., 1987, with the more succinct and provocative title *Computers and democracy: A Scandinavian challenge.*) Strong interest in the project was shown by many groups, and exposure in the pages of the MIT science publication *Technology Review* in an article entitled *Utopia: Where workers craft new technology* by Rob Howard (1985) and in a video production entitled *Computers in Context* helped significantly in making the project known around the world. Another important point of contact occurred when members of the UTOPIA project interacted with the emerging Human-Computer Interaction community, particularly with those espousing a »user-centred design« philosophy, as evidenced by, for example, Norman and Draper (1986).

UTOPIA MEETS HUMAN-MACHINE INTERACTION

> design is inevitably political, in that it includes an element of hope – a dream, however vague, containing the outlines of the society we want to live in.
>
> Guy Bonsiepe, *The invisible aspects of hfg ulm* (Bonsiepe 1999, p. 126)

Again, the aim here is not to provide a detailed historical account of this intersection, but just to note how a variety of events occurred which led to an interesting commingling of ideas and interests. Susanne Bødker had been working on her PH.D. thesis in Aarhus, entitled *Through the Interface*, which was exploring how ideas from Leont'ev's activity theory perspective might re-frame issues concerning the human-machine relation. In this approach, the interface is not the focus, rather the person attempts to work through the technology to accomplish an activity. Thus the computer is a tool or medium through which the user acts. Bødker also spent a year at Xerox PARC in 1984, with the Smalltalk group, who had an interest in designing interfaces for children to use, and were working on novel interaction mechanisms. In early 1985, two members of the UTOPIA team, Morten Kyng and Pelle Ehn, visited several sites in the US to explore the latest trends and ideas around graphic workstations and WIMP type interfaces. During that time they encountered the ideas of Direct Manipulation (Shneiderman) which fitted in well with their tool metaphor for designing interactive systems. Kyng and Ehn also visited the Human-Machine Interaction project at UCSD, led by Don Norman, and the beginnings of a conversation between the user-centred design community in HCI and the participative design community was fostered.† For example, in his chapter on Cognitive Engineering in Norman and Draper (1986), Norman refers positively to the tool metaphor of Ehn and Kyng (Norman, p. 52).

THE EMERGENCE OF PARTICIPATIVE/PARTICIPATORY DESIGN

Initially, researchers involved in projects such as DEMOS and DUE were ideologically opposed to another tradition, which on the surface appeared to share many of their interests in developing more open and participative organizational forms in the mid to late 1980s, namely the socio-technical systems perspective originating in the Tavistock Institute in London, and developed especially within the information systems area by the late Enid Mumford. This tradition was brought to Scandinavia through the work of people like Niels Bjørn-Andersen (Denmark) and Bo Hedberg (Sweden). The UTOPIA project members referred to their approach, which relied centrally on local trade union involvement, as the collective resource approach. Briefly, the key concepts of the Collective Resource Approach (CRA), as discussed in an important paper by Ehn and Kyng (1987), building on the seminal early work of their Norwegian mentor Kristen Nygaard, include:

- The desire to enhance worker control over technology.
- The centrality of the labour process.
- The need to build on the tacit knowledge and skills of labour.
- The use of computers to augment worker skills, not replace them.
- The utility of the tool rather than the machine metaphor for the computer.

† The author was involved in this exchange, as host in UCSD for the Kyng and Ehn visit, and was subsequently invited to work in Aarhus with former members of the UTOPIA team, especially Susanne Bødker and Pelle Ehn. Further insight into this interaction can be found in Bannon (1990).

- The poverty of formal models and abstractions of the work process.
- The need and desire for »user« involvement in the design process.
- The need to develop concrete representations of designs – prototypes.
- The awareness of systems design as a political and social, as well as technical process.

Their approach leans heavily on Marxist-inspired theories of society, concerning the centrality of the labour process, and its pursuit of more democracy in the workplace. What is crucial to this work, however, is its effort to go beyond the diagnosis of problems with technology in society, but actually proposing and exploring an action plan to create change. Their critique of existing system development methodologies was based on observation in practical situations, and their work involved practical attempts to change methods and procedures. While early work involved the development of information packages (courses, training materials, etc.) about workplace technologies, as we noted, the UTOPIA project went beyond this to actually propose alternative systems and work practices. Whatever one may wish to say about the actual effectiveness of these initial ideas in different settings (see Kraft and Bansler 1992, and the reply by Kyng 1993) – in terms of changed labour and business practices in companies with regard to IT systems development and implementation practices – there is no doubting that this work has had a strong influence on a number of leading research groups in several countries.

The 1985 Aarhus conference was a key factor in developing the international dimensions of the collective resource approach, and it included such people as Claudio Ciborra (Italy), Enid Mumford, Mike Fitter, Sally Hacker (UK), Rob Kling, Joan Greenbaum (USA), and Cristiane Floyd (Germany). The latter was also the key figure involved in an influential report on the developments in information systems in Scandinavia based on a tour in Denmark and Sweden made by a number of German computer scientists in the late 1980s. The resulting report entitled *Out of Scandinavia* included extensive discussion of the collective resource approach, and was re-published for an international audience in the *Human-Computer Interaction* journal (Floyd et al. 1989).

In the late 1980s a number of other liaisons were forming, with interaction between researchers based in Xerox PARC and Xerox EuroPARC (Suchman, Henderson, Moran) with the Aarhus Computer Science Dept (Kyng, Bødker, Ehn) and other Danish researchers. As the political climate changed, some of the language of the CRA approach also shifted and the term Cooperative Design began to emerge, with more emphasis on user involvement in the design process, but less explicit attention to the trade union role *per se*. The book *Design at Work*, edited by Joan Greenbaum and Morten Kyng, emerged in 1991 with an interesting mix of authors from the Scandinavian tradition, along with several others with strong links and sensibilities to this approach. This language of user involvement became a common one for both members of the Cooperative Design community and certain members of the HCI community influenced by the Scandinavian work. The first Participatory Design conference was held in Seattle, Washington, in 1990, with Lucy Suchman as Program Chair, and it included many Scandinavians as speakers (selected papers from the conference appeared in Schuler and Namioka 1993). This term of Participatory Design became more widespread in use, especially in North America, and should not be equated with the earlier Participative Design approach in Europe, headed by Enid Mumford, although there were points of commonality, and over time, some of the ideological arguments between the two groups receded in importance.

Some observers see a radical departure from the early CRA tradition in this later work by researchers of the Scandinavian school, as exemplified in the papers in the Greenbaum and Kyng collection (1991). They claim that the idea of cooperative development espoused in this collection does not continue the political commitment evidenced in early CRA work. For our purposes here, this dispute can be seen as a doctrinal one within the field, which we can leave aside for now. However, precisely because some of the ideas emanating from this work have now become so poularized and disseminated in a wide variety of settings, it may indeed be useful to critique some of the popular versions of the PD story, in order to keep some semblance of balance.

One critique (Kraft and Bansler 1992) that has been advanced is that the approach has not been very widely used in practice, even in Scandinavia. In other words, much systems development work in commercial settings is done using structured design methodologies often imported from other countries. While this is undoubtedly true, my own opinion is that many of the ideas of the school are now taught within the University system, and that there is some impact on the way systems analysts and designers pay attention to user needs and involve them in evaluating prototypes at the very least. In any event, the researchers were not really proposing an alternative complete »methodology« for system analysis and design! The current problem is that some of the »newly-baptized« proselytizers of the approach (not the researchers themselves) make claims about its original success and widespread adoption that are without empirical foundation.

Another critique (Whitaker et al. 1991) focuses on the conceptual framework underlying the approach and critiques both the melange of theoretical inspirations espoused by some in the PD school (ranging from Heidegger to Marx to Wittgenstein) and the lack of a clear research and evaluation methodology. The latter criticism is, in my view, more serious, as it is difficult to evaluate many PD projects due to the paucity of information available. The recent survey of early PD projects (Clement and Van den Besselaar 1993) and their successes and failures is itself flawed as any evaluation of the projects is carried out by the project investigators themselves, which, while not without some interest and utility, is methodologically problematic. The perspectives of other parties involved in the project are not adequately, if at all represented. For those with an interest in empirical evaluation of the action projects, the documented literature is quite small and incomplete. Despite these criticisms, we should also be aware of the significant impact the PD approach has had in areas such as HCI and in the information systems field more generally. Emphasis on practical activity, and the use of a variety of methods for »eliciting user requirements« such as Future Workshops and Wall Charting, also on the need for mock-ups and prototypes for users to experience future work situations »hands-on«, which played an important role in the work of the CRA researchers, have now become more widely used and accepted in the HCI and IT industry. The whole issue of user involvement has become much more central in the development process, if not from the viewpoint of workplace democracy, then simply in terms of building more usable and useful systems.

While the PD conferences have continued on a bi-annual basis since 1990, various members of the UTOPIA project group and authors from the Cooperative Design book have moved on in their work, extending the boundaries of their fields of systems development and human computer interaction.

THE EMERGING FIELD OF INTERACTION DESIGN

Since the early 1990s one of the key members of the UTOPIA project, Pelle Ehn, has pursued an increasing interest in the field of Design and in how it might inform IT and New Media practices. Even back in Ehn (1988) there are references to the Design field, in terms of exploring the usefulness of Design Methods approaches to building computer systems, as well as an examination of how ideas from the Bauhaus design school might still have relevance for students of new forms of computer artifacts and media. While subsequently at Lund University, Ehn and his students pushed for the recognition of *style* as an important concept in the HCI community, and encouraged efforts to collect examples of computer styles in the Qualitheque idea. While this approach did not sustain itself, the ideas were challenging and provocative. Some years later, when Ehn moved to Malmö to help setup the new University programme in media and communication, he wrote a *Manifesto for a Digital Bauhaus* (Ehn 1998) as a framework for the School, which set out an ambitious agenda in attempting to develop a new kind of graduate, one who would cross traditional divides between art, science and design, utlising the capabilities of new media in a craft-like fashion, embodying both aesthetic and ethic ideals. This evolution of concerns with issues of aesthetics paralleled a wider concern within the HCI and Design communities for new forms of rapprochement between the traditional design communities such as graphic and industrial design with the more task-oriented experimental, engineering tradition of cognitive ergonomics and human-computer interaction.

For some people, the rise of this supposedly »new« field is perplexing on a number of grounds. They argue, for instance, that HCI is already a very multidisciplinary activity, so why is there a need for a new label and new sub-grouping of the field? What, exactly, is new here? Others feel that any new research area needs to be founded on a solid conceptual foundation, and feel uncomfortable that the term »interaction design« lacks any clear and agreed-upon meaning.

While sympathizing with such concerns, we should also be aware that it is common at the beginning, and even well into the life of a research area, that there is a lack of consensus on the defining characteristics of the field – witness the lack of clarity that exists to this day in HCI as to the meaning of such foundational terms as »interface«, for example. Responding to the initial criticism above, one could argue that, while HCI is indeed multi-disciplinary, the major organs of the community are still dominated by a cognitive and engineering mentality that is viewed as closed to many Design concerns.

What Ehn has done over the years in his work – on the collective resource approach; on the tool metaphor; on the importance of tacit knowledge and skill; on the need to examine quality in use of artifacts; on the need to examine aesthetic and ethical aspcts of computer design and use; and on the need to integrate art, science and technology – has been to articulate visions of the future: Utopias. But he has gone beyond simply describing the vision and has, in each instance, also gone some way in attempting to instantiate these visions through a number of bold attempts to change practice and develop aspects of the vision in a practical manner. It is as much for these practical attempts, even if not fully successful, as in the initial outline of the vision, that he is to be lauded. On the other hand, the fact that so many of the ideas expressed by Ehn and his co-workers, going back to the 1970s, are now part-and-parcel of the thinking of the mainstream in HCI, Interaction Design and Information Systems – the value of user involvement; the need to enhance and build on human skill; the value of the tool metaphor; the need for prototyping; the importance of studying design-in-use; and the importance of both an aesthetic and ethical perspective – shows just how much of his thinking and that of his colleagues has so penetrated the community that it is difficult to believe that these ideas were not always present in the field.

CONCLUSION: AGAINST THE MAINSTREAM

It is becoming increasingly difficult to survive as an academic if one entertains unorthodox views. Throughout the world, especially in Europe in recent years, there has been a marked increase in evaluation metrics for academic promotion and tenure. While there is nothing wrong in having evaluation measures *per se*, the difficulty lies in the fact that these metrics are becoming increasingly standardized and homogenized. Only certain kinds of contributions count, only certain publications are seen as worthwhile, only certain styles of writing acceptable, etc. Most of these metrics are coming from North American sources. In sum, all of the research world is coming to look North American. This, to my mind, is a serious problem, and this attempt to narrow down what counts as success and quality needs to be resisted, before it is too late. Within its ambit, Europe has a proud tradition of scholarship, but also of academic diversity across its national borders. This attempt to reduce this diversity, and develop simple metrics applicable across disciplines and locations is deeply troubling, and is liable to lead to a sterility of thought and a loss of vision and innovation. As someone who has been fortunate to have received an education, and is still being educated, in several countries, I have benefited greatly from the diversity of viewpoints and values to which I have been exposed. In reflecting on the contribution of the distinct Nordic or Scandinavian approach to information systems outlined above in the past 40 years, one should highlight how unique its contribution has been, and how much richer our world is because of this contribution. While there is a sense in which the scientific approach is seen as universal, there are many aspects of how one carries out ones research in practice, of what questions one asks, of what values underlie the work, which are unique and particular to the place where one is living and working. Thus, as a consequence of the strong social democratic political systems in Scandinavia in the 1960s and 1970s, and the interest in industrial democracy, we saw the flowering of a set of research areas concerning human skill and the role of IT that have come to transform the debate about people and technology the world over. Now, in 2008, one finds these pressures of fitting in to the norm, and of being measured according to criteria that are external to local conditions, are increasingly persistent.

Some years ago, the noted academic James March wrote an insightful piece concerning the nature of academic communities (in this case, organizational studies), and problems and opportunities as a result of language diversity, geographical location and interdisciplinarity (March 2004). He points to both the benefits and potential drawbacks of this differentiation. By having regional fragmentation and differentiation, we can allow for a greater variety of approaches, and a certain level of isolation of ideas and concepts, which can exist and flourish outside the mainstream. He quotes the European organizational theorists Czarniawska and Sevon:

> ...the peripheral position of the Nordic countries in the last half of the twentieth century created ... a distinctive variant nurtured by being peripheral and by the unintendedly benign neglect of the establishment ... Nordic organization scholarship has been remote enough to evade the paradigm police, connected enough to influence the more vulnerable elements of the non-Nordic research community (Czarniawska and Sevon 2003, pp. 414–415).

I believe that the same is true for Nordic research in the area of information systems in the past 50 years. I can remember the shock on encountering the collective resource approach in the early 1980s, and the realization that only in Scandinavia could such an approach have been able to attract government-connected funding. Likewise, I discovered unique forums for discussion existing within the Nordic countries, such as the IRIS conferences, which also had developed a model involving younger and older members of the community in powerful and successful ways to develop and maintain professional identity and a vibrant professional community. In recent years, during my travels in Scandinavia, I have encountered some academics who wish to do away with certain local traditions and develop more standard, international conferences and educational programmes which are similar to what exists in North America. This to me is a shame, as there is real value to some of these local fora, which build on aspects of the local culture and add to the unique quality of the professional community. Whether these pressures are coming from inside or outside the community, we should be careful not to jettison our traditions in some blind faith that what is being done elsewhere is necessarily better. We can all learn from one another, but we should realize that what makes human culture so fascinating is our heterogeneity of customs and practices and, just as we are finally recognizing the importance of biodiversity in our biological world, so too we should celebrate and preserve and develop our cultural diversity, even at the level of professional communities. The value of a culturally-specific understanding, in this instance of computing, has hopefully been clearly shown in this chapter.

REFERENCES

Bannon, L. (1990). A pilgrim's progress: From cognitive science to cooperative design. *AI & Society* 4(4):259–275.

Bansler, J. (1989). Systems development in Scandinavia: Three theoretical schools. *Office: Technology & People* 4(2).

Bjerknes, G., Ehn, P., Kyng, M. (Eds., 1987). *Computers and democracy: A Scandinavian challenge*. Aldershot, UK: Gower.

Bonsiepe, G. (1999). *Interface: An approach to design*. Maastricht: Jan van Eyck Academie.

Budde R., Floyd, C., Keil-Slawik, R., Züllighoven, H. (Eds., 1992). *Software development and reality construction*. Berlin: Springer Verlag.

Bødker, S., Ehn, P., Kyng, M., Kammersgaard, J., Sundblad, Y. (1987). A Utopian experience: On design of powerful computer-based tools for skilled graphics workers. In Bjerknes, G., Ehn, P., Kyng, M. (Eds.) op.cit.

Clement, A., Van den Besselaar, P. (1993). Participatory design projects: A retrospective look. *Communications of the ACM* 36(6).

Czarniawska, B., Sevon, G. (2003). *The northern lights: Organization theory in Scandinavia*. Copenhagen: Copenhagen Business School Press.

Dahlbom, B. (Ed., 1995). *The infological equation: Essays in honour of Börje Langefors*. Gothenburg, Sweden: University of Gothenburg.

Ehn, P. (1988). *Work-oriented design of computer artifacts*. Falköping, Sweden: Arbetslivscentrum/Almqvist & Wiksell International.

Ehn, P. (1998). Manifesto for a Digital Bauhaus. *Digital Creativity* 9(4):207–216.

Ehn, P., Kyng, M. (1984). A tool perspective on design of interactive computers for skilled workers. In Sääksjärvi, M. (Ed.) Proceedings from the Seventh Scandinavian Research Seminar on Systemeering, pp. 211–42. Helsinki: Helsinki Business School.

Ehn, P., Kyng, M. (1987). The collective resource approach to systems design. In Bjerknes, G., Ehn, P., Kyng, M. (Eds.) op. cit.

Floyd, C., Mehl, W-F., Reisin, F-M., Schmidt, G., Wolf, G. (1989). Out of Scandinavia: Alternative approaches to software design and system development. *Human-Computer Interaction* 4:253–350.

Greenbaum, J., Kyng, M. (Eds., 1991). *Design at work: Cooperative design of computer systems*. Hillsdale, NJ: Lawrence Erlbaum Associates.

Howard, R. (1985). Utopia: Where workers craft new technology. *Technological Review*, 88(3):43–49. Massachusetts Institute of Technology.

Kraft, P., Bansler, J. (1992). The collective resource approach: The Scandinavian experience. In Muller, M., Kuhn, S., Meskill, J. (Eds.) PDC'92: Proceedings of the Participatory Design Conference, pp. 127–35. Cambridge, Mass: MIT.

Kyng, M. (1993). Reply to Kraft and Bansler. Electronic mail message circulated to all IRIS 15 participants, August 1993.

March, J.G. (2004). Parochialism in the evolution of a research community: The case of organization studies. *Management and Organization Review* 1(1):5–22.

Norman, D. (1986). Cognitive engineering. In Norman, D., Draper, S. (op. cit), pp. 31–61.

Norman, D., Draper, S. (1986). *User centered system design: New perspectives on human-computer interaction*. Hillsdale, NJ: Lawrence Erlbaum.

Schuler, D., Namioka, A. (1993). *Participatory design: Principles and practices*. Mahwah, NJ: Lawrence Erlbaum.

Whitaker, R., Essler, U., Östberg, O. (1991). Participatory business modeling. Research Report, TULEA 1991:31. Luleå University, Sweden.

Winograd, T. et al. (Eds., 1996). *Bringing design to software*. Reading, MA: Addison Wesley.

78

KIM HALSKOV

TRADITION AND TRANSCENDENCE

KIM HALSKOV
TRADITION AND TRANSCENDENCE

Ehn (1988) originally identified the balance between tradition and transcendence as one of the most important dilemmas in design. On the one hand, when we design, we have to take current qualifications, work organization, and work activities as points of departure; on the other hand, we also want to design something which is innovative, and which can support new activities, or support current activities in new and better ways. Winograd and Flores (1986, p. 7), in their work on a new foundation for design, talk about »tradition« in a particular fundamental sense as the background for the way people act and think beyond a cohesive cultural group or a particular set of practices, and note the particular challenge posed by a tradition being concealed by its obviousness.

A variety of design techniques and approaches which address the tradition aspect are at our disposal, including ethnographic field studies (Blomberg et al. 1993), interview (Patton 1990), and use of video (Brun-Cottan and Wall 1995). Moreover, a vast collection of techniques address the transcendence aspect, but are rooted in the existing tradition or work practices, including the use of scenarios (Carroll 1995), mock-ups (Ehn and Kyng 1991), and prototyping (Bødker and Grønbæk 1991). Additionally, there are a number of design techniques that specifically support innovation, for example Future Workshops (Jungk and Müllert 1987), use of metaphors (Madsen 1994) and interaction relabelling (Djajadiningrat et al. 2000).

Scandinavian research into digital design has predominantly focused on design for the workplace, (e.g. Ehn 1988, Greenbaum and Kyng 1991), but the use of digital technology has been dramatically extended beyond the workplace, into the domestic setting, urban spaces and other kinds of non-workplace settings (see Iversen et al. 2004). Digital technologies have become an integrated part of the critical design movement (Dunne 1999) and informative art (Redström et al. 2000), as well as of art and media (Manovich 2001).

One of the Scandinavian research tradition's contributions has been the tool perspective, which emphasizes human skills and control in the work process (Ehn 1988), and which has emerged as a critique of the system perspective, which views human actions and computer operations as analogous. In addition to the tool and the system perspectives, Kammersgaard (1985) has identified two other perspectives on human-computer interaction, namely the communication partner perspective, which considers humans and computers as equal partners in communication, and the media perspective, which views computers as analogous to other media. These four perspectives reflect the historical development of the use of information technology, as well as differences in theoretical perspectives. In a recent paper, Petersen, Iversen, Krogh, and Ludvigsen (2004) have suggested aesthetic experience as a fifth perspective on interaction, creating an awareness of interaction that »aims for creating involvement, experience, and serendipity« and »promotes bodily experiences as well as complex symbolic interaction« (Petersen et al. 2004, p. 274).

The research on aesthetic experience is part of a wave of research into experience design in the early twenty-first century, a substantial part of which is rooted in pragmatism, including the pragmatic philosophy of Dewey (1934). Based on Dewey and on Bakhtin (1993), McCarthy and Wright (2004) have identified an experience as being composed of four threads. As summarized by Mailund and Halskov (2008), an experience contains a *compositional* thread, upon which an array of elements is set together, creating a coherent whole, and a *sensual* component, that includes the design, texture and overall atmosphere, which are capable of influencing our senses. The third aspect is the *emotional*, which is to say that experiences can affect us emotionally, a factor that often plays a major role in determining the way in which we remember a given experience. Experiences include a fourth and final *spatiotemporal* thread. Both time and space play a part in an experience. For example, time may feel longer or shorter, or we may or may not derive pleasure from visiting a given place, depending on the quality of the experience. According to McCarthy and Wright, these four threads are all elements of an experience; but what, then, are an experience's particular qualities? According to McCarthy and Wright, the characteristic of an experience is that it engages the individual as a participant. It is therefore of central importance that the participant be connected to the experience through active involvement. For example, the person in question may reflect upon or interpret that which has been experienced, or perhaps even tell others about it. Referring back to the definition above, an experience may also have the particular capacity of being able to create active involvement.

In this chapter I will address issues related to tradition and transcendence in the context of digital technology in a non-workplace context, with a particular concern for experience design qualities. The chapter will take the form of a design excavation – with reference to the notion of media archaeology – of a number of experience design cases documented on www.digitalexperience.dk. To lay the groundwork for the analysis, I will start from a media research perspective.

A MEDIA RESEARCH PERSPECTIVE

Bolter and Grusin (1999) have addressed the tradition and transcendence issue from a media research perspective, and have argued that new visual media refashion earlier media, such as painting, film and television, in the same way that older media have always refashioned earlier media, for instance film may been understood as a remediation of theatre. Computer graphics, film, painting, photography, theatre, television and virtual reality are instances of technologies that are all regarded as media, each participating in a network of technical, material, social, cultural, and economic contexts. Photography as a medium consists not only of the pieces of paper or the images on the computer screen that result from the photographic process, but also the social practices of exchanging images on mobile phones, as well as the effect of sharing images on sites like Flickr. As pointed out by Bolter and Grusin (1999, p. 66), when the first general word processors appeared in the 1970s, followed by desktop computers in the early 1980s, computer technology fuelled a whole new set of cultural and social practices, constituting a new medium.

New media are often offered as improvements on older media: for instance, the digital encyclopaedia is like its print precursors, with alphabetized articles consisting of text and images, but with new features, such as video and advanced search facilities.

Remediation is, in more general terms, defined by Bolter and Grusin (1999, p. 45) as the representation of one medium in another, for example, the print version of the newspaper, *USA Today*, resembles the graphical design of a website (Bolter and Grusin 1999, pp. 40). Historically the web version of the newspaper has been a remediation of the print version, which has been subsequently followed by a remediation of the print version, illustrating the general pattern of remediation working in both directions between old and new media (Bolter and Grusin 1999, p. 48).

Bolter and Grusin (1999) distinguish between two complementary strategies – immediacy and hypermediacy – where the former is characterized by a desire to ignore the presence of the medium, whereas the latter is concerned with the medium itself. Immediacy is transparency, in the sense of the medium erasing itself, so to speak, leaving the object represented directly at hand. For instance, when you look at photographs of a person, you see the person, and in this way the new medium is an improvement or reform (Bolter and Grusin 1999, p. 59) of earlier media, such as painting. The concept of immediacy is in this respect related to the classical human-computer interaction ideals of direct manipulation and transparency. For instance, you move about a document on your desktop, and do cut and paste with a concern for the text you are writing without an awareness of the computer acting through the interface (Bødker 1991). The computer is a tool for which the awareness of the user is directed at the task at hand, not at the tool itself. In contrast to immediacy, hypermediacy makes the viewer aware of the medium, for instance by multiplying spaces and media in a process of redefining their relationship (Bolter and Grusin 1999, p. 42f).

Transparency is an ideal when it comes to designing human-computer interaction, and is closely related to the notion of a tool being ready-at-hand as opposed to being present-at-hand, where the user's awareness is directed towards the tool and the user begins to reflect on the tool. Hence, ready-at-hand and present-at-hand are parallel to immediacy and hypermediacy, but whereas a tool being present-at-hand is considered to be problematic, hypermediacy is not, per se.

In the analysis of the computer game *Myst*, Bolter and Grusin (1999, p. 95) observe that the game is a remediation of several other media: three-dimensional graphics, text, film and, not the least, the book. The game's reference to film appears during its cinematic opening credits and the subsequent scene, in which a book appears with a picture of the first scene as in a film.

The Bike Mix Machine.

The Mega Plotter.

EXPERIENCE DESIGN CASES

In this section I present a collection of experience design cases, which, in the subsequent section, will form the platform for the identification of four of the essential factors of transcendence. The following three collections of experience design cases focus on transcendence, with a particular concern for the extraordinary hypermediacy. We begin with three works by digital artist Mads Wahlberg, go on to the remediation of building façades, and end with a discussion of the transcendence of our perception of displays.

THE WORKS OF MADS WAHLBERG. The *Bike Mix Machine*, created by artist Mads Wahlberg, is a Harley Davidson motorcycle that has been converted into a drink mixer. Customers are offered the opportunity to mix their own drinks while sitting on the Bike Mix Machine. When the customer starts up the engine, the bike begins to roll on a belt, which drives a fan blowing air into the machinery and the customer's face. By using the handles, the customer can control the selection of ingredients while at the same time controlling a ball in a pinball machine integrated into the device. By controlling the ball successfully, the customer gets double up on the alcohol; otherwise, he or she only gets a soft drink. The gadget was originally presented in a 6 metre long by 3 metre wide, open container at the Music Festival in Skanderborg, Denmark, in 2006.

The Bike Mix Machine is, first of all, a combination of two familiar artefacts, the motorbike and the drink mixer, both being transformed so as to fit together in an integrated way, to form an innovative kind of drink mixer. Moreover, the motorbike has been translated to a new place, the bar setting. As in many

Retired robots from Pressalit, ready for their third age.

other works by Mads Wahlberg, scale also adds to the uniqueness of the Bike Mix Machine. The scale-related strategy has also been applied in the case of the Mega Plotter.

The *Mega Plotter* was an interactive art installation produced for the 2005 Skanderborg Music Festival. Festival attendees were able to control the plotter by using their mobile phones to dial a designated number, then using the phone's keypad to control colour, and the movements of a set of industrial paint spray guns.

The Mega Plotter is thus a transformation of the traditional plotter technology combined with mobile phone interaction.

Refrigerator Petanque is a work in progress by Mads Wahlberg, and is based on trashed industrial robots from the Danish toilet seat manufacturer, Pressalit®.

Refrigerator Petanque is a transformation of the classical game of petanque, but rather than throwing metal balls as close as possible to the piglet, the industrial robots will be throwing regular sized refrigerators at small minibar refrigerators. According to Mads Wahlberg »Refrigerator Petanque is indeed a nice way for the Pressalit robots to spend their retirement after having lifted toilet seats for more than 15 years.«

REMEDIATION OF BUILDING FAÇADES. The façade of buildings has, during recent years, become a new medium for artistic expression, informative art, entertainment, as well as company and brand communication. The term *Media façades* have become the general term for incorporating displays that are an integrated part of a building façade (ag4 2006).

The Berlin-based design firm ART+COM has developed an installation called *Duality*, which is part of a building complex at the exit of the Osaki metro station in Tokyo. As pedestrians leave the metro station, ripples of light emerge in a 6 x 6 metre LED pane; moreover the ripples extend into the water. As is the case with *USA Today*, mentioned in the introduction, here too, remediation works in both directions between old and new media: the physical ripples become virtual, which in turn interferes with the physical water ripples.

Body Movies – Relational Architecture 6 is an installation by artist Rafael Lozano-Hemmer, which was set up in Ars Electronica Festival, Hauptplatz, Linz, Austria in 2002, but originally commissioned by V2_Organisatie for Rotterdam Cultural Capital of Europe 2001 (see Bullivant 2006). The installation consists of projections on the façade of a large building, where the projections display more than 1000 portraits of people from all over the world. Two powerful 7000-watt light sources are positioned on the ground in front of the façade, bathing the projections in an intense light, thus rendering the portraits invisible. When passers-by place themselves between the light sources and the façade, their shadows reveal the portraits. The thinking behind the installation was that the passers-by would collaborate in revealing all the images, thereby bringing forth the display of a number of new portraits. It turned out, however, that Body Movies encouraged passers-by to play with each other's shadows instead (see Mailund and Halskov 2008). The installation was inspired by

Above: Duality. Below: Body Movies.

the Dutch painter Samuel van Hoogstraten, who lived from 1627–1678, and emphasizes the performative role of the observer.

Blinkenlights was an installation at an office building in Berlin's Alexanderplatz, where the upper eight floors were transformed into an 18 x 8 pixel monochrome display, by having an individually controlled lamp behind each of the 144 windows. Thus, Blinkenlights was a low resolution display used for displaying animations, developed using a custom-designed programme, Blinkenpaint, which could be submitted to a server and then later activated by one's mobile phone. Another particularly popular option was that of playing the classic game of Pong on the façade, using the keypads of two mobile phones.

TRANSCENDING OUR PERCEPTION OF DISPLAYS. Computer displays have traditionally been based on cathode ray tube and liquid crystal technologies, but experiments in art and technology have transcended our conventional understanding of a display. The fundamental quality of a display is a set of points organized as matrix, which may assume a range of visual values, for example, colours or shades of grey. But what forms can the individual pixels take? Among the answers, we find the use of air, water, and fire!

The Bubble Screen, created by Beta Tank, is a display composed of a tank of highly viscous liquid, with pixels made of individual air bubbles floating up from the bottom. The flow of air bubbles is controlled by a row of pumps that release them in a manner that makes it possible to create moving text and images which float from the bottom of the tank. A complementary strategy has been applied by SphericalRobots, which has created the 128 pixel-wide display, *Bitfall*, consisting of falling water droplets released from nozzles equipped with magnetic valves. The release of water droplets is computer controlled, enabling the creation of falling images or text. The Infernoptix *Digital Pyrotechnic Matrix* is yet another low-resolution display, of 12 x 7 pixels, in which each pixel – as the name suggests – consists of a burst of fire. The display works in different modes, including a text mode, where text may be displayed as on a scrolling text screen over which letters sweep. As opposed to the two other displays, Infernoptix actually emits light, just like a conventional CRT or LED display.

Blinkenlights. Copyright: Harald & Erhard Fotografie.

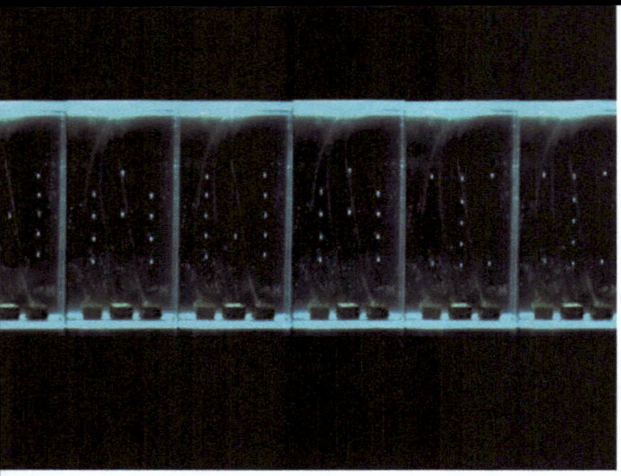

The Bubble Screen.

Circle Mirror.

Several artists, including Daniel Rozin, have been exploring the use of physical materials to create displays in which each pixel is mechanical unit, as in the case of the *Circle Mirror*. The Circle Mirror consists of 900 overlapping and individually controlled discs which have a grey-scale pattern ranging from white to solid black printed on them. Mechanically turning the disc changes the visible part of the circle, thereby changing the shade of the pixel. Circle Mirror was created as an art installation, and included a video camera so that when a person approached the mirror, he or she was reflected in it. Daniel Rozin has created several kinds of mirrors, including a *Trash Mirror*, with individual pixels made from trash collected in New York City streets.

Spoke POV is a do-it-yourself kit developed by SQUID Labs for making displays integrated into bicycle wheels. The display consists of a row of LEDs on a board mounted on one of the spokes, together with sensors, which detect when the board passes magnets mounted on the frame. BMP files imported to the board are displayed on the wheel while bicycling.

Making 3D displays has, for many years, been a challenge not only for engineers, but also for artists. *Electric moOns* is innovative kind of display, consisting of 100 balloons in a three-dimensional grid. Each balloon is attached to a string at a set of fixed (x, y) coordinates, but the string is attached to a motor, enabling the control of the position of the balloon in the z dimension, making each one a 3D pixel. Clearly, we are not talking about a general purpose dis-

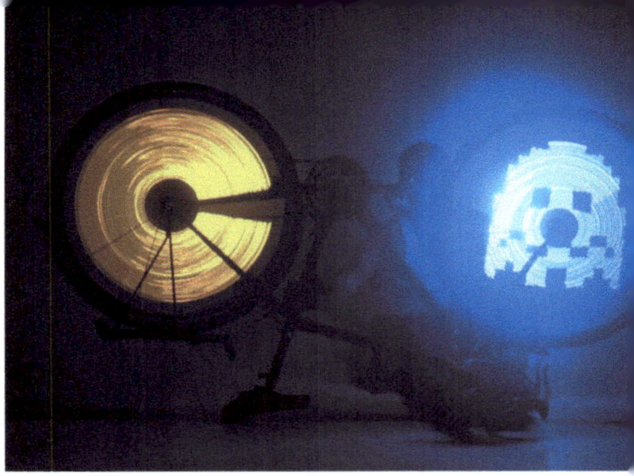

Below: *Electric moOns.*

Above: *Spoke POV.* Below: *SnOil.*

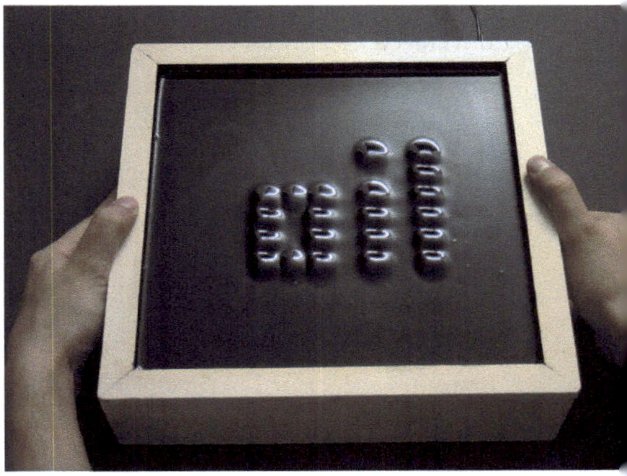

play, but an art installation, which has been exhibited at numerous festival and events.

SnOil is yet another 3D display, in this case based on ferrofluid, which is a mixture that reacts to a magnetic field. Using focused magnetic fields in a 12 x 12 grid makes it possible to control the appearance and disappearance of small bubbles or bumps in a basin filled with ferrofluid.

ELEMENTS OF TRANSCENDENCE

Most, if not all designs are, in one way or another, related to something pre-existing, and in this sense build on a given tradition, while at the same time transcending current practice. Hence, in order to understand the nature of tradition and transcendence, one needs to come to grips with how the new artefacts relate to earlier artefacts. The combination of previously unrelated elements, the transfer of technology to a new context, the use of new materials and extreme scale, are among the essential factors of transcendence.

COMBINATION. Many researchers and practitioners have argued that the combination of unrelated elements is a fundamental component in innovation. Petre (2004), quoting Langrish (1985), points out that much of creativity consists of combining existing ideas in new ways, and several of the innovation techniques developed by de Bono (1993) have at their core the combining of unrelated elements, for instance *random input*, (de Bono 1993, p. 177), which applies the selection of a randomly chosen word as a strategy for stimulating innovation. As noted earlier, The Bike Mix Machine is a combination of two familiar artefacts, the motorbike and the drink mixer, each being transformed to fit together so that, in an integrated way, they form an innovative kind of drink mixer. Moreover, the element of a pinball machine has been integrated into the device. Likewise, the Mega Plotter is a combination of two everyday objects: the plotter, and the mobile phone as an interaction device. The extraordinary effect of Duality is undoubtedly due to the combination of the virtual and the physical ripples.

NEW CONTEXT. The transfer of technology to a new context is one of the innovation strategies identified by Petre (2004) in her study of 12 engineering consultancies. As an example, she mentions the transfer of technology from unrelated fields, such as, applying robotics to medical products. Refrigerator Petanque is a somewhat more radical case of transferring robotics from an industrial context to one of play, and The Bike Mix Machine brings the bike from the road into the bar setting. Media facades are becoming increasingly common, but are also transcending our understanding of the façades of buildings, by bringing displays into a new context. Kelley (2001) uses the term cross-pollination, which in essence is about sparking innovation by bringing solutions from one domain to another, or by using a materials in a new context.

MATERIALS. Beylerian, Caniato, Dent and Quinn (2007) have compiled a collection of more than 400 smart substances, intelligent interfaces and sensory surfaces, and argue that new materials are redefining the world in which we live. The transcendence of our everyday life as we know it, from pervasive computing and ubiquitous computing (Weiser 1991), is not only a matter of computers being smaller and integrated in our physical environment, but also a result of the emergence of new materials. Duality and most of the displays introduced earlier apply ordinary materials like water, fire, and air, but in a transcendent way, whereas SnOil is made possible by a specific material, ferrofluid. Both Circle Mirror and Trash Mirror use ordinary materials, but for a new purpose.

SCALE. Scale is a significant transcending factor, which also creates opportunities for bodily interaction. Making shadow images is a common activity, but the large-scale shadows of Body Movies are definitely a transcending factor. Low resolution, together with large scale, is a recurrent characteristic of many of the displays, most notably in the case of Electric MoOns, which also may be seen as a fairly natural way of rendering 3D models.

IMPLICATIONS FOR DESIGN PROCESSES

The combination of unrelated elements, and the use of new kinds of technologies and materials are two of the key components of Inspiration Card Workshops, originally introduced by Halskov and Dalsgård (2006, 2007). An Inspiration Card Workshop is primarily used in the early stages of a design process to create design concepts that start from Technology Cards and Domain Cards. A Technology Card represents either a specific technology (e.g. ferrofluid) or an application of one or more technologies (e.g. The Bike Mix Machine). Domain Cards represent information about the domains for which we design, in terms of people, location, or aspects of the context. Technology Cards may be generated from the designers' background knowledge, or from a knowledge pool such as www.digitalexperience.dk. The Domain Cards may be generated by the designers, based on studies of the domain, or by users of the design domain. The technology cards are intended to spark innovation and to transcend the tradition current practice represented by domain cards.

The workshop itself commences with a presentation of the selected Technology and Domain Cards, followed by a phase in which the participants combine the cards on poster-sized pieces of cardboard in order to capture design concepts.

Virtual video prototyping uses virtual studio technology, with its unique potential for visualizing digital 3D objects and environments, along with physical objects, as an environment for design visualization (Halskov and Nielsen 2006). Virtual video prototyping is related to other ways of using video to create design scenarios (e.g. Mackay et al. 2000), but with the difference that, in the case of virtual video prototyping, part of the context of use or some of the future technology includes digital 3D objects. Virtual video prototyping has proved productive for testing and generating ideas and is particularly suited to addressing spatial issues, including those of scale.

In conclusion, addressing the concern for tradition and transcendence have been the starting point for this chapter. Scandinavian research into digital design has predominantly focused on transcendence and been rooted in a concern for the current work practice. This chapter has, in particular, challenged the understanding of transcendence, but primarily in the context of experience design in a non-workplace context. The combination of previously unrelated elements, the transfer of technology to a new context, the use of new materials and extreme scale, have been identified as four of the essential factors of transcendence. The concluding section indicates way of bringing these key factors into play.

ACKNOWLEDGMENT

This research has been funded by the Danish Council for Strategic Research under grant number 2128-07-0011.

REFERENCES

ag4 (2006). *Media Facades*. Cologne: daab.

Bakhtin, M. (1993). *Towards a philosophy of the arts*. Austin, TX: University of Texas Press.

Beylerian, G., Caniato, M., Dent, A., Quinn, B. (2007). *Ultra materials: How materials innovation is changing the world*. New York, NY: Thames & Hudson.

Inspiration Card Workshop.

Blomberg, J., Giacomi, J., Mosher, A., Swenton-Wall, P. (1993). Ethnographic field methods and their relation to design. In Schuler, D., Namioka, A. (Eds.), *Participatory design: Principles and practices*, pp. 123–155. Hillsdale, NJ: Lawrence Earlbaum Associates.

Bullivant, L. (2006). *Responsive environments: Architecture, art and design.* London: V&A Publications.

Bødker, S., Grønbæk, K. (1991). Design in action: From prototyping by demonstration to cooperative prototyping. In Greenbaum, J., Kyng, M. (Eds.), op. cit.

Bødker, S. (1991). *Through the interface: A human activity approach to user interface design.* Hillsdale, NJ: Lawrence Erlbaum Associates.

Bolter, J.D., Grusin, R. (1999). *Remediation: Understanding new media*. Cambridge, MA: MIT Press.

Brun-Cottan, F., Wall, P. (1995). Using video to re-present the user. *Communications of the ACM* 38(5):61–71.

Carroll, J. (Ed., 1995). *Scenario-based design: Envisioning work and technology in system development*. New York, NY: John Wiley and Sons.

Dalsgård, P., Halskov, K. (2006). Real life experiences with Experience Design. Proc. NordiCHI 2006, pp. 331–340.

De Bono, E. (1993). *Serious creativity*. New York, NY: HarperCollins Publisher.

Dewey, J. (1934). *Art as experience*. Carbondale, IL: Southern Illinois University press, reprinted in 1987.

Djajadiningrat, J.P., Gaver, W.W. & Frens, J.W. (2000). Interaction relabelling and extreme characters: Methods for exploring aesthetic interaction. Proc. DIS 2000, pp. 66–71. Brooklyn, NY: ACM Press.

Dunne, A. (1999). *Hertzian tales: Electronic products, aesthetic experience and critical design*. London: Royal College of Art.

Ehn, P., Kyng, M. (1991). Cardboard computers: Mocking-it-up or hands-on the future. In Greenbaum, J., Kyng, M. (Eds.), op. cit.

Ehn, P. (1988). *Work-oriented design of computer artifacts*. Stockholm: Arbetslivscentrum.

Greenbaum, J., Kyng, M. (Eds., 1991). *Design at work: Cooperative design of computer systems*. Hillsdale, NJ: Lawrence Erlbaum Associates.

Halskov, K., Dalsgård, P. (2006). Inspiration Card workshops. Proc. DIS 2006, pp. 2–11.

Halskov, K., Dalsgård, P. (2007). The emergence of ideas: The interplay between sources of inspiration and emerging design concepts. *CoDesign* 3(4):185–211.

Halskov, K., Nielsen, R. (2006). Virtual video prototyping. *Human-Computer Interaction* 21:199–233.

Iversen, O. S., Kanstrup, A. M., Petersen, M. G. (2004). A visit to the »new Utopia«: Revitalizing democracy, emancipation and quality in co-operative design. Proc. NordiCHI 2006, pp. 171–179. New York, NY: ACM.

Jungk, R., Müllert, N. (1987). *Future Workshops: How to create desirable futures*. London: Institute for Social Inventions.

Kammersgaard, J. (1985). Four different perspectives on human-computer interaction. DAIMI PB 203. Århus, Denmark: Department of Computer Science, University of Aarhus.

Kelley, T. (2001). *The art of innovation*. New York, NY: Random House Inc.

Langrish, J. (1985). *Innovation management: The role of creativity*. Manchester, UK: Institute of Advanced Studies, Manchester Polytechnic.

Mackay, W., Ratzer, A., Janecek, P. (2000). Video artifacts for design: Bridging the gap between abstraction and detail. Proc. DIS 2000, pp. 63–69. New York, NY: ACM Press.

Madsen, K.H. (1994). A guide to metaphorical design. *Communications of the ACM* 37(12):57–62.

Mailund, L., Halskov, K. (2008). Designing marketing experience. Proc. DIS 2008, pp. 222–229. New York, NY: ACM Press.

Manovich, L. (2001). *The language of new media*. Cambridge, MA: MIT Press.

McCarthy, J., Wright, P. (2004). *Technology as experience*. Cambridge, MA: MIT Press.

Patton, Q. M. (1990). *Qualitative evaluation and research methods*. Newbury Park, CA: Sage Publications.

Petersen, M.G., Iversen, O.S., Krogh, P., Ludvigsen, M. (2004). Aesthetic interaction. Proc. DIS 2004, pp. 269–276. New York, NY: ACM Press.

Petre, M. (2004). How expert engineering teams use disciplines of innovation. *Design Studies* 25(5):478–222.

Redström, J., Skog, T., Hallnäs, L. (2000). Informative art: using amplified artworks as information displays. Proceedings of DARE 2000, pp. 103–114. New York, NY: ACM.

Weiser, M. (1991). The computer for the 21st century. *Scientific American* 265(3):94–104.

Winograd, T., Flores, F. (1986). *Understanding computers and cognition: A new foundation for design.* Norwood, NJ: Ablex Corporation.

MARGOT BRERETON

DESIGNING FROM SOMEWHERE

– A LOCATED, RELATIONAL AND TRANSFORMATIVE VIEW OF DESIGN

MARGOT BRERETON
DESIGNING FROM SOMEWHERE
– A LOCATED, RELATIONAL AND TRANSFORMATIVE VIEW OF DESIGN

In his 1998 article, *Manifesto for a Digital Bauhaus*, Pelle Ehn introduced a vision for a program of research where the technological advances of the digital revolution would be challenged by the endeavour of expressing fundamental human conditions – values, democracy, ethics, art and aesthetic ideals (Ehn 1998). He drew upon the history of the Enlightenment and great projects seeking to unite the two sides of the Enlightenment such as the Bauhaus in order to motivate not only the cause of combining these endeavours but also to identify the challenges – that the hard and soft cultures had repeatedly demonstrated throughout history an inability to communicate.

Using the original Bauhaus movement as a case in point, Ehn describes how although a major aim of the project was to unify art and modern technology in order to create architecture and design for the modern free man and woman:

> it was at the same time diminished to a program of »hard« regular geometric white shapes in steel glass and reinforced concrete under the dictum »architecture or revolution« with the corollary that a revolution could only be avoided if the modern architects and designers were given the freedom and power to change the world. The social engagement in this version of the Bauhaus had been transformed to anti-democratic professional elitism. (Ehn 1998)

Pelle Ehn noted with caution the dialectical history of modern society, »where all development also seems to be pregnant with its opposite.« And yet he foresaw that members of the new digital generation, designing tools to explore virtual and material new worlds, might have the potential to transcend this inability of communication between hard and soft and to realize both technical and human ideals together. Design today faces the enduring challenge of how to bridge the development of technology with the expression of human ideals, not least such that people do not become enslaved to their technologies.

This chapter reflects upon the challenge of realizing an IT design to help support the human aspirations of a residential community. It is concerned with the relationships between designers, the community for whom the design is intended and the development of the design over time, or in Ehn's words, »the dialectics of tradition and transcendence – that is what design is all about.« (Ehn 1988). I pay particular attention to relationships between design and use – the design process embodies aspirations of technology for human experience and use reflects the reality of that experience.

Within the last three decades, a growing movement of people have developed design practices that have tried to incorporate the perspective of the people for whom the design is intended, often referred to as »the user«, into the design process. This movement can be seen in the light of moves since the Enlightenment to bridge human and technical ideals. While business has recognized the value of focusing on »users«, the prevailing view of design of technology coming from industry continues to see designers as the creator of technologies and the users as its recipients in a rather straightforward fashion. Suchman has described this as a designer/user opposition, an oversimplification that masks relevant social relations that cross between design and use (Suchman 2002). It is a reflection of the communication difficulty between hard and soft cultures that Ehn speaks of when relations are oversimplified and then are inherently misunderstood. One example of this might be when proxies for »the user« such as personas are employed in the design process. If taken in isolation, they can then contribute to simplifying and distancing the »user« from the designer.

Ironically, a supposed focus on »users« can present an excuse to maintain a focus on the designed object. The term »user« itself is an instrumentalist one. Many researchers have lamented their use of the term, but then continue to use it because it is convenient. The term »user« frames a person in terms of their relationship to a designed object, as the one who »uses« it. But it also limits and simplifies our consideration of a person to their role of use, and possibly their use only one particular time, such as during a product use evaluation.

Hales (1994), also cited in Suchman's argument, elaborates on the significant role that people actually undertake when they engage with technology in order to make it work. Hales argues that the »user« plays a much larger role and that there is a larger relationship between design and use than is often recognised in the making of technologies:

> Users »construct« technology; they do this both symbolically, in their »reading« of artefacts, and literally, in the articulation work that is essential before a concrete configuration of artefacts (as distinct from the generic system-products that emerge from usability labs in Silicon Valley) can serve as an adequate day-by-day supporting structure for a live practice.
> (ibid, p. 162)

In order to integrate technologies into their practices, people spend time understanding and configuring them. They in turn transform their practices through the adoption and creative use of technologies.

Looking from the perspective of the working relations that make up the design and use of technical systems, Suchman finds that in the prevailing view of technology production anonymous and unlocatable designers of technology are delivering technological solutions to equally decontextualized and consequently unlocatable users. The relations between designer and user are sparse. Suchman offers an alternative approach shifting from a view of design as the creation of discrete devices, or even networks of devices, to a view of systems development as entry into the networks of working relations – including both contests and alliances – that make technical systems possible. She argues for a shift from the claim of objective knowledge in an asituated master perspective »that bases its claims to objectivity in the closure of controversy, to multiple, located, partial perspectives that find their objective character through ongoing processes of debate.« Suchman's proposed approach recognizes the hidden work, the configuration work, the myriad boundary crossings between development and use and the meeting of different partial knowledges that are required to construct coherent technologies and put them into use. A crucial aspect of this alternative reconceptualization is that design work becomes located; »ways of being nowhere while claiming to see comprehensively« are replaced with »views from somewhere« (Haraway 1991, see also Star 1991). Suchman terms this located and relational view *located accountability.*

If, instead of viewing people as »users«, we consider how people encounter, use and incorporate designed artifacts into their life worlds, then we might instead insist on calling them people or practitioners and rethink designed objects on their terms. We might think of the object »as used«, as seen from the perspective of a person within their practices and insist on referring to people and »objects as used«, rather than to objects and their »users.«

This more holistic view of the people and their practices must in turn be reconciled with the need for designers and engineers to make detailed excursions into the technological object world (Bucciarelli 1994). Designers imagine and develop possible products through reference to all manner of their material practices and technical repertoires combined with their lived experiences and understandings of culture. The designer must be free to explore technologies and what they might become in an imagined view of people's future practices, both serious and playful. The difficulty seems to be in maintaining a rich set of relationships and discourse to link these two views.

A practice of design that transcends and fully embraces both the ethnographic human centred view and the creative synthesis view is called for. And that view must embrace a multitude of relationships between the design and the people for whom the design is intended, if it hopes to meet both technical and human aspirations.

I turn now to exploring this view of design as entry into the network of relations that make technical systems possible by drawing upon a case study of the design of community communications. This view of design implicitly recognizes design as intervention linking the before and after. Use is ongoing and design develops over time. I consider, in particular, implications for design practice and design methods.

AN EMBEDDED RESEARCH APPROACH

As a case study to motivate discussion of design relationships I refer to an ongoing project in my own neighourhood that aims to better support community communications through ICT interventions. I call the method embedded research, because I live there and am embedded within the community. The embedded research approach draws strongly on the tradition of Participatory Design (Greenbaum and Kyng 1991), which takes both an ethical and pragmatic stance that those people affected by a design outcome ought to be included in the process of design. It also draws on the more recent movement of Co-design, whose roots lie in Participatory Design and in the field of Computer Supported Co-operative Work (CSCW), which emphasises the close understanding of the situated social practices of users in informing the design of new systems (see e.g. Crabtree 2003). The embedded approach also emphasizes dwelling with the design over time and iterating and modifying the design in response community feedback and use. It draws upon a Rapid Agile Iterative Design approach used to develop Social software (Heyer et al. 2008) that has its roots in both agile software development methods, design synthesis and understanding the situated social practices of users. Using this method, a basic prototype is deployed and then iterated by examining use and obtaining ideas and feedback from its user community. The prototype grows as it supports a growing community network that is using the prototype. The kinds of user issues faced shifts as the prototyped is developed and the user community grows.

Finally, our design practice also engages in design concept development and prototyping in the broader tradition of design schools, having had visual artists, architects and product designers engaged. It is an integrative approach drawing upon a number of design traditions each of which provides a countering view to the others.

BEING EMBEDDED. Living in a community enables one to participate legitimately in that community in a myriad of ways. With children at the local school and in local clubs, by participating in local organisations and having local friendships, one is embedded into the cultures, practices and life of a community from school drop offs and local shopping, to Tupperware parties, fundraisers and birthday parties. While understanding can be gained through interviews, and we have taken this approach by interviewing community leaders, much of an understanding of a community comes from natural acts of daily participation and conversation.

I have undertaken this project with the collaboration of several colleagues, only one other of whom lives in the community. However other colleagues have spent considerable time there and without them the research would not have been possible. In this account I take a personal view as resident and design researcher.

ENTRY INTO THE NETWORK OF WORKING RELATIONS

I took a deliberate decision to begin a research project at home. I was motivated by experiences in my home community. Defamiliarising the home environment and understanding it from other viewpoints seemed a more responsible approach than inflicting our research on a disadvantaged community that we might be aiming to help, but could disappoint and from whom we might eventually withdraw. A classic problem for designers is to appreciate the design from the point of view of others, so designing for ones own community from one's own experiences therein has potential pitfalls. But I sought out other views through participation within the community and, aware of the pitfalls, resolved to see this as one of many design relationships that needs to be acknowledged and to engage researchers external to the community to also offer different views.

RESEARCH CONTEXT AND THE LOCAL COMMUNITY VIEW. The research focused on an outer suburb of the City of Brisbane, which is experiencing both the opportunities and the challenges of growth. Opportunities for business are expanding, roads are becoming more crowded, new housing estates are springing up and large residential blocks are being subdivided into smaller ones. The feel of the place is changing and for a long time the community sought to influence the character of the development taking place though petitioning the council on various developments and making concerted community responses to development applications through standard council processes. There is a desire to create a stronger social fabric within the community, to raise money for a community hall, to welcome new residents, to introduce new residents to local businesses and to provide opportunities for social engagement. However the recent issue that most stirred the community to action was a proposal by the Federal government to route a motorway through the bottom corner of the peninsular. This move was a call to action for a segment of the community that met to understand the motivations for the proposal and to develop strategies to represent local views on the issue.

RESEARCH FROM THE DESIGN INTERVENTION PERSPECTIVE. As a resident I became interested in how a community might have better means to understand, visualise and have a say in matters affecting their local places. As a researcher I was interested in how to craft global communication technologies to meet local needs and what these technologies might look like from a place-based community perspective.

There seems to be great potential for personal, public and mobile computing devices to support timely communication, creative expression and information sharing in place-based communities. Yet although the Internet is widely used for global virtual communities of interest, place-based use of the Internet seems under explored. The enduring methods of communication in our local communities are printed local newspapers that retain editorial control of contributions, physical notice boards, face-to-face meetings and contact via phone, flyers, newsletters and email. It seems likely that we do not yet sufficiently understand the nature, motivations, and interaction design needed in place-based communities in order to establish sustainable and dense webs of communication.

THREE VIEWS OF A DESIGN RESEARCH PROJECT

I reflect on the research from three perspectives, an internal view, an external view and an iterative view over time. The first approach was a participatory design approach in the tradition of community informatics, working with a community organisation in order to explore how they can take a pro-active role in engaging IT to meet their own needs. I refer to this as an *internal* view of the workings of part of the community. The second approach engaged researchers external to the project to construct a broader model of community, to probe the model and to develop design concepts for fostering community. I refer to this as an *external* view. The third approach (ongoing) is an iterative approach in which a prototype has been deployed in a community and is iterated as our understanding of its use or lack thereof grows. I refer to this as an *iterative* view.

SUPPORTING COMMUNICATIONS OF A COMMUNITY ASSOCIATION – AN INTERNAL VIEW OF COMMUNITY. The first approach to supporting community communication involved supporting the local community association. It is reported in Redhead and Brereton (2006). The issues of the day, and culture of the time, were influential in how we approached the research. The local community association had recently formed with a general mandate to improve the well being of residents in the area and in a bid to build social capital. Soon after it formed, participation grew due to the proposal to build a motorway that threatened the way of life in the suburb i.e. the common enemy model. I attended community association meetings, and joined and contributed to the community email list. It was a very effective association that attracted 1200 people to one meeting and consulted with all local state and federal politicians in the area.

Our design approach here was simply to offer to support the immediate needs of the association. The idea was to take a bootstrapping approach and to see where it might lead. The community association used face to face meetings, phone contact and a private email list of people who have attended the meetings and added their name to the list as its primary means of communication. With a need to communicate about the developments in the area we found that people who were motivated to take action largely participated in *private-strategic activity* (Redhead and Brereton, 2006). Ideas were formulated in private communications among trusted members. People used individually tailored email lists to very familiar contacts, rather than to the formal groups lists. Ideas were emailed to the wider association only once they had been tried out on trusted friends. When ready to engage the broader community, public meetings were held, with participation solicited though flyers.

At the request of the community association, we set up a local website (Bartlett, 2006) in order to allow the association to provide information to the community and to provide a shared repository for local documents. The site was designed so that anybody could upload documents to the site and committee members could post their own updates to the site. Members of the association used it for this purpose. We envisaged that by starting the design in this way we might grow the site to meet other community needs. Although a few other issues were aired to the site, use subsided as interest in the community association waned when the motorway topic went dormant. Without the community association meeting regularly and referring to the site, the website was out of sight and out of mind. The design as used was no longer relevant to the lifeworlds of the people.

Interviews with community leaders identified that long-term work on community projects is hard to sustain. Community solutions are often difficult to achieve, attracting funding requires sustained effort and many community leaders burn out (Redhead and Brereton 2006). However, within the longer dynamic of communities developing and families growing and moving in and out of the area, people still go about their daily activities. This prompted us to reflect on the various ways in which people participate in a community, aside from being involved in recognised associations. It led us to consider how to support community communications around day-to-day issues rather than only on large issues, in part in order to build a better fabric for when large issues arise. It also led us to consider how we might appropriate public space with community information so that it was seen at a glance in the community rather than being hidden away in the web.

COMMUNITY COMMUNICATION ABOUT THE DAY TO DAY – AN EXTERNAL VIEW. Although participating in a community practice informs design, it is necessary to develop representations in order to crystallize understanding and to have representational tools to think with. I am indebted to my colleague Jacob Buur, who was visiting on sabbatical and who, through a number of conversations, developed what we considered to be an informal ethnography or user experience model of living in the local area in Outer Brisbane. The model was crystallized in a diagram, which we challenged in a workshop among design researchers. Buur was working on a theory of how ethnographic representations could be used as a form of design provocation (Buur and Sitorus 2007) and developed the model as a succinct representation and provocation that could reveal our understanding of community to researchers and provoke them to challenge it.

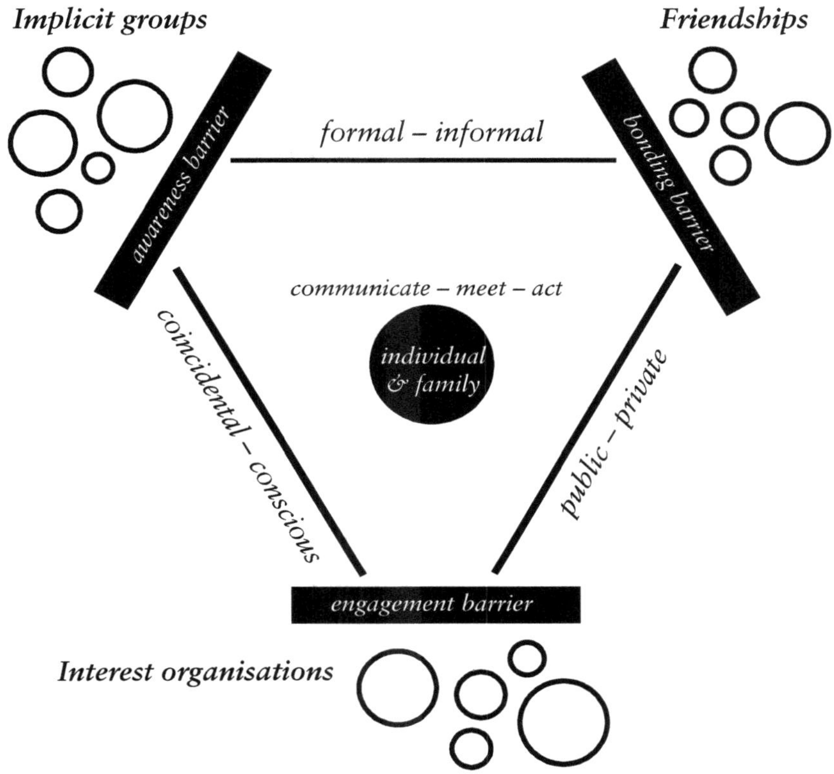

Figure 1. Belonging to Local Community. Negotiating three kinds of barriers to become part of social groups and maintain relationships.

- *Friendships are private and informal. In order to build friendships one must build bonds through shared conversations, activities, openness, and intimacy and through being supportive. Building friendships thus requires negotiating a Bonding Barrier.*
- *Implicit Groups are groups that you »automatically« become a member of by virtue of your activities. If your children go to the local school, for instance, you automatically become a member of a group of class parents. All it takes to participate is to show up. And to show up requires negotiating only an Awareness Barrier.*
- *Interest Organisations further a particular cause in the community. They include the Parents and Citizens Association, the Creek Catchment group etc. Participation is a conscious choice that requires personal engagement and enduring commitment, in effect to overcome the Engagement Barrier.*

The essence of the model was that people participate in the local community through being part of a myriad of groups, for instance taking children to school, shopping locally, volunteering at the school tuck shop, raising money for the school through the school Parents and Citizens Association, joining local bush care groups etc. The social groups vary in that they are big or small, open or closed, private or public etc. Three groupings were identified: Friendship Groups, Implicit Groups and Interest Organisations. To be a member or associated with a group requires some level of engagement and the groupings in the model are distinguished by the kind of effort that it takes to be included. We began to consider this effort as a form of »barrier« that people need to negotiate in order to belong, as described in Figure 1. Belonging to groups is one of the ways in which you establish and maintain social identity: It is both a question of how you experience your own role, and how others see you. Belonging builds on reciprocity: A balance between what you give and what you take.

THE DIALECTIC BETWEEN FIELD STUDIES AND DESIGN. The model of Community presented above was used as a provocation in a design workshop among researchers. It was presented in the context of a presentation showing various interactions in the suburb, a walk around the suburb and participants' knowledge of living in their own Brisbane communities. Part of the group explored the notion of relation building in the community – and how IT might support that. Another part worked to re-write the »theory« leading to a number of questions about if the theory was »right«: Can the barriers move? Shouldn't they be bridges? Which way do newcomers enter into the community? And how does the river serve as a barrier surrounding the community preventing relations with communities nearby. Should our design work to promote those cross community links instead?

The researchers' challenge to the field study model opened up the design inquiry to views that we either hadn't considered or were on the periphery of our thinking. The group undertook design explorations to explore how to foster community. This resulted in a series of mock up devices to help one initiate and keep track of personal friendships and an Information Pond, to encourage loitering in the local shopping centre (Figure 2) among other concepts.

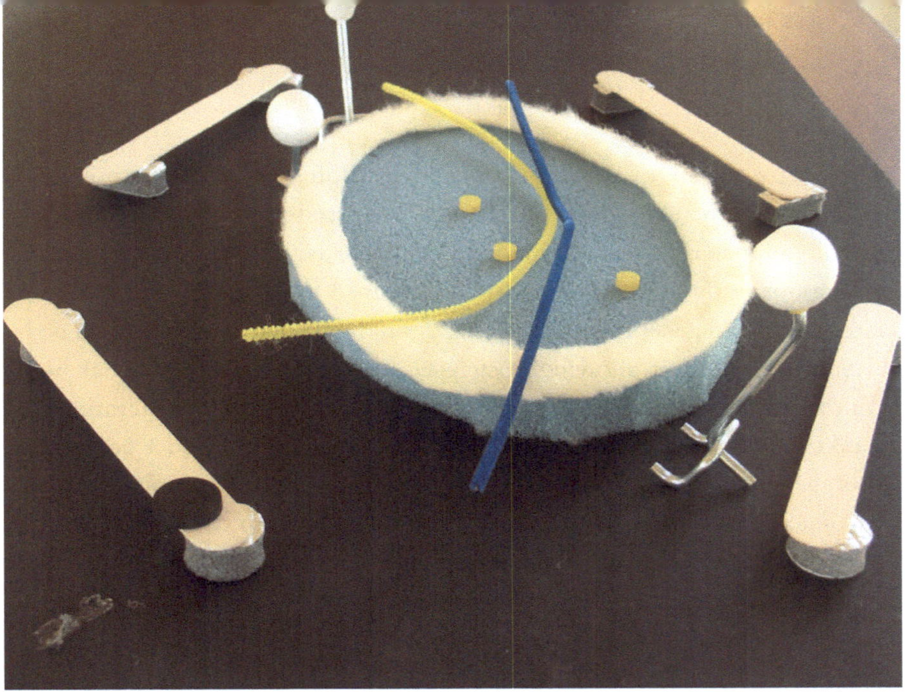

Figure 2. The Information Pond is an installation that encourages loitering in the shopping centre. People can submit information in a very easy manner for others to see. The information becomes visible for people who approach the pond.

DESIGN PROPOSALS AS A COUNTERPOINT TO ONE ANOTHER. The quality of ideas from IT researchers and designers in a workshop had quite a different character to those that come from seeking directly to support community needs. Design within the context of community action tends to focus on immediate needs such as websites. (One might argue that the latter approach is not really design at all, but I would argue that it at least sits at one end of the spectrum of design.) Workshops on how to better support a sense of place, which have been held in our area by community artists employed by Council, have led to a broader suite of achievable ideas, such as community festivals, community documentaries, multimedia representations of stories of place, signage to interesting places, playgrounds and other proposals for aspects of built environment. Due to the composition of our workshop, which consisted of IT and design researchers, it focused more upon utilizing technologies and the built environment in playful and experiential ways, leading to proposals for innovative tangible IT installations such as the information pond.

Generating a variety of concepts provided a helpful set of counterpoints for thinking about the chosen design strategy. This strategy was tempered by the repertoire of materials and technologies that were available to us and by working relations in the local community. We planned to establish a digital notice board in the local general store, drawing upon the familiar metaphor of a physical notice board, but allowing posting either from a web browser at home or in the general store. This digital prototype would allow easy iteration and rethinking. As a design research project, in contrast to a product design, this prototype would allow exploration of aspects of community posting and reading in a communal public space. It was not constrained to the form of a pond, although it was constrained to the less interesting, more readily available form of a screen! However, in time it would possibly lead to more permanent installations that take on a more interesting tangible form and structure more interesting social participation such as that proposed in the pond. Importantly when considering the use of the screen, the pond is a useful counterpoint for thinking about how the form of the screen affects its use.

AN ITERATIVE DESIGN APPROACH – BUILDING RELATIONS, LEARNING ABOUT USE AND ITERATING THE DESIGN. The digital notice-board (Redhead et al. 2007) has been designed and developed using an iterative participatory approach similar to Rapid Agile Iterative Design (RAID) approach of Heyer (Heyer et al. 2008). Using this method, a basic prototype is deployed and then iterated by examining use and obtaining ideas and feedback from its user community. Our research aim was to understand if the design could promote sustained community use, contributing to community communication.

Putting any installation into a public space requires building relationships of trust. It requires taking responsibility for the design and its use. The local general store was chosen as a location for the digital notice board because it is community-oriented, owned and run by two local families and located opposite the local state primary school. Locals sit down for a coffee and loiter awhile. The shop and school together create a community hub that people use for everyday activities such as collecting children, and for community events such as public meetings and school fetes. Schools and shops are significant hubs for both daily

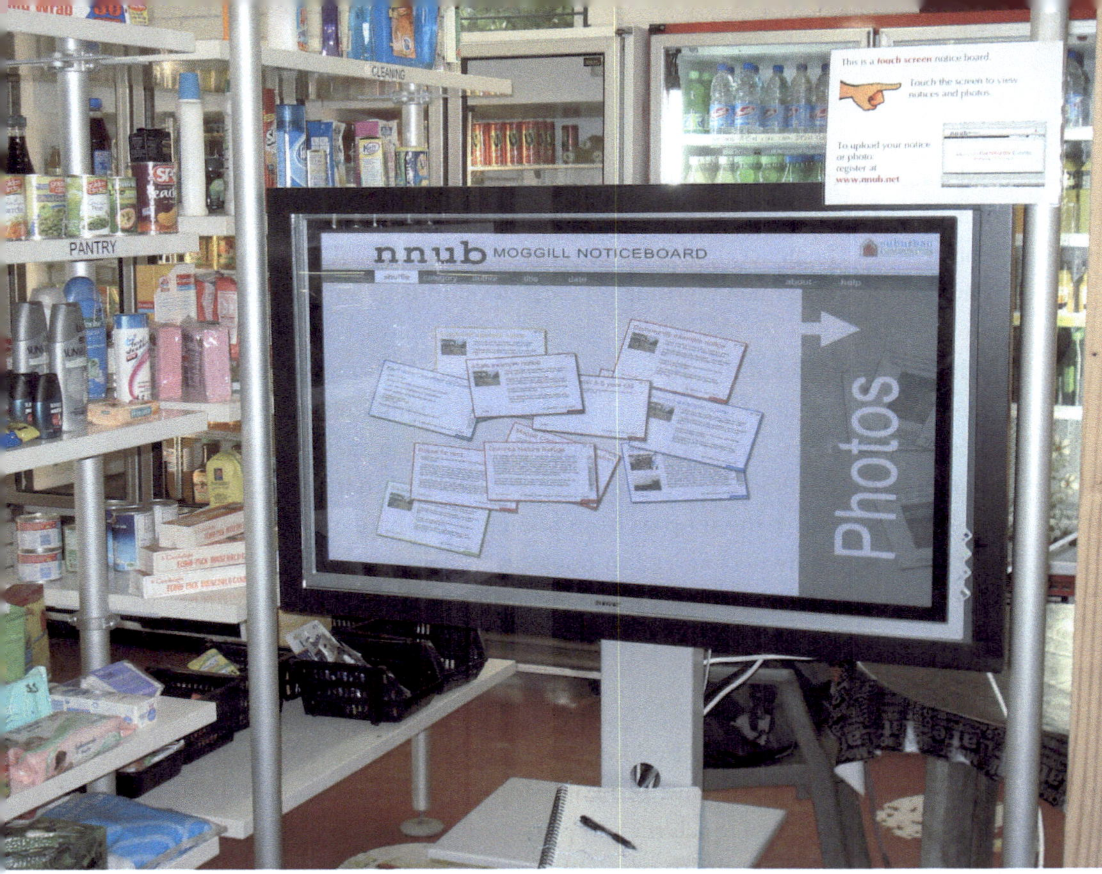

Figure 3. The community digital notice board is located in the local general store. The purpose of the notice board was to address the awareness barrier by creating a shared view of local activities and knowledge in a place passed by many local people frequently. Anyone can post a notice and posting is made as simple as possible. Notices and photos (output) are displayed to people at the store on a large interactive monitor with touch screen functionality. The public display allows browsing (no searching) through categories of notices and photos. A simple web interface allows any user to search and browse notices and photos, and registered users to upload, edit, and comment posts. A desktop computer is installed at the shop to provide web interface access and examples of use to people without computer access or knowledge. The research team administers moderation of submitted postings, solely to screen for posting of pornography and profanity. Although beginning as a simple notice-board, it would be possible, subject to community interest and use, to develop other forms of use such as community data collection and visualization of resource use, creative expression etc.

and longer-term local community activity – the Parents and Citizens Association of the local school has undertaken the task of raising funds for a community hall. The general store is frequented by the school community, nearby residents and tradesmen working on local development among others.

Although I frequented the store, I knew the owners, who work regularly in the store, only by sight and name. They appeared community minded, having a petition to stop the motorway through the suburb on their counter. After explaining the idea of a digital community notice-board that would allow people to browse notices in the shop or from home, laying bare our research interests and motives, the owners agreed to house it in their shop and so we began design work, regularly seeking their input. Interestingly the shop owners were not interested in a website, but the idea of a digital notice board captured their imagination.

In addition to gaining and building the trust of the store owners it was also necessary to develop the trust of people to use the digital notice board. Some people are reluctant to touch the screen for fear of not being able to work it in public place, (touch is used to select and enlarge notices for reading), and when people do touch it, if it doesn't work as they expect they are reluctant to try again.

By using a large screen in the local shop, it is not only easy to see, but aspects of use can be seen and demonstrated in a social space, encouraging people to try it out. Staff at the local school have used the notice board, which has led to plans to install a second notice board in the school. A notebook underneath the notice board allows people to leave feedback without having to engage with the technology. Having a notice-board prototype in a local space has revealed salutary aspects of the design as used. One friend commented, »I thought it was just a TV.« A boy commented to his friend »It doesn't work.« (Sometimes it hasn't worked.) When his friend replied, »Yes it does«, they both began touching it frantically, which suggested that certain patterns of touch could create splotches putting it into paint mode.

Initial modifications have related to practicalities such as putting a personal computer in the shop so that people can post from the shop, being able to post at the shop without registering (a procedural inconvenience that serves as a barrier to use), making registration as simple as possible, indicating the screen is interactive by touch, and decisions about moderation. The owners of the store, who work in the shop each day, have taken some ownership of the notice-board, rebooting it if it freezes for any reason and calling us to let us know if there is a problem.

They comment on how people relate to it, »I reckon if I put my plastering business up on there I'd get more work than I could poke a stick at«, and advise on what we might do differently, for example adding a notice to say that posting is free, because people assume they would have to pay to post a notice on a large fancy looking screen.

The relationship that we have with the users of the notice board is developed largely through use of notice board itself. By attending to the kind of things that people post or don't post and by soliciting comments and ideas through the notice board, we determine how to modify the design. When we meet with community groups in order to discuss the possibilities for local outreach and support for communication, the notice board as a prototype facilitates discussion. Embeddedness, through living in the same place and through many informal conversations with other residents and visitors, allows identification of potential design opportunities and discussion with other locals. It is hard to see how we could develop a realistic appreciation of the design as used without an embedded, located approach.

REFLECTIONS ON RELATIONS

I turn now to reflect upon the view of design as entry into the network of relations that make technical systems possible.

RELATIONS BETWEEN DESIGN AND USE. The significance of any intervention is determined over time and in its context of use. Redström argues that use is a kind of ongoing achievement, the results of a continuous process of encounters with objects and how one acts upon them (Redström 2006). Studies of actual use reveal that people use designs in ways not anticipated in studies of isolated use. Redström offers a more human-oriented view of design, that we could »see the process of becoming users as being a process of inviting and accepting the things that will become the building blocks of our lifeworlds.« In a critique of a literal interpretation of trying to design use, and in the process over-specifying it, Redström points instead to a path that passes on questions about use to the user, with designers using their knowledge not to answer questions with design but to leave them open, because ultimately use is not there for designers to design.

This concern with trying to over-specify use is particularly relevant to the design of devices that embed IT and software procedures. These devices often reduce people to following sequences of steps and they are closed so as to inhibit possibilities for appropriation. With design of the community notice board, the challenge has been to make it as simple as possible to use and yet to make it inviting and open to all sorts of use. The challenge is to achieve openness to all sorts of possibilities and a clarity that reveals possibilities at the same time.

Whether designing an open-source hackable kind of design, or a design of a more closed form, the designer is still aiming for people to use, appropriate or experience it in a satisfying way. Regardless of the openness of the design, designers still maintain responsibility for their design vision and for the resulting design. And they have an accompanying responsibility to understand the design as it is used as well as as it is envisioned. The debates surrounding design and use thus highlight that there is an essential dialectical relationship between them. Iterative approaches, where possible, that reveal use over time can be employed to good effect. In the implementation phases of the community communication design project, understanding the design as used has been critical to making a realistic appraisal of the design, informing how to advance the design or when to shift course.

THE RELATION BETWEEN DIFFERENT DESIGN APPROACHES. The different approaches to design over the course of the project shed quite different lights on the problem-solution frame of reference. A participatory approach from within a community organisation addressing a long-term strategic issue promoted a quite different view of community communications (private strategic activity) and a different course of design action (website to facilitate document sharing) from a broader approach that examined everyday engagement in the community (participation in a various kinds of community groupings). Representation in a simple ethnographic or user-experience model prompted questions and challenges to the design problem framing that had not been made explicit prior to employing this form of representation and engaging designers in making sense of it. See also Buur and Sitorus (2007) and Anderson (1994). Different design proposals (the information pond and the digital notice board) provided useful counterpoints for considering the social interaction that would be prompted by one versus the other.

THE RELATION BETWEEN DIFFERENT DESIGN ROLES AND DIFFERENT PARTIAL KNOWLEDGES. Within our design team itself there are several roles: Developing relationships with the community (such as the school, the local police, the shop, the council etc.); Developing design concepts; implementing concepts in software; and ongoing management of priorities and time allocation in software development. There is constant interplay between these roles and each role requires bridging work across different partial knowledges. For example, even though the noticeboard software might work as intended by the software developer and as envisioned in the design, a person using the notice board might find it doesn't operate as they expect, leading to problems with use. This leads the person who observed the use difficulty and the software developer to reflect upon the design and to consider a possible redesign. This has a flow on effect of re-assessing software development priorities, and reallocating software development time. The software developer, in developing software for the design, does so with consideration of the possible platform technologies that could be used, how suited they are to current design requirements and how well they might meet future design demands. The software developer also manages a relationship between the core design and how it is manifested in the many different web browsers and versions of web browsers that people might use to view the notice board from their home. Thus there are multiple relationships between the design, the use, the technologies, the development timeline and strategic relationships with community that need to be managed and each involves bridging partial knowledges together. We found it particularly crucial to work with a software designer/developer who is willing to negotiate and communicate these relationships between the technologies, the design and the use.

STRATEGIC DESIGN RELATIONS. The attempt to appropriate public space for community use and to design community communications is less a matter of known design process and more a matter of strategic engagement and development of relationships. It is necessary to engage strategically and collaboratively with local business leaders and political leaders and to work out aligned interests. The role of the designer becomes one of fostering appropriate engagements and championing and guarding core values that underlie the design philosophy, in this case, democratic civic engagement.

IN CONCLUSION. Taking a relational view of design over time draws into focus the way that design relationships are constituted, the myriad relationships that make design possible and the rich understanding of design that can be derived from multiple, located, partial perspectives.

ACKNOWLEDGEMENTS

I thank the editors for very helpful comments on drafts. I am indebted and thankful to my colleagues Jacob Buur, Fiona Redhead, Andrew Dekker, Ian MacColl and Keiran Bartlett, the local general store, local community association and participants in the design workshop.

REFERENCES

Anderson, R. J. (1994). Representations and requirements: The value of ethnography in system design. *Human-Computer Interaction* 9:151–182.

Bartlett, K. (2006). Exploration of the effect on community collaboration and interaction with the introduction of a community website. Masters Thesis, University of Queensland.

Bucciarelli, L. (1994). *Designing engineers*. Cambridge, Mass.: MIT Press.

Buur, J., Sitorus, L., (2007). Ethnography as design provocation. EPIC Ethnographic Praxis in Industry Conf. Proc., pp. 146–157.

Crabtree, A., (2003). *Designing collaborative systems: A practical guide to ethnography*. Secaucus, NJ: Springer-Verlag.

Ehn, P., (1988). *Work-oriented design of computer artifacts*. Stockholm: Arbetslivscentrum.

Ehn, P., (1998). Manifesto for a Digital Bauhaus. *Digital Creativity*, 9(4):207–216.

Greenbaum, J., Kyng, M. (Eds., 1991). *Design at work: Cooperative design of computer systems*. Hillsdale, NJ: Lawrence Erlbaum Associates.

Hales, M. (1994). Where are designers? Styles of design practice, objects of design and views of users in CSCW. In Rosenberg, D., Hutchison, C. (Eds.) *Design issues in CSCW*, pp. 151–177. Secaucus, NJ: Springer Verlag.

Haraway, D. (1991). *Situated knowledges: The science question in feminism and the privilege of partial perspective*. New York: Routledge.

Heyer, C., Brereton, M., Viller, S. (2008). Cross-channel mobile social software: An empirical study. Proc. CHI 2008, pp. 1525–1534. New York, NY: ACM Press.

Redhead, F., Brereton, M. (2006). A qualitative analysis of local community communications. Proc. OzCHI, pp. 361–364. DOI: 10.1145/1228175.1228245.

Redhead, F., Dekker, A., Brereton, M., MacColl, I. (2007). Nnub: Getting to the nub of neighbourhood interaction. International Workshop on Social Interaction and Mundane Technologies, Melbourne 26th-27th Nov. http://www.mundanetechnologies.com/goings-on/workshop/melbourne/papers/RedheadDekkerBreretonMaccoll.pdf Accessed April 29 2008.

Redström, J. (2006). Towards user design? On the shift from object to user as the subject of design. *Design Studies* 27:123–139.

Star, S. L. (1991). Invisible work and silenced dialogues in knowledge representation. In Eriksson, I., Kitchenham, B., Tijdens, K. (Eds.) *Women, work and computerization*, pp.81–92. Amsterdam: North Holland.

Suchman, L. (2002). Located accountabilities in technology production. *Scand. J. Information Systems*, 14(2):91–105.

JEANETTE BLOMBERG

ON PARTICIPATION AND SERVICE INNOVATION

JEANETTE BLOMBERG
ON PARTICIPATION AND SERVICE INNOVATION

INTRODUCTION

There has been a rapid rise in the global service economy. Today nearly two-thirds of all economic activity in the developed countries derives from the service sector (e.g., healthcare, education, travel, entertainment, IT and business process outsourcing) and employment in service industries is growing throughout the world (Chesbrough and Spohrer 2006). Enabling the recent growth in the service sector are advances in ICT (Information and Communication Technologies) which facilitate new divisions of labor through which work and workers are more easily be distributed around the globe. As products commoditize, businesses expand their service offerings to attract new customers and grow their revenue. For example, automobile manufacturers offer warranty, repair, insurance, and navigation services as companions to the purchase of a car, while telecommunications companies give away cellular phones in exchange for long term service contracts. The rise in the service economy invites reflection on design approaches relevant to *service innovation*, including the applicability of *participatory design* with its focus on interactions between designers and users.

WHAT ARE SERVICES?

Before exploring the applicability of participatory design approaches to service innovation, let's examine what is often meant by the term services. While many definitions of services have been proposed (Fitzsimmons and Fitzsimmons 2005, Gronroos 1990, Zeithaml and Binter 1996), perhaps in its simplest form a service can be thought of as any act in which a provider and recipient co-create value together. For instance, a teacher and student co-create value when the student attends a lecture delivered by the teacher. The value of the service is influenced by the student's participation and is not determined by the teacher's performance alone. In another example, a financial advisor provides a service when discussing income and investment positions with a client in light of recent market trends and, based on input from the client, makes recommendations for the sale of certain financial assets.

For the purposes of my argument what is important to note in these examples is that the provider of the service relies on the recipient to establish the value of the service. Students cannot learn what is being taught unless they engage in some way with the content of the teacher's lectures. Likewise financial advisors cannot make meaningful recommendations unless their clients provide them with information such as income, risk tolerance or future financial commitments. In many service exchanges the engaged parties devote a significant amount of time conferring and negotiating before the service is actually delivered, making refinements or customizations to the standard offerings and specifying the manner in which the service will be performed. The character of provider–recipient interactions has major impact on the quality and appeal of the service.

The opportunity for the provider and recipient to engage in interactions, even if at times technologically mediated, is essential for the realization of value in the service exchange. It is important that we consider whether those interactions occur in the context of a relationship built up over time between the provider and recipient or are defined solely on the basis the specific encounter itself. Gutek (1995:4) makes this distinction by identifying two types of service transactions, those structured as *relationships* and those structured more as *encounters*. Those services that are delivered over time by the same provider offer opportunities to cultivate relationships, while those that are conveyed in a single, discrete transaction afford little possibility for relationships to be developed or sustained. As an example of this distinction remember when it was commonplace in the developed world for healthcare services to be delivered by a family doctor who treated the same set of patients for years, getting to know them in the process. Now consider that today many people receive healthcare in a clinic setting where the treating doctor is determined by availability and not prior history with the patient. In the first instance, the healthcare service is shaped by the knowledge that the doctor has about long standing patients, while in the second the doctor must rely on documentation or what can be learned in a single visit to understand the family and health history of any given patient.

Gutek (1995:7) argues that when »...provider and customer can draw on the store of shared knowledge, relationships become more efficient over time« as each interaction builds on previous ones. Making a related point, Mathiassen and Sørensen (forthcoming, p. 9) exploring the circumstances under which one or the other type of transaction might be preferable state that: »Encounters (not relationships) ensure efficiency, speed and uniformity of services« and »... ha[ve] a predefined context. In contrast, relationships are ... aimed at more complex service needs.« As such, routine healthcare services such as vaccinations might adequately be delivered as encounters, where more complex healthcare services might not be so amenable and would benefit from deep knowledge of the patient.

Opportunities for relationship formation are often influenced by the period of time over which services are contracted. For example, the services of an architect designing a house may continue for a number of weeks or months as the house is designed and built, providing time for the architect to get to know the lifestyle, likes and dislikes of clients. Similarly, in IT outsourcing services, where one company contracts with another to provide IT support (e.g. help desk services, applications management, or IT security), contractual agreements are typically in place for years, providing ample opportunity to establish strong (or troubled) relationships. Service providers know the risks of »getting off on the wrong foot« with their outsourcing clients and invest a great deal of attention to the initial phase of service contracts where the two companies »transition« to a state where the provider is able to assume full responsibility for the contracted services (Kreeger 2007). Mistakes made during this critical period can have a lasting impact on the long term relationship. It is important to note for our discussion that services are defined in part by the quality and type of the interactions occurring between client and service provider.

INNOVATION IN SERVICES

Given the rapid expanse of the service economy worldwide, it is somewhat surprising that little investment has been made in research devoted to service innovation (Chesbrough 2005, Thomke 2003). Gallouj (2002) notes that modern economies are not typically regarded as economies of innovation *in* services and that investment in innovation by service firms is not proportional to their contribution to the global economy. Instead investment remains primarily focused on technology and product innovation. While there are current efforts to change this situation (Davis and Berdrow 2008, Glushko 2008), we might ask why there has been so little investment in service innovation.

One factor that might help explain the lack of investment in service innovation is that products and technologies (the typical focus of R&D) have been decentered in service exchanges with value determined not by the product or technology alone, but through the interactions and exchange between providers and recipients. Vargo and Lusch (2004, 2006), in outlining their »service dominate logic,« insist that customer *interactions* actually drive value co-creation and that goods (or technology) are sidelined as »appliances« enabling the delivery of service. Bryson et al. (2004) make a related point suggest that one of the important distinctions between products and services is that the *relationship* has become a resource in itself and value is enhanced by extending the scope, content and process of the relationship. This suggests that efforts to innovate in services must focus attention on interactions and relationships, not simply on technologies and products.

Gutek (1995:6) arguing for the importance of innovation in »social mechanisms« to improve service performance, insists that what is needed is »... change in the way interactions between customers and providers are structured.« Shifting the focus of innovation to interactions, relationships and processes demands a research agenda and profile that diverge from what has defined much R&D to date with the resources predominately directed toward engineering, material science and computer science.

While noting the need for a change in the focus of service innovation toward interactions and relationships, we cannot ignore the fact that advances in information and communication technologies have aided the growth in new services. Developments in search algorithms, back office storage technologies and high speed connectivity have enabled the rise of internet search services. Continued progress in these and other enabling technologies promises to expand service offerings in areas like GPS mapping services, real time analytics and remote medical diagnosis. The role of enabling technologies is undeniable as a component of many innovative new services. However, service innovation extends far beyond the scope and limits of the technology design and development, highlighting interactions and relationships between service providers and recipients. As such the door seems to be wide open for a (re)introduction of participatory design (PD) approaches to service innovation with its emphasis on techniques

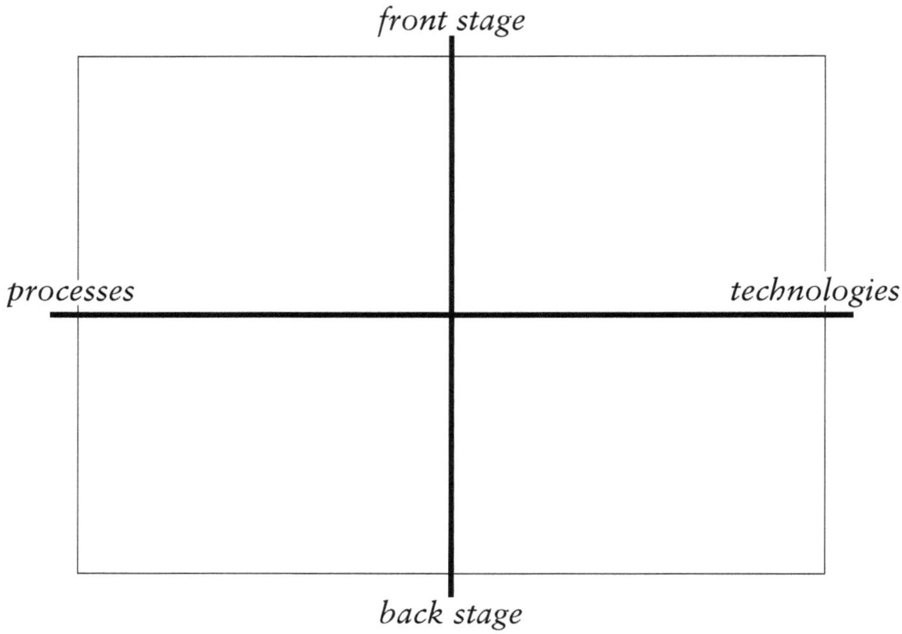

Figure 1. Schematic service innovation framework.

to support interactions between designers and users and on opportunities to learn about different domains of knowledge.

SERVICE INNOVATION FRAMEWORK

I would now like to introduce a service innovation framework to help identify opportunities for participatory approaches to service innovation. The delivery of services typically entails both *front stage*, direct interactions with clients and *back stage*, behind the scenes, facilitating activities (Bitner et al. 2008, Glushko and Tabas 2008, Teboul 2006). These client interactions and facilitating activities involve both enabling *technologies* and the *processes* that shape how the services are delivered†. The service innovation framework (Figure 1) depicts the

† I use the term *process* here to reference not only formal workflow processes, but informal practices and activities that constitute and characterize service encounters and service delivery.

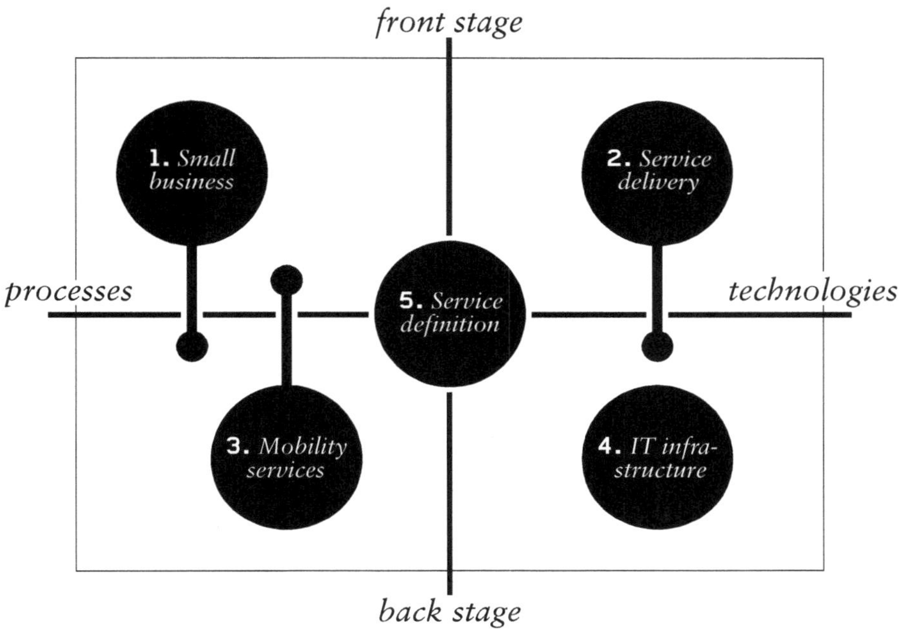

Figure 2. Five project profiles plotted on the service innovation framework.

intersection between the front and back stage and technologies and processes; and points to different focus areas for innovation in services – greater emphasis on enabling technologies or processes, or similarly, more stress on the front or back stage activities. These distinctions are not intended to suggest that service innovations are either process or technology innovations or that they concern only the front stage or back stage as they always involve integration across these dimensions.

FRAMEWORK DISCUSSION

Five service innovation research projects will be used to illustrate different opportunities for service innovation. These projects, as plotted on the service innovation framework in Figure 2, differ in their emphasis on *processes* versus *technology* design and *front stage* versus *back stage* activities. It should be noted that while each project differed in emphasis, none completely ignored the other dimensions of service innovation, recognizing that change in any area

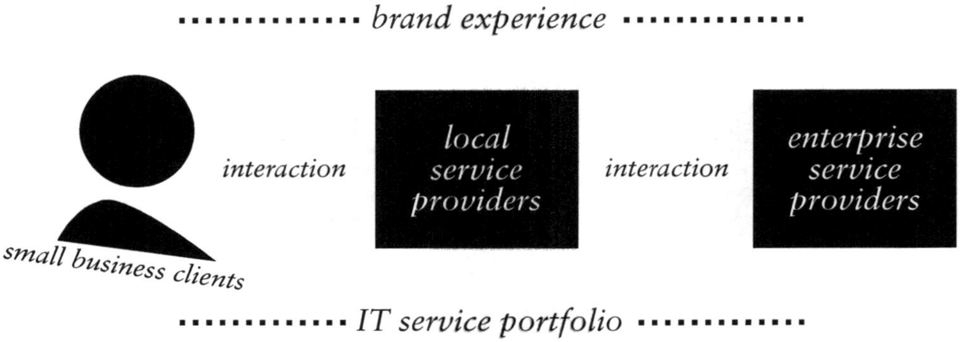

Figure 3. IT services for small business.

had implications for the others. This mutual shaping of technology and organizational practices and processes has been well established in the literature (e.g. Akrich 1992a, 1992b, MacKenzie and Wajcman 1985, Orlikowski 1992, 2000, Suchman et al. 1999)

PROJECT 1: IT SERVICES FOR SMALL BUSINESS
(PROCESS INNOVATION/FRONT STAGE AND BACK STAGE ACTIVITIES)

This research project explored the design of a new business model for delivering IT services to small businesses (<100 employees) and focused on innovation in both front and back stage processes. Because small businesses typically have few employees with IT expertise they frequently rely on outside providers for technology services. Our study examined how small businesses currently acquired IT support with the aim of informing the design of a new business model for selling and delivering technology services. The overall vision of the new business model was to improve the interactions customers had with local IT service providers by leveraging the technical and process knowledge and expertise of the large enterprise. Our research showed that small businesses preferred service providers who offered a range of support options, including timely expertise in solving their specific IT problems, knowledge of their current IT environment and configuration and access to advisors they could trust to assist in making IT decisions.

These findings had implications for the type of transactions most valued by small businesses receiving particular IT services. Valuing interactions with service providers that were built on trusted *relationships*, it was only in routine services that small businesses were content with more impersonal interactions structured as encounters. Our focus on interactions between the enterprise and the local service provider, and between the local provider and the client (Figure 3) led to the design of new process innovations supporting the new »go-to-market« business model which aimed to bring the back stage processes of technology standardization of the large enterprise to the front stage interactions with the small business clients. The local service providers acted as intermediaries fitting the standard service offerings to the local context of the small business. In a similar way, the new business model took advantage of one-off innovations occurring through interactions between local service providers and their clients by packaging standard service offerings in the back stage activities of the enterprise and then redistributing them to a network of affiliated local providers. The local providers, in turn, could make these new offerings available to their clients. In this case service innovation was occurring at the points of interaction between local providers and the enterprise and small business customer and local providers. The enabling technologies were not the site of innovation, although implicated in how the services were designed and delivered.

Project 2: Service delivery portal (technology innovation /front stage activities)

This research project was directed at service innovation in front stage technologies to enable sustainable client-provider relationships in IT outsourcing. In particular, the effort involved the design of a web portal to facilitate interactions between IT service delivery teams and their clients (see Figure 4). The portal development effort was initiated to increase client access to service performance metrics and, in so doing, allow greater information transparency (Blomberg 2008). The targeted users of the first version of the portal were executive level employees in both the service provider and client organizations. A key element

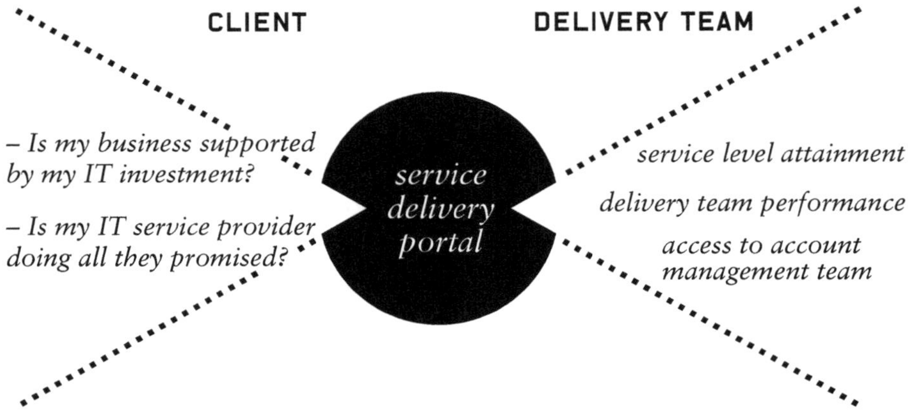

Figure 4. Service delivery portal.

of the portal design was the provision for presenting »real time« IT performance information to clients. This design direction oriented the research toward an investigation of how IT service performance information was currently made available to executive level clients.

Based on our interviews and observations of IT executives within the provider and client organizations, we concluded that while providing accurate and timely performance information was of value, what was more important were opportunities for service providers and clients to »negotiate« the meaning of performance information and thereby develop both immediate and longer term plans to mitigate problems and, as appropriate, expand the scope of the engagement. For example, we found that IT performance measures and reporting formats evolved throughout the outsourcing engagement, in response to adjustments in the contract that required additional performance measures, or to requests from the client to present performance measures in different formats (e.g. bar charts instead of or in addition to tables) to facilitate specific IT decisions they faced at any given time. It is often in the interest of the provider to comply with these requests even if they are not specified in the original contract for the purpose of strengthening the relationship with the client and for the benefit of the long term health of the account.

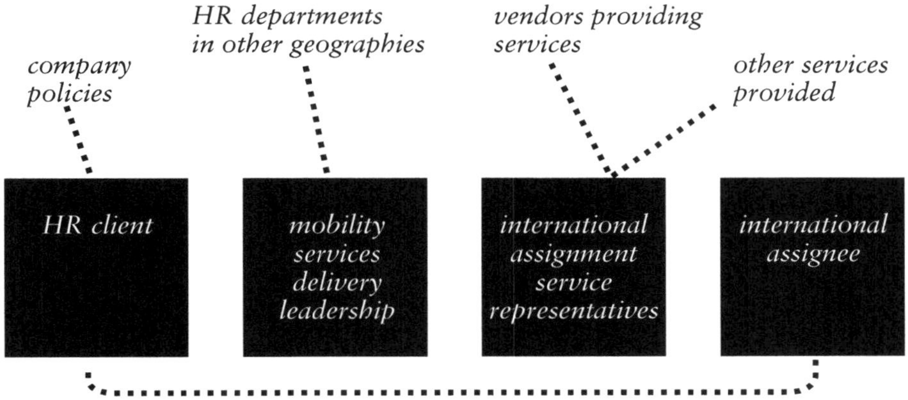

Figure 5. Principal actors in delivery of mobility services (schematic).

We argued that the portal design needed to support easy modifications to reporting formats, as they were worked out over time by trial and error and through repeated interactions with the client. We also recommended that it should be possible to easily import performance data displayed on the portal to spreadsheets and other applications to facilitate real-time interactions with clients in face-to-face meetings or over the phone. In these ways our design innovations centered on enhancements to the portal technology that would better support interactions to facilitate the negotiation of the meaning of performance data, and not just on enabling the reporting of performance information.

Project 3: Mobility services (process innovation /back stage activities)

This third project specifically focused on innovation in the back stage processes of a global delivery center. The aim was to innovate on how services were delivered from a global delivery center in Manila to improve employee retention and customer satisfaction. The service offering of interest was »mobility services« (see Figure 5) where service representatives provided relocation support to employees on international assignment. These employees were temporally being transferred to another country and required assistance with such things as locating housing, schooling for children and healthcare services; understanding tax regulations, applying for drivers licenses, setting up bank accounts and acquiring language training. Our interest was in developing recommendations for both modest and more »transformational« changes to delivery center processes to improve both the quality of the services delivered and the experiences of the delivery center employees.

Areas where we identified a potential for change involved the adoption of different strategies for pairing service representatives with international assignees and revisions in the division of labor among the mobility service delivery team, including support for rotational assignments among delivery center employees. We focused our innovation on redesigning the work so that service employees could increase their scope of responsibility, gain experience outside mobility services and better understand how their contributions were situated in the global matrix of clients and services. It was our view that innovation in these *back office processes* would be critical in making improvements in the quality and effectiveness of the mobility services and the working conditions of the mobility service representatives.

Project 4: IT infrastructure (technology innovation/back stage activities)

The focus of this project was on innovation in back office technologies to enable the design and delivery of more effective and higher quality services. This IT infrastructure project was aimed at developing new architectures for capturing, sharing and analyzing service information. These new IT architectures, it was argued, would make service data available in multiple locations and would permit analytics on a range of data sources and types (e.g. proposal and design documents, technology performance, financial execution, employee staffing). Focusing on innovation in the underlying technical infrastructures would enable the design of new front stage services and provide improvements in the effectiveness of existing offerings.

In this particular example, the innovation is directed at change to the IT architecture that would allow data to be collected and analyzed to calculate costs (and therefore price) of IT services more accurately, based on the actual delivery costs. Lacking a consistent data source across engagements, the current IT infrastructure did not support the calculation of actual costs of service delivery – expenditures in people, time and technology. Access to these data, enabled by the new architecture, would also allow consideration of new front stage services such web-enabled, self-service solution design, where clients could explore the benefits of different IT solution configurations. This example highlights how innovation in back office technologies can promote new back stage process improvements and front stage technology and process innovation.

Project 5: Service Definition (process and technology innovation/ front stage and back stage activities)

This research project focused on both process and technology innovation and included considerations of both front stage and back stage activities. Our objectives were twofold; first, to design new tools to support the solution definition and costing of IT outsourcing services, and second, to innovate in organizational processes of the engagement teams, including the work of arriving at »accurate« cost estimates. Both the technology and process innovations were directed at the engagement phase of work where the service provider, often responding to a request for proposal (RFP) from the client; designs, costs and prices the IT services solicited in the RFP. Nominally the engagement phase ends when the client either accepts or rejects the provider's proposal for how the service will be delivered and the price that will be paid.

When we began our study, the engagement phase of IT outsourcing was depicted as a highly sequential linear process (see Figure 6, top). Our research revealed, however, that the work was better characterized as interactive and iterative (see Figure 6, bottom). Those involved in different phases of the work (e.g. requirements review, developing the cost case or due diligence) worked in parallel, providing each other with relevant information along the way and interacting, from time to time, to interpret client documents and clarify interdependencies. We pointed out that interactions and information exchange was occurring within, and across, activities and groups, and throughout the overall engagement process (Bailey et al. 2008). These observations were relevant to both the

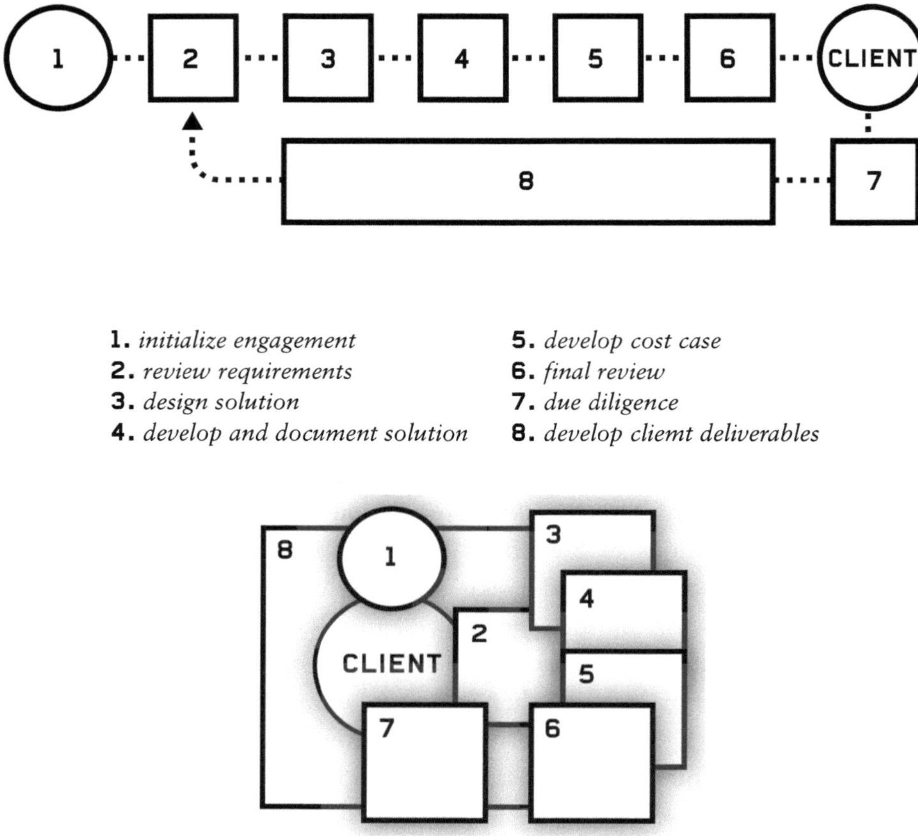

Figure 6. Engagement phase process. Top: Linear. Bottom: Iterative.

design of *back stage technologies* to support the work of costing and pricing and changes in the *processes* to aid collaboration and coordination among the engagement team.

These five examples illustrate that service innovation occurs across the service innovation framework, while at the same time noting that change in one area has implications for the others. Indeed much has been written about the mutual shaping of technology and organizational processes (Akrich 1992a, 1992b, Bijker et al. 1987, Blomberg 1988, Cefkin et al. 2007, Orlikowski 1992, 2000), and these projects illustrate that service innovation requires consideration not only of the connections between technology and organizational process, but also between front stage activities where providers and service recipients interact directly and back stage activities which enable and shape service encounters, relationships and interactions.

ON PARTICIPATION

I began this chapter by pointing out that services were co-created through interactions between service providers and recipients, noting that in some cases those interactions were mediated by technology (e.g. automated cash machines, internet search engines and airline reservation sites). The crucial point was that services involve the participation of clients (customers or users) in value co-creation interactions. Participatory design explicitly relies on designers and users working together to define project goals and design new technologies, attending to implications for new ways of working.

It seems to me that participatory design is relevant to service innovation in two distinct ways. The first is the rather straightforward application of participatory design approaches to the design of new service offerings whether they be front or back stage technologies or processes. The second proposes that participatory design principles should be considered as actual design elements of new service offerings. The argument is that by incorporating participatory design principles in how services are defined and delivered the value co-creation interactions between service providers and recipients would be strengthened. In this sense the well known principles and practices of participatory design (Schuler and Namioka 1993, Greenbaum and Kyng 1991, Kensing and Blomberg 1998) that provide the context for designers and users to work together would have direct relevance to service innovation where service providers and clients interact to co-create value. As such participatory design principles and practices can be viewed as relevant both to our approach to service innovation and to the characteristics of new service offerings.

Let's briefly review some of the guiding principles and practices of PD before we explore their relevance to service innovation and, in particular, to the five projects described above.

MUTUAL RESPECT FOR THE DIFFERENT KNOWLEDGE. Participatory design has long recognized the importance of *mutual respect for different knowledge* that participants bring to the design effort. Those who take part in PD projects (e.g. developers, users, managers, researchers, customers) bring unique experiences and perspectives to their interactions with each other. Respecting these differences and the value they provide helps ensure that everyone is heard. This is particularly important when disparity in authority or organizational position among participants might weaken the contributions of some who are essential to the success of the project.

OPPORTUNITIES TO LEARN ABOUT OTHERS' DOMAIN OF KNOWLEDGE. Mutual respect for knowledge differences must be coupled with the *opportunities to learn about others' domain of knowledge.* Allocating time and identify contexts in which participants can interact so each can learn from the others and help shape the project and its outcomes has been recognized as important for PD projects.

JOINT NEGOTIATION OF PROJECT GOALS. The quality and degree of participation in PD projects is shaped by whether *project goals are jointly negotiated.* Participants are more likely to buy-in to the project and feel a sense of shared commitment if they help define the goals and have a voice in the outcomes. Joint negotiation of project goals also improves the likelihood that all participants benefit in some way from participation. Lacking this willingness, sustaining the level of commitment needed for effective participation is difficult.

TOOLS AND PROCESSES TO FACILITATE PARTICIPATION. Finally, participatory design has developed *tools and processes to facilitate participation*, including future workshops, design games, prompted reflections, cardboard mock-ups, and case-based prototypes (Kensing 1987, Ehn 1989, Greenbaum and Kyng 1991, Trigg et al. 1991, Blomberg et al. 1996, Grønbæk et al. 1997). As Kensing and Blomberg (1998, p. 176) state: »These tools and technologies avoid the overly abstract representations of traditional design approaches and allow workers and designers to more easily experiment with various design possibilities in cost effective ways.«

These principles and practices have enabled those involved in participatory design projects to create a balance between what Ehn (1989) has called *tradition* and *transcendence*, recognizing the simultaneous desire to respect the way things are today and to look for ways to go beyond the status quo for the benefit of all.

To further explore the relevance of PD to service innovation each of the five projects described above will be examined from the standpoint of how they either adopted a participatory approach to service innovation or incorporated participatory principles in new services offerings.

PROJECT 1: IT SERVICES FOR SMALL BUSINESSES. Local IT service providers were involved in the design of new processes for interacting and engaging with both the enterprise providing IT solutions and brand recognition and the small business clients. Although not specifically adopting PD tools and techniques, local IT providers had opportunities to help shape the new business model in workshops and design meetings. But more importantly the processes of the new business model recognized the value of local providers having specific knowledge about their small business clients and the importance of clients knowing enough about their IT providers, particularly their service technicians, to trust the advice they were given. The new processes reinforced the value of service providers gaining knowledge about their clients, including characteristics of their existing IT infrastructure and levels of IT expertise among employees. This knowledge enabled interactions between provider and customer and helped enable the development of trusting relationships.

PROJECT 2: SERVICE DELIVERY PORTAL. Service delivery client executives were not directly involved in the portal design. In fact the developers who led the initial design of the portal had little understanding of the views of either the client or service provider executives who were the targeted beneficiaries of the new capabilities enabled by the portal. The research on current interactions between client and service provider executives challenged the assumed perspective of the developers, emphasizing the important role of interaction and negotiation among providers and clients to interpret the meaning of service performance information. In alignment with participatory design principles, recommendations were made to support interactions between providers and clients which we understood to be critical for the development of shared and actionable understandings of performance metrics. As part of the new portal technology we stressed the importance of providing a context for ongoing interactions between providers and clients and avoiding features that might impede or undermine the formation and maintenance of long lasting relationships between providers and clients.

PROJECT 3: MOBILITY SERVICES. A participatory approach was critical for the success of this project because of the multiple stakeholders who would be affected by any changes to back office processes. Among them were delivery center employees, enterprise process owners, international assignees, human resource departments responsible for employees on international assignments and the researchers. The success of the project was tied to our ability to balance the realities of the Manila delivery team context with the desire of our sponsors to create more standardized processes across the enterprise. Importantly, the clients for mobility services, both the international assignees and the human resource departments contracting for mobility services, contributed their views to the redesign effort. Without the support of each of these constituencies it would have been difficult, if not impossible, to bring about meaningful change. But in addition, some of the changes recommended aligned with participatory design principles. For example, it was suggested that service representatives be provided with greater knowledge of the context and varied experiences of the assignees they were charged with supporting. The representatives were typically young college graduates from the Philippines beginning their first job, whereas assignees were typically seasoned employees of the enterprise, often married, with children and a mortgage, and almost always in a senior position in the enterprise relative to the representative. A better understanding of issues faced by the assignees as they made the transition to the new country would assist representatives in providing the service. In addition, we recommended that the work and organization of mobility services be more visible to both the assignees and the HR departments contracting for this service. This, we argued, would ameliorate some of the misunderstandings that occurred when services were not delivered as expected or desired.

PROJECT 4: IT INFRASTRUCTURE. There was little recognition of the value of participatory approaches in a project focused on IT infrastructure innovation. The view was that innovation in the underlying architecture was only indirectly connected to end users or the recipients of service. However, we showed how design decisions made at the infrastructure level carried implications for the tools that are built on top of the IT infrastructure and ultimately on the processes and activities that are enabled. We had the opportunity to increase the awareness of those involved in these back stage technology projects that social and technical infrastructures are inextricably tied (Star 1999, Star and Ruhleder 1996). While there was the expectation that the new IT architecture would enable significant changes to the processes of cost and price determination in IT outsourcing engagements, this did not extend to actually involving those involved in these activities in discussions of the underlying architecture design. It may be that intermediaries are needed to navigate the intricacies of infrastructure configurations in relation to what front stage services they support.

PROJECT 5: SERVICE DEFINITION. Surrogates for those currently involved in the engagement phase of IT outsourcing (i.e. enterprise employees responsible for maintaining existing costing and pricing tools) were directly involved in the design of the new tools to support service costing and pricing. But more importantly, our research of actual engagement phase practices underscored the importance of iterative interactions among members of the engagement team who were involved in various aspects of the solution definition, costing and pricing. The sequential, linear view, where work was handed off as it passed from one phase to the next was challenged by a careful examination of the work and instead we exposed the need for tools and processes that supported comparing perspectives, identifying dependencies and providing easy access to each others' work products and expertise. PD principles emphasizing opportunities to learn about the others' domain of knowledge and jointly developing project goals were particularly relevant to the tools and processes that support the work of service definition.

CONCLUSIONS

In his »Manifesto for a Digital Bauhaus« Ehn (1998) called for a *critical* stance to information and communication technology. Today we find ourselves in a world dominated by services that are remaking global connections as work and workers flow more easily from one part of the world to another. Now, perhaps more than ever, we need a strategy and approach for bringing the multiplicity of interests and viewpoints that are implicated in new services and service economies to the fore. What better way to continue the balancing act of navigating between tradition and transcendence than by adopting participatory sensibilities in the services we design and by adopting participatory approaches to service innovation? In my view there is a genuine opportunity in current theorizing about services for notions of co-creation of value to challenge the artificial lines often drawn between production and consumption, seller and buyer, citizen and government, employee and employer. We really are in this together and we need move beyond mere recognition to find ways of enabling conversations across old divides. The work that Ehn and many others began nearly 40 years ago, of redefining boundaries between users and designers, workers and employers, researchers and developers, has been joined by those of us involved in service innovation.

REFERENCES

Akrich, M. (1992a). The description of technical objects. In Bijker, W. E., Law, J. (Eds.) *Shaping technology/Building society: Studies in sociotechnical change.* Cambridge, MA: MIT Press.

Akrich, M. (1992b). Beyond social construction of technology: The shaping of people and things in the innovation process. In M. Dierkes, M., Hoffmann, U. (Eds.) *New technology and the outset: Social forces in the shaping of technological innovations*, pp. 173–190. Boulder, CO: Westview Press.

Bailey, J., Kieliszewski, C., Blomberg, J. (2008). Work in organizational context and implications for technology interventions. Proceedings of Human Factors in Organizational Design and Management (ODAM 2008). Sao Paulo, Brazil. March 2008.

Bitner, M. J, Ostrom, A. L., Morgan, F. N. (forthcoming). Service blueprinting: A practical technique for service innovation. *California Management Review*.

Bijker, W., Hughes, T., Pinch, T. (Eds., 1987). *The social construction of technological systems: New directions in the sociology and history of technology*. Cambridge, MA: MIT Press.

Blomberg, J. (1988). The variable impact of computer technologies on the organization of work activities. In Greif, I. (Ed.) *Computer-supported cooperative work: A book of readings*, pp. 771–782. San Mateo, California: Morgan Kaufmann.

Blomberg J. (2008) Negotiating meaning of shared information in service system encounters. *European Management Journal* 26(4):213–222.

Blomberg, J., Suchman, L., Trigg, R. (1996). Reflections on a work-oriented design project. *Human-Computer Interaction* 11(3):237–265.

Bryson, J. R., Daniels, P. W., Warf, B. (2004). *Service worlds: People, organizations and technology*. New York, NY: Routledge.

Cefkin, M., Thomas, J. O., Blomberg, J. (2007). The implications of enterprise-wide pipeline management tools for organizational relations and exchanges. Proceedings of Group 2007.

Cefkin, M., Kreeger, L. (2008). The client within: A meta-dynamic service system model. Proceedings of ServSig 2008.

Chesbrough, H. (2005). Toward a science of services. *Harvard Business Review* 83:16–17.

Chesbrough, H., J. Spohrer (2006). A research manifesto for services science. *Communications of the ACM* 49(7):35–40.

Davis, M. M., Berdrow I. (2008). Service science: Catalyst for change in business school curricula. *IBM Systems Journal* 47(1):29–40.

Ehn, P. (1989). *Work oriented design of computer artifacts*. Hillsdale, NJ: Lawrence Erlbaum Associates.

Ehn, P. (1993). Scandinavian design: On participation and skill. In Schuler, D., Namioka, A. (Eds.) *Participatory design principles and practices*, pp. 41–78. Hillsdale, NJ: Lawrence Erlbaum Associates.

Ehn, P. (1998). Manifesto for a Digital Bauhaus. *Digital Creativity* 9(4):207–216.

Ehn, P., Kyng, M. (1991). Cardboard computers: Mocking-it up or hands-on the future. In Greenbaum, J., Kyng, M. (Eds.) *Design at work: Cooperative design of computer systems*, pp. 169–195. Hillsdale, NJ: Lawrence Erlbaum Associates.

Fitzsimmons, J. A., Fitzsimmons, M. J. (2005). The nature of services. In Fitzsimmons, J. A., Fitzsimmons, M. J. *Service management: Operations, strategy, and information technology*, pp. 17–35. New York, NY: McGraw-Hill.

Gallouj, F. (2002). *Innovation in the service economy: The new wealth of nations*. Cheltenham, UK: Edward Elgar.

Glushko, R. J. (2008). Designing a service science discipline with discipline. *IBM Systems Journal* 47(1):15–28.

Glushko, R. J., Tabas, L. (2008). Bridging the »front stage« and »back stage« in service system design. Proceedings of the 41st Hawai'i International Conference on System Sciences.

Greenbaum, J., Kyng, M. (1991). *Design at work: Cooperative design of computer systems*. Hillsdale, NJ: Lawrence Erlbaum Associates.

Gronroos, C. (1990). *Service management and marketing: Managing the moment of truth in service competition*. Lexington, MA: Lexington Books.

Grønbæk, K., Kyng, M., Mogensen, P. (1997). Toward a cooperative experimental system development approach. In Kyng, M., Mathiassen, L. (Eds.) *Computers and design in context*, pp. 201–238. Cambridge, MA: MIT Press.

Gutek, B. (1995). *The dynamics of service: Reflections on the changing nature of customer/provider interactions*. San Francisco, CA: Josey-Bass.

Kensing, F. (1987). Generation of visions in systems development: A supplement to the toolbox. In P. Docherty et al. (Eds.) *Systems design for human development and productivity: Participation and beyond*, pp 285–301. Springer Verlag.

Kensing, F., Blomberg, J. (1998). Participatory design: Issues and concerns. *Computer Supported Cooperative Work: The Journal of Collaborative Computing* 7(3–4):163–165.

Kreeger, L. (2007). Inside outsourcing: A grounded theory of relationship formation within a nascent service system. Doctoral dissertation, Antioch University, Dissertation abstracts international, AAT 3285363.

MacKenzie, D., Wajcman, J. (Eds., 1985). *The social shaping of technology*. Open University Press: Milton Keynes.

Mathiassen, L., Sørensen, C. (forthcoming). Towards a theory of organizational information services. *Journal of Information Technology*.

Orlikowski, W.J. (1992). The duality of technology: Rethinking the concept of technology in organizations. *Organization Science* 3(3):398–427.

Orlikowski, W. (2000). Using technology and constituting structures: A practice lens for studying technology in organizations. *Organization Science* 11(4):404–428.

Schuler, D., Namioka, A. (1993). *Participatory design: Principles and practices*. Mahwah, NJ: Lawrence Erlbaum.

Star, S. L. (1999). The ethnography of infrastructure. *American Behavioral Scientist* 43(3):377–391.

Star, S. L., Ruhleder, K. (1996). Steps to an ecology of infrastructure: Design and access for large information spaces. *Information Systems Research* 7(1):111–134.

Suchman, L. Blomberg, J., Orr, J., Trigg, R. (1999). Reconstructing technologies as social practice. In Lehman, P., Wakeford, N. (Eds.) Analyzing virtual societies: New directions in methodology. Special issue of *American Behavioral Scientist* 43(3):392–408.

Teboul, J. (2006). *Services is front stage.* Palgrave Macmillan.

Thomke, S. (2003). R&D comes to services: Bank of America's pathbreaking experiments. *Harvard Business Review*, April 2003:70–79.

Trigg, R. H., Bødker, S., Grønbæk, K (1991). Open-ended interaction in cooperative prototyping: A video-based analysis. *Scandinavian Journal of Information Systems* 3:63–87.

Trigg, R., Blomberg, J., Suchman, L. (2002). Working artifacts: Ethnomethods of the prototype. *British Journal of Sociology* 53(2):163–179.

Vargo, S. L., Lusch, R. F. (2004). Evolving to a new dominant logic for marketing. *Journal of Marketing* 68:1–17.

Vargo, S. L., Lusch, R. F. (2006). Service-dominant logic: What it is, what it is not, what it might be. In Lusch, R. F., Vargo, S. L. (Eds.) *The service dominant logic of marketing: Dialog, debate and directions*, pp. 43–56. Armonk, NY: M.E. Sharpe.

Zeithaml, V. A., Binter, M.J. (1996). *Service marketing.* New York, NY: McGraw-Hill.

GIORGIO DE MICHELIS

THE PHENOMENOLOGICAL STANCE OF THE DESIGNER

GIORGIO DE MICHELIS
THE PHENOMENOLOGICAL STANCE OF THE DESIGNER

Design today is becoming more and more cooperative and multi-disciplinary, becoming more and more complex. Design is complex because it involves several diverse disciplines; because its object is manifold; because finally its beneficiaries, its stakeholders, are in the same moment (1) sources of knowledge for the designers, (2) those who will evaluate its outcome and (3) those who will transform it into a part of their place. Designers should, therefore, become aware of the changes impacting design, reflecting on their practice to better understand how it can become effective and capable again to answer the needs and desires of its stakeholders. In this chapter I propose a sort of deconstruction of design, where its object is clearly distinguished by its outcome, and the interplay between them is used to characterize its complexity. My approach assumes a phenomenological stance, i.e., a position allowing a »return to the very things«, looking at what there is in front of a person's eyes and not at that thing's existence. This position is well rooted in the European philosophy of the twentieth century and is embedded in a thread of studies by scholars in fields like CSCW, HCI and Interaction Design.

THE GROWING COMPLEXITY OF DESIGN

Design today is becoming more and more cooperative and multidisciplinary: the figure of the designer/artist as the unique author of the designed opus has already disappeared. It is only kept alive by the media, which are always searching for stars to be mythicized, and by the designers themselves who need to cultivate their excessive ego; on the other hand, it is becoming the norm that not only designers (urbanists and architects and/or industrial designers and/or graphic designers and/or interaction designers, …) participate in a design process but also human scientists (psychologists, anthropologists, economists) and technologists (software and hardware engineers). This means that the partiality of the viewpoint of any participant in the design process emerges more clearly: any designer, whatever his/her competence is, has a partial and limited view of the design evolution and its expected outcome. The problem is that cooperation among people with different cultural and disciplinary backgrounds is only possible if each of them is able to recognize the contributions of the other participants and to appraise and integrate them in the design process. And this is not what designers generally do. In Bruce Nussbaum's March 2007 talk, »Are designers the enemies of design?« (Nussbaum 2007), at Parsons, the New School for Design in New York, the curator of the conversation on innovation at *Business Week*, accused designers of not being able to understand that today they must design with people and of being irritated by the fact that everyone today is designing:

> The process of design, the management of the design process, are changing radically. Egos and silos are coming down, participation is expanding, tools are widespread and everyone wants to play … The emerging question is therefore: how do [designers] … switch gears from designing for to designing with?

Moreover, the designed things are always more complex, since the effectiveness of the services delivered by ICT (Information and Communication Technologies) applications depends on the way they are situated in space in order to deliver, on the contrary, buildings and objects offer flexible and ad hoc services if they are augmented by dynamic, self-regulated features. We could regard this as a new occurrence of the typical combination of creative design (shaping spaces) and engineering (efficiently realizing them), but the question seems to me to be more subtle: we still have a combination of creativity and rational development in the design of spaces and we should have the very same combination again in the design of their dynamic behavior. Finally we should have a combination of creativity and rational development in merging spatial and behavioral design. This means that far from a solution to the above problem, design today still faces, fragmented in each of its moments, the problem of integrating creativity and rational development. For example, in his already quoted talk at Parsons, Nussbaum also accused designers of not designing for sustainability, creating things that last, that can be reused many times, or that easily recycle:

> Let's take your favorite toy, designed by one of today's design gods, Jonathan Ive and his team at Apple – the iPod. Apple does fantastic things with materials. Amazing things. And it has recycling programs for its products. But what it doesn't do is prioritize cradle-to-cradle design. It doesn't design a long-cycle product that you can open and upgrade over time. It doesn't design a process that encourages the reuse of materials again and again. It doesn't demand sustainability.

Finally, as the designed thing couples spatiality and dynamicity, becoming intrinsically flexible, the future stakeholders† play a relevant role, both in its design process and in its experience once it has been delivered. During design, both what stakeholders know on the practice to be supported and their beliefs, expectations and desires play a decisive role, as it has been strongly affirmed by participatory design (Ehn 1990) to grant the utility and usability of its outcome. On the other hand, as meta-design has brought to our attention (Fischer and Giaccardi 2004), complex things will be more effective if they can be configured by stakeholders, discovering the best ways to use them in a sort of »design

† In this chapter we will generally use »stakeholders« instead of »users«, in order to underline that design impacts not only those who will use the designed thing but also those who are interested in it and/or have made an investment on it. It is important to have a broader viewpoint on the design process and to also take into account that at the customer/beneficiary side there is a mix of different opinions, needs and desires.

after design« phase. On one hand there is a difference between stakeholder participation during and after design, on the other, design itself and, therefore, the way stakeholders participate in it change if what is designed must be flexible and adaptable. In particular, its aesthetics value changes, since what people perceive does not only depend on the designer's creativity.

The three remarks above together offer a partial view of the high complexity reached by design today:‡ design is complex because it involves several diverse disciplines; because its object is manifold, characterized, as it is, by different aspects with different quality criteria; because finally its beneficiaries, its stakeholders, are in the same moment (1) sources of knowledge for the designers, (2) those who will evaluate its outcome and (3) those who will transform it into a part of their place. The above problems, therefore, are not deriving from faults and/or flaws of designers and they should not feel responsible for them, but they should also not attribute to other the responsibility of the difficulties design encounters today.

What can, and must, be asked of them is to become aware of the changes impacting design, avoiding the arrogance of having the solution to its problems and reflecting on their practice to better understand how it can become effective and capable again to answer the needs and desires of its stakeholders.

It has been Donald Schön's contribution to bring »reflection« into the centre of an understanding of what professionals like designers do. *The Reflective Practitioner* (Schön 1983) is directed against technical rationality as the grounding of professional knowledge, opposing an alternative epistemology of practice to it »in which the knowledge inherent in practice is to be understood as artful doing« (ibid). The notions of reflection-in-action and reflection-on-action are central to Donald Schön's arguments. The former is sometimes described as »thinking on our feet«, since it involves looking at our experiences, connecting

‡ The debate on design has been very rich in the last 15 years. Among the many contributions, let me quote Mitchell (1993), Brown and Duguid (1994), and Nelson and Stolterman (2003).

with our feelings and attending to our theories in use. It entails building new understandings to inform our actions in the situation that is unfolding. The practitioner can experience surprise, puzzlement, or confusion in any uncertain or unique situation. We can link this process of thinking on our feet with reflection-on-action. This is done later – after the action. The act of reflecting-on-action enables the practitioners to spend time exploring why they acted as they did, what was happening in the team and so on. In this way they engage with the situation. They do not have a full understanding of things before they act, but hopefully they can avoid major problems while »testing the water.«

The combination of reflection in action and on action radically transforms practitioners, since they become people continually coupling action and reflection. If we go back to designers and to the problems they meet with the growing complexity of their practice, we see that the latter are strictly related to communicating with people having diverse competencies, cultures, needs and desires. This is impossible if the involved participants are not reflecting on what they do: the individual creators can avoid using words to explain what they do[†] but designers involved in a collaboration to design a building or a system for a specific community of stakeholders can't be silent, since their contribution to the joint effort depends on their ability to explain their proposals and to understand those of others.

If design today requires collaborating designers, then it requires reflective designers. It makes sense, therefore, to ask: What is, or should be, the viewpoint from which designers observe and reflect? What should be their stance? It should be immediately clear, in fact, that what matters here is not the act of reflecting *per se* (even if we could agree that reflecting designers are in any case preferable to designers following only their instinct and intuition). What is needed is a reflection, on the one hand, which supports the ability to investigate and take into account the complexity of the ongoing design and, on the other,

† Alberto Burri, the Italian painter, refused to answer to questions about the sense of his paintings, »Words don't mean anything to me. What I want to express, appears in my paintings.« (Gendel 1954).

which cares about the interactions with other people, both as speakers and as listeners, and therefore is based on listening to other voices and can speak to people from different cultures.

Thus, the stance we are looking for is one that allows designers to keep awareness of the whole and of the particular, of the object of their design and of the partiality of the contributions they and others give to it, recognizing and crossing the mobile boundaries which separate their action domain from that of other participants.

DECONSTRUCTING DESIGN

As written above, the main thing that reflective designers do is to pay continuous attention to their practice, i.e. to design, in order to discover new problems in it, new facets and new ways of behaving. This open-minded attitude is counter-intuitive since, as designers, they know what to do in any moment of the design process and how it makes sense. The practice of reflective designers is permeated with an irreducible duplicity: they behave as experts and look at their practice as if new patterns of behavior could be discovered.

As any practitioner, in fact, designers embody a (frequently tacit) view on design in their practice: they look at design as they always have and interpret their practice on the basis of the categories through which they characterize the different facets of it. When they collaborate with other people who are colleagues or customers, their view on design extends to them so that the designers know what they are doing and what their role is in the design process. The designers introduce changes in the way they perform, in the repertoire they use, knowing if, for some specific character of what they are performing, they are occasionally breaking the silently fixed rules guiding design practice; or if they are experimenting with a change of repertoire as a step towards innovating it. The designers' image of the way they perform is relentlessly affected by their pre-understanding of design: their prejudices affect the way they view their practice, but new experiences question well-established ideas and beliefs.

Re-considering their idea of design, renovating the understanding of their practice is of paramount importance for reflective designers when, as we have recalled in the previous section, the sense of their practice seems lost if problems and contradictions arise.

»What is design?« is the first question for the reflective designer. What we need is not a new definition of design, but an opening path which spreads new light on its nature.

As an experience, design is characterized by the fact that the people participating in it deal with something that does not yet exist, but the future existence of it is their principal concern. The not yet existing thing† that will be its outcome takes form in the design process through the actions and interactions of its participants, but it is absent during the design process. Its place is taken by the object of design that designers create and manipulate day by day: the practice of a designer can, in fact, be characterized by its object. Despite the fact that we generally use the same name for both the object of design and its outcome, the former is not its latter: they are irremediably diverse.

What, then, is the relationship between the object of design and its outcome? On the one hand, the thing being the outcome of the design process will be the embodiment of the design object, but it can't be reduced to it (a thing exceeds the intentions of the people dealing with it, even when they have designed it); on the other hand, the object of design is not just a thing: it is constituted by all the (inscribed) things the participants create, import and/or modify during the design process. Its constituents are all interrelated: they form a web characterizing them as different representations, versions, views and details of the object of design.‡

The object of design is continuously changing during the design process, since day by day new constituents are created and existing ones are changed or sometimes destroyed: the creative process characterizing design is well reflected by the continuous changes of the web of things constituting its object. From this viewpoint, considering design as the development of the best solution to a problem, as the engineering traditions seem to do, is reductive and cannot fully capture its complexity.

† In a short essay published in *Poetry, Language, Thought* (Heidegger 1971) Martin Heidegger recalls that the German word »ding« (sharing its root with the English word »thing«) was used to name the governing assembly in ancient Germanic societies, made up of the free men of the community and presided by lawspeakers. It should be noticed that also the Latin word for thing, »res«, occurs in »res publica« (»republic« in English). So things are the issues governing assemblies take into consideration, the issues raising public concern. The word »thing«, therefore, does not indicate genericity, absence of specification, but impossibility of specification. Things are not without interest: on the contrary, they are what merit our attention. Things are matters of concern because they can't be reduced to any specification: things exceed the way we classify them and are open to discovery and surprise (see Latour and Weibel 2005).

‡ Here, as well as in the following pages, we will use *thing* to indicate something in the physical space. The outcome of a design process, its embodiment, is a thing, but also any constituent of the design object taken per se, detached from the object whose is a constituent is a thing, while we reserve *object* to make reference to the appropriation of a thing by people.

During the design process any »move« in the process is either aligning some constituents or dis-aligning them or both, so that the dis-alignment is always limited but never absent. From the viewpoint of the plurality of people participating in the process, alignment stabilizes achievements through a shared view of what has been done, while dis-alignment innovates, breaking the web of constituents of the design objects.

All the words that are spent during the design process contribute to shape the web linking the things constituting the object of design to each other, so that they contribute to give sense to it.

Design appears, from the above viewpoint, as the basic practice where human beings experience not yet existing things. The multiple constituency of its object has a not yet existing thing that has to be continuously evoked in the discourse/conversation accompanying design as a counterpart. Listening to what other people – designers with different backgrounds and cultures, users and/or stakeholders – bring to design is therefore the basis for enriching the object of design. On the other hand, the quality of design depends on its ability to transfer the richness of its object into the thing being its outcome. From this viewpoint multi-disciplinarity, stakeholder participation and opening the designed thing to the experience of its stakeholders are different aspects of a good design practice.

Constituents are not what designers are designing but each one in the design process allows participants to interact with the object and to discuss its different features. Objects do not exist *per se*, but only through their several, diverse constituents. Even when what has to be designed is something physical, such as a building, a chair or a machine, its embodiment when it comes into existence, remains just one constituent among others. The object of design, let me repeat again, is not its outcome, its embodiment: the latter may be less rich than the process of bringing it into existence; other constituents may light up its sense or evoke qualities that it does not adequately embody already.

Once design has ended, and its outcome is delivered, a completely different story begins: the story of people experiencing the outcome of design. It is during this story that users appropriate the outcome of design, reinventing their behavior and practice. The intentions of the designers, the values they wanted to give to the thing designed, are not automatically transferred to it: users are free to make their experiences with the outcome of design discovering the possibilities it offers to their behavior and practice, beyond what designers had thought and imagined. Even if users participate in the design process, the latter can't determine what will happen once the outcome of design is delivered: it depends on the quality of the design process if the outcome will be coherent with the designers' aims. Appropriation is again performed creating an object, i.e. a web of things allowing stakeholders (inhabitants) to consider the objectified thing as part of their space of possibilities. Here space is used in a metaphorical sense, but not by chance: as recalled, for example, by Harrison and Dourish (1996), the objectification of spaces and things we do in our everyday experience transforms the *space* we inhabit in our *place* and characterizes the things populating it through the possibilities for action and interaction they offer to us (a space is our place if we are at home in it, knowing what we can do in it and how). But, it can't reduce the things from being »matters of concern«

(Heidegger 1971), to their specific functions. The object people associate to a thing has – again – a multiple constituency, where each constituent, characterized by its spatiotemporal coordinates and by the people who created it, offers a partial view of the thing and of its potential for action and interaction. The irreducibility of a thing, its complexity, therefore mirrors the multiple constituency of the object we create experiencing it.

What we have briefly sketched – for a more complete account, see Telier (2008) – is a picture of design practice, where design is characterized for its being a complex collective endeavor aiming to create some*thing* new, that other people will later appropriate. Playing with it, a designer will open herself to a new reflection on her practice, and therefore to a new way of practicing design which is able to deal with its growing complexity.

CONCLUSION: THE PHENOMENOLOGICAL STANCE OF THE DESIGNER

Following a recent tradition, that had one of its pioneers in Pelle Ehn (1990), I have searched in the European philosophy of the twentieth century, and in particular in its phenomenological and hermeneutical schools, the solid grounds for my »de-construction« of design[†]. It was the *linguistic turn*, through which Richard Rorty (1979) interpreted the inspiration that was common to quite different authors as Ludwig Wittgenstein (1922, 1953), Martin Heidegger (1962, 1971) and John Dewey (1934, 1938), that appeared to have the right perspective for me for refreshing our understanding of design. Going back to the very essence of any human practice, as well as of any fact of human life, is not possible directly, since our understanding is always mediated by language, and limited by it. We need, therefore, to reach the very essence of design by going beyond language, understanding how what is said couples with what is done. The linguistic turn, in fact, shows the fallacy of thinking that we can

† I use here the word *deconstruction* in a rather lazy sense. My excursus on design is a deconstruction in the sense that it tries to observe it without prejudices and looks for its constitutive elements and aspects. I hope that readers with a philosophical background will forgive me for it.

access facts apart from the propositional structure of the language, and that we can construct any assertion without making reference to other assertions. We are therefore trapped in language and there is no way to discover a direct correspondence between our thoughts and the world out of them. There is not a language proper to nature. Knowing does not mean »representing«, »copying« reality but coping with it, with its challenges and questions. The answers of nature are always indirect, bounded by the structure of our questions: the world is the totality of facts not of things (Wittgenstein 1922). It is made of the constraints we encounter in our struggle for knowing, foreseeing and controlling the events of our life. I was searching the grounds for my work in philosophy because it helped me to go beyond the rather naïve realistic assumption that design has to do with transforming matter in order to build things which have some pre-defined spatial and/or behavioral qualities that permeate the current debate on design. Such a simplistic view does not allow for understanding of the distance between the designers' intentions and the outcome of their practice, the ambiguity permeating their collaboration with other practitioners, how difficult it is to transfer the richness of the design process into the designed thing and the impossibility for them to limit the stakeholders in their appropriation of the designed thing.

On the contrary, basing my analysis on philosophy I could see the interplay between the mutual irreducibility of objects of design and design outcomes and the clear-cut distinction between the design process and the story beginning after the delivery of its outcome to the stakeholders: designers appear to me to be immersed in a process where their aims cannot be automatically transferred to the outcome of their work which, when it comes into existence, will have a new life where they can only have a minor and peripheral role.

In my view, the practice of design is intertwined in an inextricable way with the threads of conversations within the design team (with the richness of their diverse cultures) and between designers and stakeholders, without any possibility of granting the alignment between what is said and what is done. Words give sense to the designed thing, bringing forth its being a matter of concern, and not defining its nature in functional and/or behavioral terms; the object of design gives sense to the ongoing conversations. Even the problem of knowledge sharing among all the participants in the design process cannot be fully understood in the realistic perspective: if design is transforming matter, then what is needed is to grant that participants share as much knowledge as possible about the planned/ongoing transformation, but the interplay between the knowledge created and shared and the evolution of the object of design is lost. Knowledge sharing is therefore reduced to a new occurrence of the »bounded rationality« problem (Simon 1957), losing the fact that it is a constitutive move of the design process and not an auxiliary activity necessary to overcome its limits.

I call the position from which I look at design a *phenomenological stance*. This term has been used to characterize a position allowing a »return to the very things«, looking at what there is in front of a person's eyes and not at that thing's existence. From the phenomenological stance things are accessible only through language: their very nature appears only beneath the words we spend on them, it manifests itself to the extent that the words we are sharing cannot be subject to different interpretations. The phenomenological stance enables us to keep our minds open enough to live any experience in its wholeness, trying to set aside any prior thoughts, conceptions or judgments about it. In doing so, a person will be placing the phenomenon in époché; by working with the description of the experience the researcher focuses on searching for its essence, its most invariable parts, as it is located within a context. The essence, therefore, is the very nature of what is being questioned.

It has to be underlined that the phenomenological stance should not be reduced to any phenomenological school in philosophy: without entering into the subtleties of the discussions among its most relevant representatives and making reference to the work of Richard Rorty (1979), we can place in the phenomenological stance not only Edmund Husserl (2001) and Martin Heidegger (1962), but also Ludwig Wittgenstein (who claimed in the *Tractatus*: »The world is everything that is the case« – Wittgenstein 1922, 1.1 and in the *Philosophical Investigations*: »The meaning of a word is its use in the language« – Wittgenstein 1953, p. 43), John Dewey (1934, 1938), the exponents of contemporary hermeneutics Hans-Georg Gadamer (1989) and Paul Ricoeur (1981), the deconstructionists as Jacques Derrida (2003) and Jean Luc Nancy (1992), just to name a few. I know that in some ways it is arbitrary to make broad generalizations like I do here, but I hope that the reader will understand my aim to indicate as broad a perspective as possible.

What unites all these philosophers, holding for the rest very different philosophical positions and frequently conflicting between each other, is their refusal of any assumption that what we experience is part of an external reality that we can access directly. When we speak of the »phenomenological stance«, we make reference to a viewpoint which distinguishes a thing from any object we may see in it, even while recognizing that the thing appears after the objects we see in it and not besides them. The phenomenological stance gives us tools to approach everyday life by returning to concrete things and occurrences rather than the abstractions describing them.

From now on we will use the term object to name experienced things, embodying the deep relationship with words that Ponge has richly characterized (1972). Objects, in fact, allow the things created and imported in the design process and their relation with its outcome, the designed thing, to be investigated: they have a transient life, limited socially and spatially by the human experience in which they appear.

In design practice the naïve assumption we are contrasting in these pages generates some misunderstandings that can dramatically affect the quality of design.

If what the designer delivers to their stakeholders is the object they have designed, the designer cannot pay attention to the mutual irreducibility between it and the thing being its outcome. The designer will therefore disregard one of the major aspects of the complexity of design: the fact that it is not a linear process where the transformation of intentions into outcomes is straightforward. Why should the designer listen to the stakeholder, or need to collaborate with other practitioners? The arrogance of designers that Nussbaum (2007) was denouncing is strongly grounded on the realistic assumption that design brings things to existence in accordance with the designer's intentions. Reflective designers fight against their potential for arrogance by being humble and continuously questioning their practice: the phenomenological stance appears to me a good candidate for hosting them.

As said before, this chapter is immersed in a thread of studies where scholars of CSCW, HCI and Interaction Design have been working for more than 20 years, and it is strongly indebted to them. Let me recall the most relevant contributions characterizing this thread. Winograd and Flores (1986) dedicate the first part of their book to phenomenology and hermeneutics. They bring the reader to a new understanding of human experience and of the role of computers in it. It's a radical shift from the dominant naïve acceptance of a rationalistic and realistic approach to knowledge of modern science. The Language-Action perspective, characterizing the interplay between conversing and acting in human experience, opened a new horizon for the study of computer-based systems.

The discussion about *Understanding Computers and Cognition* declined after the mid nineties, but its influence has continued as shown by two different books – Paul Dourish's *Where the Action is* (2001), and Claudio Ciborra's *The Labyrinths of Information* (2002). Dourish proposes a phenomenological foundation for embodied interaction, offering new insights into the interplay between language and action. The book not only begins its presentation of embodied interaction by drawing on the contribution of *Understanding Computers and Cognition*, but continues in line with the theoretical style of their book, grounding its discourse on analysis and design of computer-based technologies on a careful reading of some texts of the phenomenological/hermeneutical school of European philosophy.

Claudio Ciborra uses the customer–performer cycle, proposed for the first time in *Understanding Computers and Cognition* and later developed in Action Workflow, to explain the Customer Relationship Management (CRM) strategy at IBM (where Flores and Winograd's ideas were taken into account). He also pays tribute to them for inspiring him to carefully read Heidegger's philosophy. Another thread of works reading philosophy to understand technology and/or design, intertwining frequently with the one opened by Winograd and Flores, has its root in Pelle Ehn's *Work Oriented Design of Computer Artifacts* (1990) and its last contribution in A. Telier's *Making Design Take Place* (2008). This work should be considered as a partial account of Telier's book, where her findings are recalled in a tendentious way.

ACKNOWLEDGEMENT

This chapter is a side effect of my participation in the Atelier project and, later, in the writing of the book of A. Telier with the title *Making Design Take Place*. My thanks go therefore to all the members of the Atelier team and, in particular, to the colleagues who are hidden with me behind the name A. Telier: Thomas Binder, Pelle Ehn, Giulio Jacucci, Per Linde, Ina Wagner. To all of them goes my tribute, for the many discussions and joint work where these ideas emerged and took shape. This is also the right occasion to say that for nearly 20 years the work of Pelle Ehn has been a reference point for my research and I feel lucky for having had the occasion to collaborate with him in the last few of them. The responsibility of what is written in the above pages is, in any case, only mine.

REFERENCES

Brown, J.S., Duguid, P. (1994). Borderline issues: Social and material aspects of design. *Human-Computer Interaction* 9(1):3–36.

Ciborra, C. (2002). *The labyrinths of information*. Oxford: Oxford University Press.

De Michelis, G. (1998). *Aperto, molteplice, continuo*. Milano: Dunod Italia.

De Michelis, G. (2007). The contribution of the Language-Action Perspective to a new foundation for design. In Erickson, T., McDonald, D. W. (Eds.) *HCI Remixed*, pp. 293–298. Cambridge, MA: MIT Press.

Derrida, J. (2003). *The problem of genesis in Husserl's philosophy*. Translation by M. Hobson. Chicago, IL: The University of Chicago Press.

Dewey, J. (1934). *Art as experience*. New York, NY: Minton, Balch.

Dewey, J. (1938). *Logic: The theory of inquiry*. New York, NY: Henry Holt and Company.

Dourish, P. (2001). *Where the action is: The foundation of embodied interaction*. Cambridge, MA: MIT Press.

Ehn, P. (1990). *Work-oriented design of computer artifacts*. Hillsdale, NJ: Lawrence Erlbaum Associates.

Ehn, P. (1998). Manifesto for a Digital Bauhaus. *Digital Creativity* 9(4):207–216.

Fischer, G., Giaccardi E., et al. (2004). Meta-design: A manifesto for end-user development. *Communications of the ACM* 47(9):33–37.

Gadamer, H-G. (1989). *Truth and method*. Translation by J. Weinsheimer and D.G. Marshall. New York, NY: Crossroad.

Gendel, M. (1954). Burri makes a picture. *Art News*, 3(28):67–69.

Harrison, S., Dourish. P. (1996). Re-place-ing space: The role of place and space in collaborative systems. Proceedings of the 1996 ACM Conference on Computer supported cooperative work, pp. 67–76. New York, NY: ACM Press.

Heidegger, M. (1962). *Being and time*. Translation by J. Macquarrie and E. Robinson. London: SCM Press.

Heidegger, M. (1971). *Poetry, language, thought*. Translation by A. Hofstadter. New York, NY: Harper & Row.

Husserl, E. (2001). *Logical investigations, Vols. One and Two*. Translation by J.N. Findlay. Edition with translation corrections and with a new Introduction by D. Moran. With a new Preface by M. Dummett. London: Routledge.

Latour, B., Weibel, P. (Eds., 2005). *Making things public: Atmospheres of democracy*. Catalogue of the Exhibition at ZKM – Center for Art and Media – Karlsruhe, 20/03-30/10 2005. Cambridge, MA: The MIT Press.

Merleau-Ponty, M. (1996). *Phenomenology of perception*. Translated by C. Smith. London: Routledge.

Mitchell, W. J. T. (1993). *Redefining design: From form to experience.* Van Nostrand Reinhold.

Nancy, J.L. (1992). *Corpus.* Paris: Métailié.

Nelson, H. G., Stolterman. E: (2003). *The design way: Intentional change in an unpredictable world.* Englewood Cliffs, NJ: Educational Technology Publications.

Nussbaum B. (2007). Are designers the enemy of design? Talk given at Parsons, New York, in March, www.businessweek.com/innovate/NussbaumOnDesign/.

Ponge, F. (1972). *The voice of things.* Translation by B. Archer. New York, ny: McGraw & Hill.

Ricoeur, P. (1981). *Hermeneutics and the human sciences: Essays on language, action and interpretation.* Translation by J. B. Thompson. Cambridge: Cambridge University Press.

Rorty, R. (1979). *Philosophy and the mirror of nature.* Princeton, NJ: Princeton University Press.

Schön, D. (1983). *The reflective practitioner: How professionals think in action.* New York, NY: Basic Books.

Simon, H. (1957): A behavioral model of rational choice. In *Models of man, social and rational: Mathematical essays on rational human behavior in a social setting*, pp. 261–273. New York, NY: Wiley.

Telier, A. (2008). Design things. Unpublished manuscript.

Winograd, T., Flores, F. (1986). *Understanding computers and cognition: A new foundation for design.* Norwood, NJ: Ablex.

Wittgenstein, L (1922). *Tractatus logico-philosophicus.* German text with an English translation en regard by C.K. Ogden; with an introduction by Bertrand Russell. London: Routledge.

Wittgenstein, L. (1953). *Philosophical investigations.* Edited by G.E.M. Anscombe and R. Rhees, Translated by G.E.M. Anscombe. Oxford: Blackwell.

BILL GAVER

DESIGNING FOR HOMO LUDENS, STILL

BILL GAVER
DESIGNING FOR HOMO LUDENS, STILL

»All work and no play makes Jack a dull boy«
– popular saying

The advent of graphical interfaces, more than 20 years ago, revolutionised the way we think about computers. The desktop metaphor had such a complete inner logic that it seemed to dismiss offhand the tedious call-and-response interfaces that had prevailed. The computer as concept expanded from a tool to a virtual environment, from a clumsy machine to a place for exploration and experimentation. Research on interaction also expanded, as people sought new perspectives from which to understand this newly-discovered territory – from cognitive, to perceptual, to ethnographic and anthropological. As our appreciation of computing's potential grew, so did our appreciation of the aspects of humanity it mirrors.

Now we are in the midst of another revolution, as computers become part of our everyday lives. Computers are no longer at the cutting edge of popular imagination (that mantle has passed to bio- and nanotechnology), but they are now making more profound societal changes, as commodities on sale at local superstores, than they ever did when they were confined to the laboratory or workplace. This coming of age is changing the nature of computers as surely as, and arguably more profoundly than, icons and mice, the World Wide Web and even the advent of the PC itself. The point is not that computers are becoming ubiquitous or ambient or disappearing altogether. Nor am I saying that interaction will be tangible, or that the virtual will merge with the physical. These things may happen, but they're symptoms — attempts to shortcut technologically the challenges we face. The real revolution is that computing is leaving the confines of task-oriented, focused, rational work, and joining us in our homes, on the street, at parties, on lonely mountaintops – everywhere, in short, where we leave work behind to do the things we really want to do.

The effects of this new revolution will, I believe, be as radical as the move to graphical interfaces, causing us to rethink computers, research and even ourselves. However, we have been slow to appreciate the implications of technology's incursion into our everyday lives. As computing has emerged from the office and laboratory, it seems to have brought along values of the workplace:

concerns for clarity, efficiency and productivity; a preoccupation with finding solutions to problems. It is as if digital devices can mirror only the work required to achieve an ordinary life – a typically ethnomethodological perspective – and not the joyful, poetic and spiritually rewarding aspects of the life we might achieve. In this work-oriented vision, internet-enabled refrigerators will automatically update our shopping lists. We will use our microwave ovens to do our banking as well as to heat ready-made meals. Mobile devices will allow us to coordinate our schedules, download information, update records on the move. We will be surrounded by technology devoted to taking care of our everyday chores, giving us the leisure to pursue whatever activities we really value.

But what if technologies helped us pursue those activities now, directly, rather than merely helping us get the chores done? What if computing helped us pursue our lives, not just our work?

»We are here on Earth to fart around.«
– Kurt Vonnegut

The idea of Homo Ludens – humans defined as playful creatures (Huizinga 1950) – is an antidote to assumptions that technology should provide clear, efficient solutions to practical problems. From this perspective, we are characterised not just by our thinking or achievements, but by our playfulness: our curiosity, our love of diversion, our explorations, inventions and wonder. An aimless walk in the city centre, a moment of awe, a short-lived obsession, a joke – all are defining and valuable facets of our humanity, as worthy of respect as planning, logic or study. Play is not just mindless entertainment, but an essential way of engaging with, and learning about, our world and ourselves — for adults as well as children. As we toy with things and ideas, as we chat and daydream, we find new perspectives and new ways to create, new ambitions, relationships, and ideals. Play goes well beyond entertainment: it's a serious business.

»Play« means different things to different people, however. When Huizinga (1950) wrote that »civilization is, in its earliest phases, played«, he was linking the evolution of rituals and ceremonies, of the rules of diplomacy and those of warfare, to the contests and competitions that characterise games. Competitive play is not the same as the more fluid and self-determined play that I am advocating here. My view is closer to that of the artist Alan Kaprow, who contrasts play with games:

> [A] critical difference between gaming and playing cannot be ignored. Both involve free fantasy and apparent spontaneity, both may have clear structures, both may (but needn't) require special skills that enhance the playing. Play, however, offers satisfaction, not in some stated practical outcome, some immediate accomplishment, but rather in continuous participation as its own end. Taking sides, victory, and defeat, all irrelevant in play, are the chief requisites of game. In play one is carefree; in a game one is anxious about winning. (Kaprow 2003, p. 122)

Play, of the sort that might provide a relief from our obsession with work, is not the same as games or pre-programmed entertainment. Not only are these forms of »play« fundamentally goal-oriented, but in striving for a defined outcome they impose rules about the right and wrong ways to go about things. Most computer games are as rule-based and outcome-oriented as an air traffic control system. The interfaces for MP3 players are as concerned with utility and usability as any spreadsheet. Entertainments themselves are designed with the same concern for efficiently and predictably producing a result – an »experience« – as any online marketing site is for producing a sale. As Kaprow puts it: »The real substance and stimulus of our ›fun market‹, particularly in entertainment and sportive recreation, are superstars, record sales, popularity ratings, prizes, getting somewhere first, catching the biggest fish, beating the house at Las Vegas. Some fun!« (Kaprow 2003, p. 122). Pursuing such an instrumental version of »fun« does not help provide an alternative model for computing. On the contrary, it co-opts play into the same single-minded, results-oriented, problem-fixated mindset that we have inherited from the workplace.

Figure 1. The Pillow, by Tony Dunne, glows in response to ambient electromagnetic radiation. It may be greeted as an aesthetic object, a new kind of radio, or as a tool for electronic voyeurism.

In order to truly leave work behind, we need to embrace an open-ended, self-motivated form of play. This is an engagement that has no fixed path or end, but instead involves a wide-ranging conversation with the circumstances and situations that give it rise. Rules may emerge and goals may be sought, but these will be provisional inventions, makeshift tools to help the advance of curiosity and exploration. Such play may be purely physical, but often it will have conceptual components as well, as we assign different meanings to things or try out various roles ourselves. Most of all, it will be unpremeditated, evolving according to intrinsic motivation and moment-by-moment interpretation. For it is this lack of imposed structure and outcome that distinguishes play from work, and which separates systems that can truly support play from those that masquerade as playful while, at core, reproducing the demands and tensions of instrumental labour.

»These things are fun and fun is good.«
– Dr. Seuss

What sorts of computational device might appeal to Homo Ludens? Early forays found pleasure in exploring unusual values, beyond the boundaries of »normality« embodied in computing of the time, encouraging people to engage with the world in unaccustomed ways.

The *Pillow* by Tony Dunne (Dunne 1999, Dunne and Gaver 1997; see Figure 1) is an early example. This is a clear inflatable pillow, enclosing a translucent plastic block with holes cut in it, exposing patterns of colour as they play over an LCD screen. As the light suffuses the object, it creates a much softer, more imprecise display than we usually associate with computers. But the Pillow isn't just an aesthetic object; it is a strange form of radio in which lighting reflects bits of electromagnetic information from radio stations, passing taxis or nearby baby alarms. And more than a radio, it is a poser of sociocultural questions, pointing out the degree to which our homes, and even our bodies, are permeated by wireless communications. It casts its viewers as meditative voyeurs, providing them with a gentle electronic experience while subtly eliciting unease about the communications that feed it. It is an object which invites a relationship, not as a pet, but perhaps as a sort of computational alien sharing one's home (Dunne 1999).

Unorthodox values were also explored in the proposals that Heather Martin and I developed for the Alternatives project (Gaver and Martin 1999). Funded by Hewlett Packard, the Alternatives project was part of the Appliance Design Studio, a collaborative investigation of information appliances. In investigating the field, Heather and I found ourselves uninspired by contemporary examples, and developed a series of sketch proposals to expand the group's thinking. For instance, the *Dawn Chorus* (Figure 2a) was a birdfeeder that would use oper-

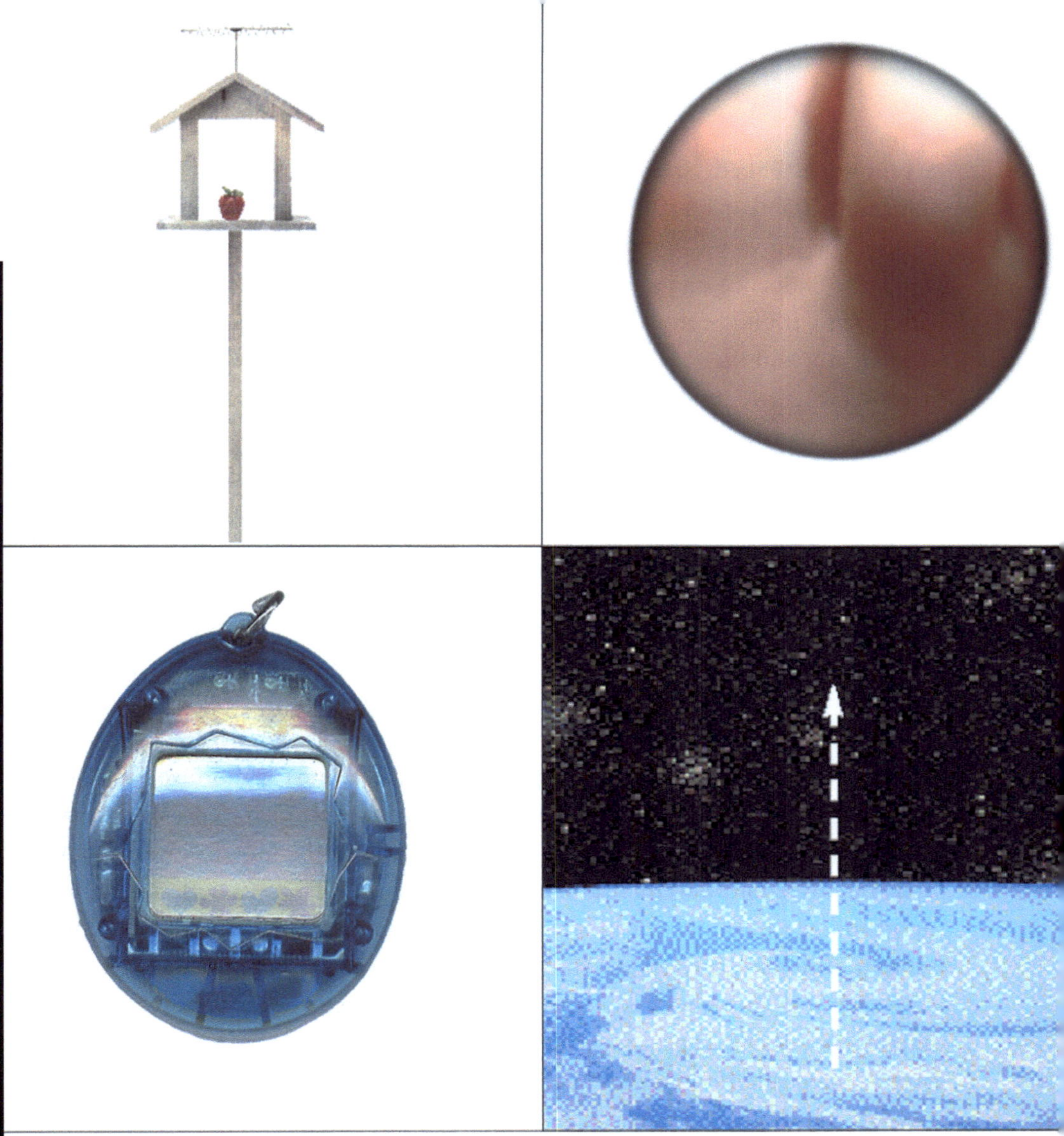

Figure 2. Several of the »Alternatives« proposals. From top to bottom, left to right: a) Dawn Chorus; b) Intimate View; c) Telegotchi; d) Prayer Device.

ant conditioning principles to teach local songbirds new tunes. The *(De)tour Guide* would be an audio-only device using GPS and an electronic compass to lead people through the city – and to support them in getting lost for a predetermined interval. The *Intimate View* camera (Figure 2b), later developed as a prototype, linked separated lovers by allowing them to capture and transmit small, highly magnified pictures to encourage moments of intensely shared focus. The *Dream Communicator* allowed distant lovers to use sounds or speech to influence one another's dreams. Finally, the *Telegotchi* was an electronic pet with no buttons that relied on psionic communication for happiness (Figure 2c), and the *Prayer Device* (Figure 2d) would be found on streets, like a new sort of telephone booth, waiting to transmit one's voice to the sky. The appeal of many of these proposals, in part, was that they didn't demand belief so much as a suspension of disbelief. They encouraged an attitude of speculation that in itself might be enjoyable.

Designing for uncommon activities and strange orientations is attractive in expanding the repertoire of computing beyond comfortable assumptions about people and their concerns. There are, however, risks in such an approach. Catering to marginal constituencies is itself liable to be perceived as a niche pursuit, with little relevance to mainstream concerns. Designs arising from such a practice can appear comical if optimistic, and alarmist if more sober. They can seem the products of sophomoric transgression, intended to provoke scandal as a means for garnering attention. None of these difficulties is insurmountable, but all require careful negotiation. More seriously, however, designing for unorthodox values doesn't inherently avoid the prescription that comes with more traditional approaches. After all, designing for unusual orientations suggests that one embodies and supports the implicit logic behind them, and this implies mandating appropriate activities and interpretations. No matter how bizarre the result, designs that seek to reify experience in this way will not truly support self-motivated play.

More recent examples of ludic design focus less on the novelty of the values they support and more on exploring a different conception of interaction itself. They let go of the idea of desirable goals or outcomes to the point that one can say they aren't »for« anything at all. Instead, they create situations that people can explore and interpret for a variety of reasons and from diverse frames of reference. As goals are relinquished, so are notions of problems to be solved or preferred courses of interaction to be encouraged. Instead, designs are better thought of as offering resources to people to make use of as they see fit.

This does not mean that such designs are completely open-ended or that they do not privilege certain topics or issues. On the contrary, one of the responsibilities of the designer is to highlight areas that are richly suggestive. The trick is to do this without implying preferred interpretations or courses of action, instead stepping back to allow people to find these for themselves.

Figure 3 (above). The Drift Table.
Figure 4 (below). The Plane Tracker.

For example, the *Drift Table* (Gaver et al. 2004a; Figure 3) is a small (1 m^2) coffee table with a circular view port on top, through which can be seen slowly scrolling aerial photography of the British countryside. The weight of objects on the table controls the direction, speed and apparent height the Table's virtual travel. Adding weight causes the table to speed up and »descend« towards the landscape below, while shifting weight around its centre controls the direction. A small screen on the side of the table shows the current location, and a built-in electronic compass ensures the images are aligned with the actual countryside. Containing almost a terabyte of high-resolution aerial photography of England and Wales, the Drift Table allows almost endless exploration of the countryside. But how one might interact with it, where one might go, and why one might go there are all left undefined. Some people stay close to home, looking at otherwise inaccessible views of their neighbourhood. Others take longer journeys, periodically checking progress and rearranging weights over the course of hours until they reach a destination chosen for its personal significance, or historical import, or current topicality. Still others simply let the table wander, seeing where it ends up after a day's random use or a night's uninterrupted travel. All are equally valid responses to the table, all are personally determined and understood, and none are privileged by the table's design. The Drift Table instantiates a form of play that is open, provisional, and personally motivated.

The *Plane Tracker* (Figure 4) is another example of a design that creates an evocative situation without enforcing a particular point of view. The Tracker is a freestanding, polyhedral cabinet with a screen on the front and a large angular aerial on the top. This device decodes radio signals from passing aircraft and uses this information to create imagined flights around the globe, shown onscreen as aerial imagery that flows smoothly from origin to destination. We designed the Plane Tracker to serve several possible narratives. The original intention was to compensate people for the noise of passing air traffic, but we also thought it might encourage a felt appreciation of the home's connections with far off locations through the aircraft passing overhead. The design also seemed of potential relevance to particular interest groups – plane spotters, for instance, or people worried about the environmental impact of flying. Like many of our designs, it seemed to create a richly evocative situation that could be approached at a number of levels and from a number of perspectives. The fact that it didn't tell any one story clearly, but might fit into many, appealed to us. It seemed to also appeal to the volunteers who lived with it for several weeks as well. With a home directly under the flight path into Heathrow Airport, we expected them to orient to the Tracker around issues of noise and disruption. Instead, they engaged with it in many different ways: as a window onto places they had been or wanted to go, as a spur to wanderlust or an uneasy reminder of the environmental effects of air travel, as a puzzle to be solved, an aesthetic object and an alternative to television. Again, the Tracker supported all these engagements, but none were directly suggested. It simply created a situation that people could explore conceptually, finding their own meanings and significances over time.

It should be clear that, whether exploring new values or setting up situations, the examples above are intended to be pleasurable in ways that go beyond mere entertainment. Each design raises issues and asks questions, ranging from the effects of pervasive electromagnetic communication, to the ethics of taming nature, the value of drifting, the status of spiritual experiences, or the implications of connecting the globe via air travel. They raise these issues, but don't provide answers. Instead, they offer avenues for people to experience life from new perspectives, and to consider hypotheses about who we might be or what we might care about. They hint at possibilities for technologies that we could use in our everyday life, not to accomplish well-defined tasks, but to expand in undefined directions. Open-ended and personal, they encourage us to play – seriously – with experiences, ideas and other people.

»...work is play for mortal stakes...«
– Robert Frost

What does designing for Homo Ludens imply for our methodologies? How can we invent and develop systems that legitimise wonder, even encourage it? How do we encourage people to meander, rather than to accomplish tasks with speed?

First, scientific approaches to design need to be complemented by more personal, idiosyncratic ones. It is difficult to conceive of a task analysis for goofing around, or to think of exploration as a problem to be solved, or to determine usability requirements for systems meant to spark new perceptions. Instead, designers need to use their personal experiences as sounding boards for the systems they create. Balancing this, they need to engage in, and often lead, a conversation with the people for whom they are developing, lest their designs become purely self-indulgent. Traditional requirements capture or ethnographic methods may be useful in this, but more ambiguous, open-ended forms of engagement can also produce inspiring results.

For instance, *Cultural Probes* (Gaver et al. 2004b, Gaver et al. 1999) are collections of provocative tasks designed to elicit inspirational responses from volunteers. Materials vary from maps to be annotated with labels or pictorial stickers, such as those used in the original Presence probes (Figure 5a), to a device for recording dreams (5b), a diary for describing nighttime sounds (5c), or a camera modified for taking self-portraits (5d), all developed in later projects. At their most prosaic, Probe materials can resemble stylised questionnaires (see Boehner et al. 2007), but more uncompromising versions thwart easy interpretation, disrupting stereotyped roles and requiring active sense-making both from researchers and the researched. The returns from such materials are neither clear nor definitive, but they are evocative, allowing researchers to create semi-factual narratives about the communities for whom they are designing and to develop design ideas that further these stories.

Second, designing for Homo Ludens means allowing room for people to appropriate technologies. Playing involves pursuing one's inner narratives in safe situations, through projective interpretation and action. If computational devices channel people's activities and perceptions too closely, then people have to live out somebody else's story, not their own (c.f. Wejchert 2001). This might be an interesting possibility – as Dunne (1999) suggests, people might approach computational devices the way they do cinema, borrowing the identities and values they suggest for a short period of time – but in general we should give people the ability to own technology, to bring it into their own complex life stories.

We have explored two primary tactics for encouraging interpretative appropriation. The first, embodied by the Drift Table and Plane Tracker described earlier, involves creating situations that suggest topics for consideration based on the resources they provide, while standing back from offering clear recommendations about how such situations should be construed.

In contrast with the self-effacing approach taken in the Drift Table and Plane Tracker, a second strategy is to exaggerate the content and authority of interpretations offered by systems. This may serve as a provocation for people to assert their own understandings as a correction. For example, the *Home Health Horoscope* (Gaver et al. 2007) uses sensor data collected from around the home to make inferences about the household's general wellbeing, communicating its conclusions in daily »readings« automatically generated from sentences found in online horoscopes. The combination of overly specific outputs, with the language of a medium that is often entertained rather than believed, seems to encourage volunteers to engage with the topics suggested by the system while insisting on their own interpretations. For instance, when the system suggests that the household is too busy they might protest that they enjoy being active, and when it encourages them to go out more they might consider it merely sarcastic.

This does not mean that such designs are completely open-ended or that they do not privilege certain topics or issues. On the contrary, one of the responsibilities of the designer is to highlight areas that are richly suggestive. The trick is to do this without implying preferred interpretations or courses of action, instead stepping back to allow people to find these for themselves.

Figure 3 (above). The Drift Table.
Figure 4 (below). The Plane Tracker.

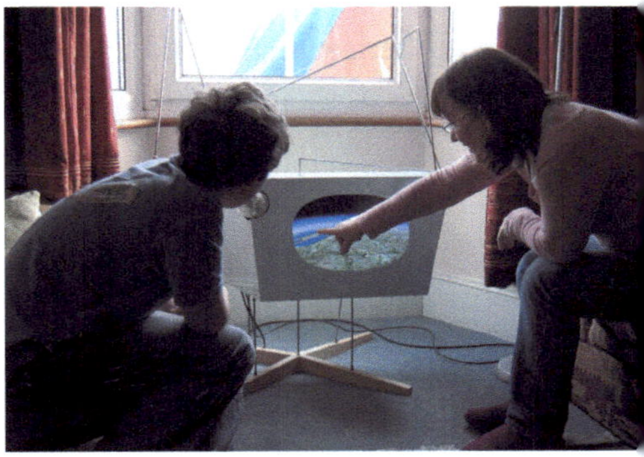

For example, the *Drift Table* (Gaver et al. 2004a; Figure 3) is a small (1 m^2) coffee table with a circular view port on top, through which can be seen slowly scrolling aerial photography of the British countryside. The weight of objects on the table controls the direction, speed and apparent height the Table's virtual travel. Adding weight causes the table to speed up and »descend« towards the landscape below, while shifting weight around its centre controls the direction. A small screen on the side of the table shows the current location, and a built-in electronic compass ensures the images are aligned with the actual countryside. Containing almost a terabyte of high-resolution aerial photography of England and Wales, the Drift Table allows almost endless exploration of the countryside. But how one might interact with it, where one might go, and why one might go there are all left undefined. Some people stay close to home, looking at otherwise inaccessible views of their neighbourhood. Others take longer journeys, periodically checking progress and rearranging weights over the course of hours until they reach a destination chosen for its personal significance, or historical import, or current topicality. Still others simply let the table wander, seeing where it ends up after a day's random use or a night's uninterrupted travel. All are equally valid responses to the table, all are personally determined and understood, and none are privileged by the table's design. The Drift Table instantiates a form of play that is open, provisional, and personally motivated.

proposals were, for instance when implementation is difficult or the ideas too simple to warrant the effort. But usually it is more satisfactory to deploy such designs as prototypes to witness their completion through use.

Here again, the approach to studying designs in use benefits from a divergent, personal approach rather than the convergent, objective one advocated by traditional scientific perspectives. After all, designs are not hypotheses to be tested simply as true or false, successful or unsuccessful. They may be approached at multiple levels, ranging from the aesthetic to the conceptual and the personal to the cultural. They may be experienced by the same person at different times, by different people and groups of people, and in different settings and circumstances. If there is no reason to privilege one particular account, it may be more informative to consider several. For instance, in my group we have recruited a variety of commentators, including ethnographers, documentary filmmakers, screenwriters and journalists, to describe how people engage with our systems. The result is a many-voiced narrative rather than a singular judgement, affording a rich, contextualised understanding of our designs that nonetheless permits evaluative judgements to be made.

> »We can't say we game not to game.«
> – Alan Kaprow

Last, and most important, pleasure comes before understanding, and engagement before clarity. Designing for Homo Ludens requires a new focus that seeks intrigue and delight at all levels of design, from the aesthetics of form and interaction, to functionality, to conceptual implications at psychological, social and cultural levels. This implies that designers cannot stand back, pronouncing as experts on situations they do not engage with personally. Instead, they need to seek a kind of empathy with the people and places for which they design, while maintaining their own sense of self. Technologies should not only reinforce pleasures that people know, but they should suggest new ones as well. Designers cannot simply efface themselves while seeking to fulfil people's articulated desires. Instead, we need to enter into a conversation with the situations for which we design, allowing ourselves both to affect and be affected by the interaction. Such a conversation will, of necessity, be situated and particular, multi-levelled and evolving – just like any good conversation is. And this implies that theories, those attempts to analyse and abstract from the messy complexity of lived experience, will have limited purchase and provide limited support. In the end, designers themselves need to be Homo Ludens. We need to recognise that we are playful creatures, and that our work depends on our play.

A lot has changed since I wrote the first version of this essay. Then, it was a manifesto. Now it is more of a report. Then, it seemed this style of design was a niche activity, belonging mainly to interaction designers. Now it appears that the perspective taken here – that technologies and the methods used to develop them need to embrace more open-ended forms of exploration and recognise wider ranges of human experience – is increasingly shared many researchers from a growing number of disciplinary perspectives. In the early essay, I wrote we were »on the brink« of a revolution in computing. Now it seems we are over the brink and well into a transformation of research methods, concepts, and practices: a »new paradigm« (see Harrison et al., 2007) for understanding technology. If we are lucky, this new paradigm won't work – it will play.

ACKNOWLEDGEMENTS

I am grateful to Jake Beaver, Anne Schlottmann and Jakub Wejchert for their comments and suggestions. This is a revised and expanded version of an article that appeared in *i3 Magazine* No. 12, June 2002.

REFERENCES

Boehner, K., Vertesi, J., Sengers, P., Dourish, P. (2007). How HCI interprets the probes. Proc CHI '07. New York: ACM Press.

Dunne, A. (1999). *Hertzian tales: Electronic products, aesthetic experience and critical design*. London: RCA:CRD Research Publications.

Dunne, A., Gaver, W. (1997). The Pillow: Artist-designers in the digital age. Conference Companion for CHI '97.

Gaver, W.W., Dunne, A., Pacenti, E. (1999). Cultural Probes. *interactions* vi(1):21–29.

Gaver, W., Martin, H. (2000). Alternatives: Exploring information appliances through conceptual design proposals. Proceedings of CHI '00 (Den Haag). New York: ACM Press.

Gaver, W., Hooker, B. (2001). The Presence Project. London: RCA:CRD Research Publications.

Gaver, W., Bowers, J., Boucher, A., Gellerson, H., Pennington, S., Schmidt, A., Steed, A., Villars, N., Walker, B. (2004a). The Drift Table: Designing for ludic engagement. Proc. CHI '04 Design Expo. New York: ACM Press.

Gaver, W.W., Boucher, A., Pennington, S., Walker, B. (2004b). Cultural Probes and the value of uncertainty. *interactions* xi(5):53–56.

Gaver, W., Sengers, P., Kerridge, T., Kaye, J., Bowers, J. (2007). Enhancing ubiquitous computing with user interpretation: Field testing the Home Health Horoscope. Proc. CHI '07.

Harrison, S., Tatar, D., Senger,s P. (2007). The three paradigms of HCI. Proc. alt.chi.

Huizinga, J. (1950). *Homo Ludens: A study of the play-element in culture.* Boston: The Beacon Press.

Wejchert, J. (2001). The dreaming. *Informatik/Informatique* 5.

ERIC ZIMMERMAN

GAMING LITERACY

– GAME DESIGN AS A MODEL FOR LITERACY IN THE 21ST CENTURY

ERIC
ZIMMERMAN
GAMING LITERACY
– GAME DESIGN AS A MODEL FOR LITERACY IN THE 21ST CENTURY

INTRODUCTION: LITERACY AND GAMES FROM THE INSIDE-OUT

Gaming Literacy is an approach to literacy based on game design. My argument is that there is an emerging set of skills and competencies, a set of new ideas and practices that are going to be an increasing part of what it means to be literate in the coming century. This chapter's proposal is that game design is a paradigm for understanding what these literacy needs are and how they might be addressed. I look at three main concepts – systems, play and design – as key components of this new literacy.

Traditional ideas about literacy have centered on reading and writing – the ability to understand, exchange, and create meaning through text, speech and other forms of language. A younger cousin to literacy studies, *media literacy* extended this thinking to diverse forms of media, from images and music to film, television and advertising. The emphasis in media literacy as it evolved during the 1980s was an ideological critique of the hidden codes embedded in media. Media studies scholars ask questions like: Is a given instance of media racist or sexist? Who is creating it and with what agenda? What kinds of intended and unintended messages and meanings do media contain?

Literacy, even media literacy, is necessary but not sufficient for one to be fully literate in our world today. There are emerging needs for new kinds of literacy that are simply not being addressed, needs that arise, in part, from a growing use of computer and communication networks (more about that later). Gaming literacy is one approach to addressing these new sorts of literacies that will become increasingly crucial for work, play, education, and citizenship in the coming century.

Gaming literacy reverses conventional ideas about what games are and how they function. A classical way of understanding games is the »magic circle«, a concept that originates with the Dutch historian and philosopher Johann Huizinga (1950). The magic circle represents the idea that games take place within limits of time and space, and are self-contained systems of meaning. A Chess king, for example, is just a little figurine sitting on a coffee table. But when a game of Chess starts, it suddenly acquires all kinds of very specific strategic, psychological and even narrative meanings. To consider another example, when a Soccer game or *Street Fighter II* (Capcom, 1992) match begins, your friend suddenly becomes your opponent and bitter rival – at least for the duration of the game. While many social and cultural meanings certainly do move in and out of any game (for instance, your in-game rivalry might ultimately affect your friendship outside the game), the magic circle emphasizes those meanings that are intrinsic and interior to games.

Gaming literacy turns this inward-looking focus inside-out. Rather than addressing the meanings that only arise inside the magic circle of a game, it asks how games relate to the world outside the magic circle – how game playing and game design can be seen as models for learning and action in the real world. It asks, in other words, not *What does gaming look like?* but instead, *What does the world look like from the point of view of gaming?*

It's important to be very clear here: gaming literacy is not about just any kind of real-world impact – it is a specific form of literacy. So for the sake of specificity, here are some things that gaming literacy is *not*:

- Gaming literacy is not about »serious games« – games designed to teach you subject matter, such as eighth-grade algebra.
- Gaming literacy is not about »persuasive games« that are designed to impart some kind of message or social agenda to the player.
- Gaming literacy is also not about training professional game designers, or even about the idea that anyone can be a game designer.

Gaming literacy is *literacy* – it is the ability to understand and create specific kinds of meanings. As I describe it here, gaming literacy is based on three concepts: *systems*, *play* and *design*. All three are closely tied to game design, and each represents kinds of literacies that are currently not being addressed through traditional education. Each concept also points to a new paradigm for what it will mean to become literate in the coming century. Together they stand for a new set of cognitive, creative and social skills – a cluster of practices that I call *gaming literacy*.

I like the term »gaming literacy« not only because it references the way that games and game design are closely tied to the emerging literacies I identify, but also because of the mischievous double-meaning of »gaming«, which can signify exploiting or taking clever advantage of something. Gaming a system means finding hidden shortcuts and cheats, and bending and modifying rules in order to move through the system more efficiently – perhaps to misbehave, but perhaps to change that system for the better. We can game the stock market, a university course registration process, or even just a flirtatious conversation. Gaming literacy, in other words, »games« literacy, bending and breaking rules, playing with our notions of what literacy has been and can be.

SYSTEMS

To paraphrase contemporary communication theory, a system is a set of parts that interrelates to form a whole. Almost anything can be considered a system, from biological and physical systems to social and cultural systems. Having a systems point of view (being *systems literate*) means understanding the world as dynamic sets of parts with complex, constantly changing interrelationships – seeing the structures that underlie our world and comprehending how these structures function.

As a key component of gaming literacy, systems can be considered a paradigm for literacy in the coming century. Increasingly, complex information systems are part of how we socialize and date, conduct business and finance, learn and research and conduct our working lives. Our world is increasingly defined by systems. Being able to successfully understand, navigate, modify and design systems will become more and more inextricably linked with how we learn, work, play and live as engaged world citizens.

Systems-based thinking is about process, not answers. It stresses the importance of dynamic relationships, not fixed facts. Getting to know a system requires understanding it on several levels, from the fixed foundational structures of the system to its emergent, unpredictable patterns of behavior. Systems thinking thereby leads to the kinds of improvisational problem-solving skills that will be critical for creative learning and work in the future. In part, the rise of systems as an integral aspect of our lives is related to the increasing prominence of digital technology and networks. But systems literacy is not intrinsically related to computers. The key to systems literacy is about a shift in attitude, not about learning technological skills.

If systems are a paradigm for an emerging form of literacy, what is the connection to games? Games are, in fact, essentially systemic. Every game has a mathematical substratum, a set of rules that lies under its surface. Other kinds of media, art, and entertainment are not so intrinsically structured. Scholars debate, for example, the essential formal core of a film – is it the script? The pattern of the editing over time? The composition of light and shadow in a frame? There is not one correct answer. But with games, there is the clarity of a formal system – the rules of the game. This formal system is the basis of the structures that constitute a game's systems. More than other kinds of culture and media which have been the focus of literacy in the past, then, games are uniquely well-suited to teach systems literacy.

To play, understand, and – especially – design games, one ends up having to understand them as systems. Any game is a kind of miniature artificial system, bounded and defined by the game rules that create the game's magic circle. Playing a game well to see which strategies are more effective, analyzing the game's rules to see how they ramify into a player's experience, and designing a game by playtesting, modifying the rules, and playtesting again, are all examples of how games naturally and powerfully lend themselves to systems literacy.

PLAY

Games are systems because at some level they are mathematical systems of rules. But if games were just math, we would never have the athletic balletics of Tennis, the bluffing warfare of Poker, or the deep collaboration of *World of Warcraft* (Blizzard, 2004). Play is the human effect of rules set into motion, in its many forms transcending the systems from which it emerges. Just as games are more than their structures of rules, gaming literacy is more than the concept of systems. It is also play.

There is a curious relationship between rules and play. In the classical sense of a game as a magic circle, rules are fixed, rigid and closed. They are logical, rational and scientific. Rules really don't seem like much fun at all. But when rules are taken on and adopted by players who enter the magic circle and agree to follow the rules, play happens. Play in many ways is the opposite of rules: as much as rules are closed and fixed, play is improvisational and uncertain. Yet in a game, these two opposites find a common home – gameplay paradoxically occurring only because of game rules.

In *Rules of Play*, Katie Salen and I define play as *free movement within a more rigid structure* (Salen and Zimmerman 2004). Imagine play as the »free play« of a gear or steering wheel: the loose movement in an otherwise rigid structure of interlocking parts. The free play of a steering wheel is the distance it can move without engaging with the drive shaft, axle and wheels – the more rigid utilitarian structures of the car. This free play only exists because of the more inflexible, functional structures of the automobile. Yet it also exists *despite* those structures. A joke, for example, is funny because of how it plays with the structures of language, creating subtle ironies, or double-meanings, or vulgar inappropriateness. The free play humor of a joke exists in opposition to the more rigid structures of earnest, ordinary language – yet is utterly dependent on these very structures for its play.

Yet play is far more than just play *within* a structure. Play can *play with* structures. Players don't just play games; they mod them, engage in metaplay between games and develop cultures around games. Games are not just about following rules, but also about breaking them, whether it is players creating homebrew rules for *Monopoly* (Charles B. Darrow, 1933), hacking into their favorite deathmatch title, or breaking social norms in classics like Spin the Bottle that create and celebrate taboo behavior.

Although play exists outside of games, games do provide one of the very best platforms for understanding play – from free play within a structure to the transformative play that reconfigures that structure. Any instance of a game is an engine designed to produce play, a miniature laboratory for studying play *qua play*.

So why is play an important paradigm for literacy in the coming century? Systems are important, but if we limit literacy to structural, systemic literacy, then we are missing part of the equation. When we move from systems to play, we shift focus from the game to the players, from structures of rules to structures of human interaction. Games as play are social ecosystems and personal experience, and these dimensions are key aspects of a well-rounded literacy.

As our lives become more networked, people are engaging more and more with structures. But they are not merely inhabiting these structures – they are playing with them. A social network like Wikipedia is not just a fixed construct like a circuit diagram. It is a fuzzy system, a dynamic system, a social system, a cultural system. Systems only become meaningful as they are inhabited, explored, and manipulated by people. In the coming century, what will become important will not be just systems, but *human* systems.

A literacy based on play is a literacy of innovation and invention. Just as systems literacy is about engendering a systems-based attitude, being literate in play means having a *ludic attitude* that sees the world's structures as opportunities for playful engagement. What does it mean to play with institutional language, with social spaces, or with processes of learning? When these rules are bent, broken and transformed, what new structures will arise?

Play emerges from more rigid systems, but it does not take those systems for granted. It plays with them, modifying, transgressing, and reinventing. We must learn to approach problem-solving with a spirit of playfulness; not to resist, but to embrace transformation and change. As a paradigm for innovation in the coming century, play will increasingly inform how we learn, work, and create culture.

DESIGN

>> The notion of design connects powerfully to the sort of creative intelligence the best practitioners need in order to be able, continually, to redesign their activities in the very act of practice. It connects as well to the idea that learning and productivity are the results of the designs (the structures) of complex systems of people, environments, technology, beliefs, and texts.

The New London Group (1996)

If gaming literacy were simply about systems and play, it would be a literacy based on games, not game design. But design, the third component of gaming literacy, is absolutely key, and in many ways helps bring the traditional idea of literacy as understanding and creating meaning back into the mix. There are many definitions of design, but in *Rules of Play* Katie Salen and I describe design as *the process by which a designer creates a context, to be encountered by a participant, from which meaning emerges* (Salen and Zimmerman 2004).

Design as the creation of meaning invokes the magic circle: designers create contexts that in turn create signification. Although design comes in many forms, from architecture to industrial design, games happen to be incredibly well-suited for studying how meaning is made. Outside the game of Rock Paper Scissors, a fist can mean many things. But inside the game, that gesture is assigned a highly specific significance, a defined meaning within the lexicon of the game's language. The creation of meaning through game design is wonderfully complex. A game creates its own meanings (blue means enemy; yellow means power-up), but also traffics with meanings from the outside (horror film music in a shooter means danger is coming; Poker means a fun evening with friends).

For a game designer, the creation of meaning is a second-order problem. The game designer creates structures of rules directly, but only indirectly creates the experience of play when the rules are enacted by players. As a game unfolds through play, metaplay and transformative play, unexpected things happen, patterns that are impossible to completely predict. In this way, design is not about the creation of a fixed object. It is about creating a set of possibilities.

The audience is always at least one step removed from the designer. Games embody this aspect of design in a very direct and essential way; even the most straightforward game of Chess or *The Sims* (Maxis Software, 2000) is about players exploring the possibilities that they are given by a designed object. In a game, design mediates between structure and play; a game system is designed just so that play will occur.

Over and above game design's affinity for the process of making meaning, it is also radically interdisciplinary. Making a game includes creating a formal system of rules, while also designing a human play experience for a particular cultural and social context. Game design involves math and logic, aesthetics and storytelling, writing and communication, visual and audio design, human psychology and behavior, and understanding culture through art, entertainment and popular media. For video game design, computer and technological literacy become part of the equation as well.

As an exploration of process, as the rigorous creation of meaning, and as a uniquely interdisciplinary endeavor, game design represents multimodal forms of learning that educators and literacy theorists have been talking about for years, perhaps most significantly in the publications of the New London Group (I've quoted them at the start of this section above). Game design, as the investigation of the possibility of meaning, truly gets at the heart of gaming literacy, and ties together systems, play, and design into a unified and integrated process.

CONCLUSION: A PLAYFUL WORLD

As we move into the early years of the twenty-first century, the world is becoming increasingly transformed by communications, transportation and information technology that is shrinking our globe, making it a place of cultural exchanges both constructive and destructive. Existing models of literacy simply do not fully address reality in the world today.

Gaming literacy is certainly not the only way to understand the emerging literacy needs I have identified. But games and game design are one promising approach, making use of a cultural form that is wildly popular and wildly varied, both incredibly ancient and strikingly contemporary. And intrinsically playful as well.

So how does one take action to promote gaming literacy? At Gamelab, the independent game development company I founded in 2000 with Peter Lee, we have begun a number of gaming literacy projects. We are building Gamestar Mechanic – funded by the MacArthur Foundation and created in collaboration with the Games, Learning and Society group at the University of Wisconsin-Madison – a computer program that will help youth learn about game design by letting them create and modify simple games. A year ago, we announced the creation of the Institute of Play. With Katie Salen as the Executive Director, the Institute will promote gaming literacy through educational programs and advocacy.

What does gaming literacy mean for game players and game makers? The good news is that games, so often maligned, have much to offer our complex world. And not just so-called »serious games« with explicit educational goals, but any game. Gaming literacy can help us feel good about what we do by playing games, making games, studying games, modding games and taking part in gaming communities. As literacy scholar James Paul Gee likes to say, »video games are good for your soul.«

Gaming literacy turns the tables on the usual way we regard games. Rather than focusing on what happens inside the artificial world of a game, gaming literacy asks how playing, understanding, and designing games all embody crucial ways of looking at and being in the world. This way of being embraces the rigor of systems, the creativity of play, and the game design instinct to continually redesign and reinvent meaning.

It's not that games will necessarily make the world a better place. But in the coming century, the way we live and learn, work and relax, communicate and create, will more and more resemble how we play games. While we're not all going to be game designers, game design and gaming literacy offer a valuable model for what it will mean to become literate, educated and successful in this playful world.

CODA: NO ESSAY IS AN ISLAND

The ideas in this chapter are not just my own, but are part of a growing conversation that can be heard across universities, commercial game companies, grade school classrooms, nonprofit foundations, and in other places where game players, game makers, scholars, and educators intersect.

Although I have been a game designer and game design theorist for more than a decade, I began to rigorously connect game design and literacy through my interaction with the GAPPS group (now called GLS), a collection of scholars at the University of Wisconsin-Madison that includes Jim Gee, Rich Halverson, Betty Hayes, David Shaffer, Kurt Squire and Constance Steinkuehler. I was privileged to be invited to a series of conversations with this stimulating crew about games and literacy sponsored by the Spencer Foundation. In 2006, during the third of these three meetings, the term »gaming literacy« emerged from our conversations as a concept that could reference growing connections between games, learning, literacy, and design.

I am greatly indebted to game designer, scholar and educator Katie Salen for our ongoing collaborations, including the textbook *Rules of Play: Game Design Fundamentals* (Katie also attended that third Spencer meeting). My ideas on game design and learning have also been shaped by my work with the amazing staff at Gamelab, especially my co-founder Peter Lee, and former Gamelab game designers Frank Lantz and Nick Fortugno. Connie Yowell at the MacArthur Foundation has also been instrumental in bringing together scholars, artists, educators, and designers to exchange ideas, including the commission of important foundational research by the polymedia scholar Henry Jenkins. The specific formulations in this chapter were first instantiated in a talk I gave at Vancouver's Simon Frasier University, in January 2007, and this chapter received valuable feedback from Jim Gee, Katie Salen, Kurt Squire, and Constance Steinkuehler.

So thanks, everybody. I go to this trouble to highlight some of my sources in order to emphasize the newness of these ideas and the collaborative way that they are emerging from a thick soup of scholarship, debates and collaborations. This kind of dialogue is very much in the spirit of gaming literacy itself and I encourage you to take part in the conversation as well. Some of the best places to get involved include the Games, Learning and Society conference held annually at the University of Wisconsin-Madison (www.glsconference.org), the Serious Games Initiative (www.seriousgames.org), the Education SIG of the International Game Developers Association (www.igda.org/education) and the ongoing dialogs about digital media literacy at the Macarthur Foundation website (http://community.macfound.org/openforum).

REFERENCES

Huizinga, J. (1950). *Homo Ludens*. New York, NY: Roy.

Salen, K., Zimmerman, E. (2004). *Rules of play*. Cambridge, MA: MIT Press.

The New London Group (1996). A pedagogy of multiliteracies: Designing social futures. *Harvard Educational Review* 66(1):60–92.

JOHAN REDSTRÖM

DISRUPTIONS

JOHAN
DISRUPTIONS
REDSTRÖM

INTRODUCTION

There seems to be something about the expressiveness of digital technologies that has to do with disruptions. Consider analogue to digital signal conversion as an example. Whereas it might be the goal of such processes to hide the resulting artefacts, it is nevertheless a matter of cutting a continuous flow up into sequences of discrete events. The same, of course, holds for how a computer tracks what the user does. If we look to the expressions of such processes, the issue of how these discrete events and pieces are created is central, that is, how disruptions are introduced through sensor systems, sampling procedures, compression algorithms, etc.

Also in more high-level discourses on how technology presents itself to us, we find that disruptions play a rather central role. As in phenomenology: the notion of breakdown, when a tool reveals itself to us not as an instrumental extension of our intentions but as thing in itself. As in art: the use of poetic devices such as estrangement to disrupt normal conduct and expose aspects of how we relate to things and situations. And in between: everything from waiting for the traffic signals to turn green and dishwashers to finish, to conversations being disrupted by calling mobile phones.

In what follows I will look at how we deal with disruptions in interaction design. The basic reason for doing so is the somewhat paradoxical situation that while disruptions seem to be something intrinsic to the digital, they are typically something interaction design aims to eliminate. I will argue that the idea – or ideal – of a continuous interaction between man and machine is one out of several options and thus perhaps not the »natural« strategy we typically seem to think.

GENEALOGIES OF CRITIQUE

> Criticism of society is ultimately revolution; there you have criticism taken to its logical conclusion and playing an active part. A critical attitude of this type is an operative factor of productivity; it is deeply enjoyable as such, and if we commonly use the term »arts« for enterprises that improve people's lives why should art proper remain aloof from arts of this sort? (Brecht 1957)

The task of design research to stake out the possible is not only about what has not yet been done, but also about that which has already been created which could be done differently. This creates a rather peculiar situation for design research in that our way of acknowledging the work we build on often turns out as a critique of the same.

The history of user-centred design illustrates this situation quite well with its many twists and turns in developing ever richer conceptualisations of both use and user. For instance, although psychological experiments performed in order to »defend human attributes in the age of the machine«, to use Norman's phrase (1993), have been instrumental in uncovering hidden assumptions and misconceptions about use and users, such approaches have also been criticized for taking a far too narrow perspective on both people and their practices. Another historical illustration is how the early Design Methods movement became criticised for an overly rationalistic and formal approach to understanding and appreciating design work, when the very purpose of that formalisation was to introduce new kinds of representations in order to open up the design process for collaboration and external participation (e.g. Alexander 1984, Jones 1984, 1992).

In this way we seem to move one, not only by advancing but importantly also by disrupting previous lines of design work. Maybe it is because design has to deal with so many variables that many of them are hidden and that it is only when we highlight some of them we also notice others. Maybe it is because there indeed is progress and that the questions we can, and are allowed to, ask changes as our field grows.

A more recent addition to this genealogy of critiques within what we may now call interaction design concerns aesthetics (cf. Udsen and Jørgensen 2005, Hallnäs and Redström 2002). If we consider aesthetics to be about the expressions and expressiveness of things, then it is quite clear that there are always aesthetical choices present also in the design of technology – be that they may not be explicit but rather silently assumed. Any design, including the design of technological systems, involves a range of decisions related to how the design in question will present itself to us.

Just as the shape of things in certain ways is a matter of aesthetics, so are the forms of use. When dealing with computers, it is not necessarily the external shape of the objects as such that is in focus, but rather the expression of its functions and how they unfold over time through use. Commenting on the experience of designing the ELEA 9003 mainframe in the 1950s, Sottsass remarked that »one ends up conditioning the man who is working, not only his direct physical relationship with the instrument, but also his very much more penetrating relationship with the whole act of work« (Sparke 1982, p. 63).

Because of the central importance of forms of use when it comes to technology, an important task for interaction is to uncover the aesthetical design issues we do not notice as such, as they have become hidden not only by deliberate decisions but also by habits and institutionalised ways of developing technology. Thus, it is, to some extent, a matter of reclaiming certain issues now often understood as just technical or functional concerns as also being a matter of aesthetics. This might be one reason why the emerging aesthetics of interaction to such a great degree seem to engage in a critique of use and usability. Eventually, an aesthetics of interaction need not be critical to functionality and usability as such, but for the time being there seems to be a need not only for developing new positions, but for deconstructing established ones.

EFFICIENCY AND THE FEAR OF FAILURE

» The good object can offer only one unambiguous solution: the type. (We all have the same telephone without longing for an individual design. We wear similar clothes and are satisfied with a small degree of difference within this restriction.)

The optimal form demands mass production. Mechanization also means economy.

The Bauhaus attempts to produce the elements of the house with this economy in mind – therefore to find the single solution that is best for our times. It applies itself to this task in experimental workshops, its designs prototypes for the whole house as well as the teapot, and it works to improve our

> entire way of life by means of economic production which is only possible with the aid of the prototype. (Moholy-Nagy 1923)

The problem with discussing hidden assumptions is of course that they are not that present in the literature expressing the position in question. At times, however, they rise to the surface. Consider this characterisation of the man-machine interface by Krippendorff (2006, p. 9):

> Interfaces constitute an entirely new kind of artifact, a human-technological symbiosis that cannot be attended to without reference to both. For designers, a key concern is that interfaces are understandable. User's understanding need not be »correct« as intended by the producer, engineer, or designer of the technology. It needs to go only as far as needed for users to be able to interact with that technology as naturally and effortless as possible, without causing disruptions and reasons to fear failure. User-friendliness is a popular term that describes interactive understanding and seamless or uninterrupted use. Usability is another word for much the same interface quality.

Krippendorff presents a typical picture of how the man-machine interface has been addressed in design, and especially how it has been developed within human-computer interaction (HCI). Though more popular terms such as »user-friendliness« have a stronger presence outside the research field, its expression of ideals related to natural, efficient and effortless interaction holds true also for much of this research.

With respect to an understanding of technical perfection as efficiency, disruptions become a kind of failures. Disruptions are shortcomings of technology and design that will vanish as optimisation proceeds. Because of this attitude, designers may easily bracket disruptions, thinking that they eventually will disappear entirely when we get the design right (Johansson 2007). However, in case there indeed is something important about disruptions in the design of the digital, and in case they indeed are hidden in – and by – design practice, they ought to turn up as problems in use. And they do.

The disruptive character of the digital reveals itself in many ways ranging from the pixilation of live images sent over networks, to the sometimes short but distinct interruptions we experience as the computer accelerates its hard disk back from rest, connects to a server, etc. But it also shows in the interferences between how interaction with a computer has been designed and the often disrupted and fragmentary nature of work and life. A small experiment: next time you are in a meeting and you need to coordinate the next meeting using the calendars in your computers (and the computers are not already up and running) – watch what happens. Even if you just put your computer to rest and do not have to start it, the effects are quite visible.

Even if we no longer have to live with batch-programming and the downtimes of time-sharing systems, contemporary users of complex business intelligence systems, systems for forecasting and analysing huge data sets, etc., frequently have to plan for sometimes long periods of waiting for computing to take place. And the practice of file-sharers to initiate the download of very large files in the evening in order to take advantage of the reduced network traffic load and to be able to have the result in the morning, is after all not that different from batch-programming from a user's point of view. Even the effects of time-sharing might still be experienced when connecting to popular websites, such as news sites when there has been a significant event. Or indeed what happened to me just *now*: my computer says it needs to restart because of a security update … (two minutes later) … It seems that even massively improved technology still has not eliminated these disruptions. And maybe it never will.

But how did it come to the point where we do not think we have to design disruptions? To start unpacking this idea and ideal about what interacting with computers should be like, let us go back to the time before this approach to computer use was developed, back to when continuous interaction was introduced as the »new« approach to computer use.

In the early days of computing, computation was comparably very slow, making the issues of time in computer use quite visible. In many ways a question of temporal form, the need to optimise the use of computational power had to be balanced against the capacity of its human operators and the need for a rational work practice. As a response, notions such as batch programming, and then conversational, time-sharing and later so-called interactive modes of use were developed. Based on estimates and an analysis of both human's and computer's information-processing capacities, Simon once proposed three different modes of use (1966, p. 48):

> a user might be given the alternatives of (1) operating in a conversational mode, (2) operating with a ten to twenty minute turnaround time, or (3) submitting tasks that will be processed in, say, a day. [...] It will not only be useless, but absolutely harmful, (1) to provide service that is slower than conversational, but gives faster than ten minute's turnaround, and (2) service that is slower than ten to twenty minutes, but of the order of magnitude of an hour. [...] *It would be harmful, also, to provide unpredictable service in any mode.*

Over time, the massive increase in computing power resolved many of these design problems eventually making the »interactive« modes more common. An interesting aspect of this history is how it highlights the close relation between the temporal character of computation and the concrete form of the acts of using it – and by extension how their combination influences how use will unfold over time. Especially in the early modes of use, the gaps – or swaps – between different acts and activities and their relation to computational processes are clearly visible. Indeed, one design issue was how to deal with waiting in relation to a rational work practice.

Whereas batch programming and time sharing were responses to a situation where computing power was limited, interactive computing is to some extent a response to the opposite situation, a situation where it increasingly is the user's capacities that defines the limits of the efficiency and capacity of this »coupled« man-machine information-processing system. Indeed, this is a central reason for the increasing interest in understanding users evident in early human-computer interaction studies. Hints in this direction are available quite early on in the design of computer use acts. Simon (1966, p. 51) again:

> The reflections in this paper have centred around the notion that in designing a man-computer system, both human user and computer can be specified in terms of the same parameters – principally, processing rate and memory swap time – although man and computer will have quite different numerical values for each parameter. Viewing a man-machine system as a more or less symmetric structure in which the machine initiates tasks for the man just as the man initiates tasks for the machine suggests approaches to the control of time-sharing systems quite different those typically taken in the past.

The point with this brief historical overview is not to discuss the history of HCI, but to illustrate that the development of »interactive computing« did not only happen because of an increasingly user-centred approach to design, but essentially because of a continuous expansion and optimisation of the capacity of the man-machine information-processing system. To a significant extent, the modes of using computers stem from the properties of the computational material and how to make the most out of it. This is why the first sentence in the quote from Krippendorf (2006, p. 9) above is so important: »Interfaces constitute an entirely new kind of artifact, a human-technological symbiosis that cannot be attended to without reference to both.«

Though the origin of such a symbiosis can be traced to the technical development of computers, its influence on work and life have caused alternative and often critical approaches to emerge. Because of this history, a central aspect of any such approach is therefore the re-interpretation, or conceptualisation, of the computer something else than just a »computer«, for instance as a *tool* (e.g. Ehn 1998), a *medium* (e.g. Liestøl et al 2003) or a *material* (e.g. Löwgren and Stolterman 1998, Redström 2005). This is an important tactic used to shift the balance between looking at use from the perspective of technology and considering technology on basis of its use.

Turning back to temporal form in general, and to disruptions and interactive computing in particular, let us now inspect one of the design paradoxes that this development seems to have caused. Suchman (1987, pp. 10f) wrote that:

> The technical definition of »interactive computing« ... is simply that real-time control over the computing process is placed in the hands of the user, through immediate processing and through the availability of interrupt facilities whereby the user can override and modify the operations in progress.

According to Suchman's account, the possibility to interrupt computational processes is a key to the real-time control of the machine. Turning back to Krippendorff's (2006, p. 9) description, interruptions are instead something to be eliminated by design:

> It needs to go only as far as needed for users to be able to interact with that technology as naturally and effortless as possible, without causing disruptions and reasons to fear failure. User-friendliness is a popular term that describes interactive understanding and seamless or uninterrupted use.

It seems disruptions are at the same time central to interaction, and something interaction design should aim at eliminating. The easy way out here is of course to dismiss the issue since the two quotes obviously deals with two different kinds of disruptions: wanted and unwanted ones. Whereas the first concern the user's control over the machine and how »use« at least in principle might take precedence over »computing« when it comes to structuring its temporal form, the second is about technical perfection understood as efficient and error-free operation.

The slightly more interesting option, however, is to assume that they do have something to do with each other and that while disruptions have become something we avoid, they do have an interesting potential when it comes to the aesthetics of interaction. Another reason for adopting such a perspective is, of course, that distinctions such as the one between wanted and unwanted disruptions is not likely to hold.

Before exploring the design potential of disruptions, however, we probably have to say something more about why disruptions have become something we think should be eliminated by design. Besides the argument from the history of computer use sketched above, there are at least two other possible reasons worth examining. The first one concerns the spreading of a kind of economical thinking across many domains of life and is very much related to the story above; the second reason concerns the issue of how »immaterial« artefacts may become present in our lives.

In industrial production and its management, disruptions are generally something to be avoided as all available resources, including the time of people, are being optimised. As ideas about economical and instrumental rationality spreads to domains outside its industrial and management office origins, also its ideals diffuse. Virilio (1995, p. 135) argues that:

> the gradual spread of a SOCIOPOLITICAL CYBERNETICS that tends to eliminate not only the weak, but also the component of free will in human work, promoting, as we have seen, so-called »interactive user-friendliness.« This is just a metaphor for the subtle enslavement of the human being to »intelligent« machines; a programmed symbiosis of man and computer in which assistance and the much trumpeted »dialogue between man and the machine« scarcely conceal the premises ... the total, unavowed disqualification of the human in favor of the definitive instrumental conditioning of the individual.

Today, people might be expected (and expect themselves) to be »efficient« not only at work, but also in life in general. For instance, quite frequently people might use the very same devices (time-managers, calendars, etc.) to plan and structure their »free« time as they use at work. Given such an expanding influence of economical rationality, it would not be too surprising if our interactions with technology were designed along similar lines – especially as many of these ideas have their origin in technology development and the notion of technical rationality. It is, however, important to remember that such ideas have been part of industrial design from the start, as can be seen in the quote from Moholy-Nagy (1923) opening this section.

Disruptions have, however, also been a hidden issue in design approaches not necessarily subscribing to such technical and economical rationality. Here, the reasons for avoiding disruptions differ. One reason stems from the notion that computational technology in some ways can, or must, be considered »immaterial«, i.e. that what makes it into what it is, is not present to us the way ordinary objects are. As a consequence, interfaces must be used to access the results of computation and communication and it is by means of such interfaces that we aim to prevent people from literally losing touch with their knowledge and skills. We need not dwell upon the particular properties of such »immaterial« technologies here, but it is important to understand that such issues are an important reason to find ways of making computational things more continuously present to us in order to make them more accessible and even graspable.

Historically, the ambition to design and create such a continuous presence, however, seems to have been resolved by means of continuous interaction with the machine, resulting in an overall design that frequently demands its users full attention. That is, creating presence by means of immersion rather than expression. However, the design strategy of continuous interaction to meet the needs for making computational things present to users has been challenged. Within areas such as mobile technologies and ubiquitous computing, existing computer interface paradigms have been challenged on basis of the need to accommodate short bursts of interaction and more fragmented forms of use. Here, disruptions have become a more central design concern, which we will have to return to later.

DIS-COVERED DISRUPTIONS

> There is indeed such a thing as »order« in art, but not a single column of a Greek temple fulfills its order perfectly, and artistic rhythm may be said to exist in the rhythm of prose disrupted. Attempts have been made by some to systematize these »disruptions.« They represent today's task in the theory of rhythm. We have good reasons to suppose that this systemization will not succeed. This is so because we are dealing here not so much with a more complex rhythm as with a disruption of rhythm itself, a violation, we may add, that can never be predicted. If this violation enters the canon, then it loses its power as a complicating device. (Shklovsky 1925)

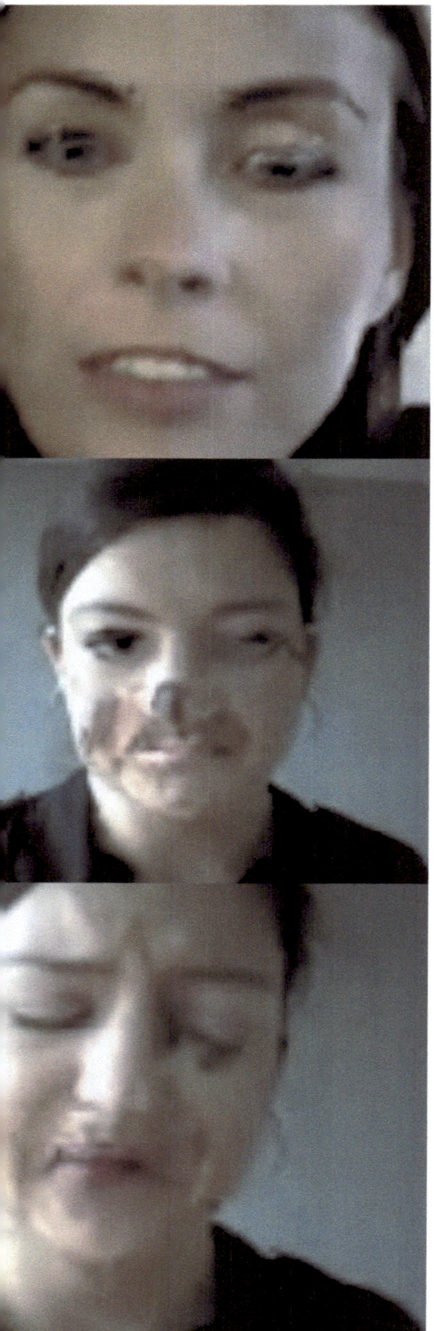

ONLINE PHOTOGRAPHY

Besides the more theoretical exploration of the expressions of disruptions presented here, I also made some more practical experiments. One such series of experiments were made around a notion of »online photography«, that is, a kind of digital photography made possible by remote cameras communicating over the Internet. Here, the many layers of space and time intersect and interact causing glitches and disruptions in both time and space. For instance, where and when is a picture taken when the photographer is in one part of the world, and the camera and subject in another?

In particular, I became interested in how we appear as we »meet« online, in video-conferences for example. Not only do such technologies introduce disruptions of actual space and time by enabling us to communicate »anywhere, anytime«, they also make us lose control of how we appear to others because of the disruptions introduced through the properties of network connections, data compression etc. You don't see these transformations of your appearance yourself, as the feedback image you can see represent the images sent, and not the ones the other part receive. Thus, as a »sender«, you do not see the glitches introduced, and as a »receiver«, you do not see the original image. And so the photographer can not really see what the person being portrayed actually looks like, adding a certain kind of complexity to the already socially rich category of the »portrait«. These images are three such portraits of friends of mine.

The word digital stems from the latin word for finger, *digitus*, the practice of counting using the fingers and, by extension, the use of discontinuous values to represent information. Of particular interest to us here is how digital technology is characterised by its representation also of continuous streams of information as sequences of discrete elements. In a way, this technology gains its power through the introduction of disruptions.

These digital disruptions are meant to disappear as technology becomes increasingly perfected, but at least in the early stages of development they are clearly visible. Just take a look at a picture taken with a digital camera five years ago. There are, however, examples especially from art that instead of hiding such characteristic properties underneath the surface aim at exposing them. One such example is to be found in Glitch music, Cascone (2000, p. 13) comments:

> While technological failure is often controlled and suppressed – its effects buried beneath the threshold of perception – most audio tools can zoom in on the errors, allowing composers to make them the focus of their work. Indeed, »failure« has become a prominent aesthetic in many of the arts in the late 20th century, reminding us that our control of technology is an illusion, and revealing digital tools to be only as perfect, precise, and efficient as the humans who build them. New techniques are often discovered by accident or by the failure of an intended technique or experiment.
>
> The medium is no longer the message in glitch music: the tool has become the message. The technique of exposing the minutiae of DSP [Digital Signal Processing] errors and artifacts for their own sonic value has helped further blur the boundaries of what is to be considered music, but it has also forced us to also to examine our preconceptions of failure and detritus more carefully. (ibid, p. 17)

Glitch music is located within a rich history of musical experimentation, and especially related the line of work initiated by Schaeffer's *musique concrete*

(1966), but it also relates to a range of artistic work investigating digital technologies. Thus, there are also examples of glitch aesthetics in digital photography and film. A somewhat related example is the work with JPEG compression and images widely spread over the Internet by the German photographer Thomas Ruff. In his work, images of catastrophic events such as 9/11, or pornographic images downloaded from the Internet, are treated by repeated compressions to create results sometimes almost resembling impressionistic paintings.

How information is distributed and presented on the Internet has inspired a range of artistic work on the relation between for instance code and protocols, and what is meant to be presented to the user. Some early examples of web-based art include the *Shredder* by Mark Napier, an alternative browser presenting fragmented versions of webpages based on their HTML code, and the *Web Stalker* by I/O/D which strips away what the user is typically meant to see, instead exposing structures created by links and files.

As evident from Cascone's remark above, this work on deconstructing digital technology is closely related to other such movements within design. For instance, the work of Kennedy and Violich on surfaces and material presence in architecture clearly relates to the issues discussed above (Kennedy 2001, p. 9):

> The smooth, seamless cladding of modernism presents an abstraction of architecture's materiality: the primacy of the idea of surface results in the concealing of the particular qualities of its constituent materials. Despite this abstraction, of precisely because of it, plugs, ports and other points of contact that interrupt the seamless surface gain a new visibility and importance as materials. [...] Infrastructure and materiality intersect at the molecular level. When a material surface itself becomes a source for the transmission of light, heat, colour or information, material properties can be understood as dynamic infrastructure with inherent variable spatial effects. [...] Cladding materials that appear to be solid become potentially permeable, not only through the cracks and junctures of their seems and joints, but also through their newly transmissive surfaces.

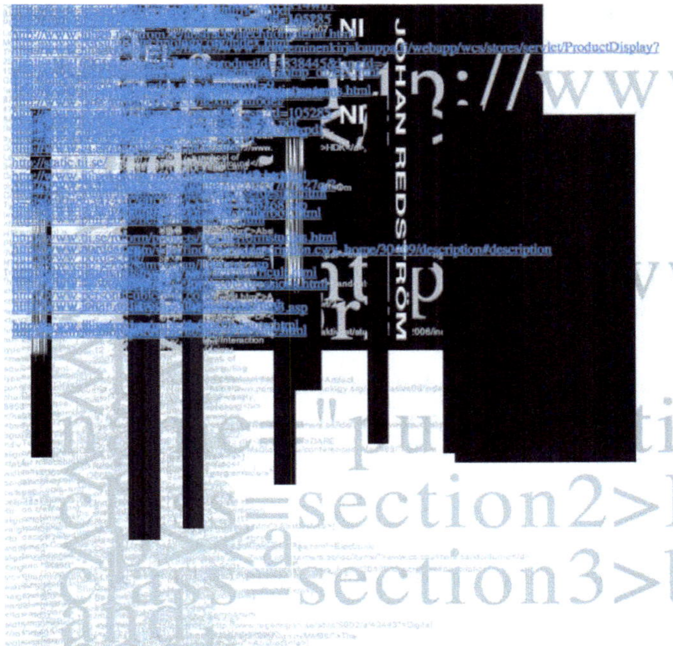

Shredder (screenshot). Mark Napier, 1998.

Importantly, this exploration of material presence does not stop with the materials as such, but extends into their forms of use as well, in this case into disruptions also at programmatic levels (Kennedy 2001, p. 20):

> Today, materials, building components and even programmes arrive preformed as »products« to the site or to the imagination. The role of the architect is not so much to form these entities as it is to deform them from their standard applications and invent for them new definitions and uses.

Turning towards issues of use, another line of inquiry of relevance stem from the observation that disruptions of normal conduct often causes people to stop and reflect upon something they otherwise would have taken for granted. In design theory, it is often discussed on basis of Heidegger's (1927) distinction between present-at-hand (*vorhanden sein*) and ready-to-hand (*zuhanden sein*), and the notion of breakdown (*Zusammenbruch*) (cf. e.g. Ehn 1988). Used as a poetic technique, it is, however, also connected to the notion of estrangement developed by Shklovsky (1990), and the use of a alienation effect by Brecht (1957): »Before familiarity can turn into awareness the familiar must be stripped of its inconspicuousness; we must give up assuming that the object in question needs no explanation. However frequently recurrent, modest, vulgar it may be it will now be labelled as something unusual.«

The notion of breakdown, i.e. when a tool becomes present to its user as a detached object possible to reflect upon and not the, in some sense, invisible extension of himself that it normally is, has been used several times to illustrate a basic difficulty in design to at the same time both change and keep aspects of a given practice in a new design. Ehn (1988, p. 77) expressed this issue as a dialectic between »tradition and transcendence«:

> On the one hand, to design so as not to breakdown or make obsolete the understanding and readiness-to-hand the users have acquired in the use of the already existing artefacts. The new artefacts should be ready-to-hand in an already existing practice.
>
> On the other hand, to break down the understanding of the already existing situation and make it present-at-hand, is to make reflection about it possible, and hence to create openings for a new understanding and alternative designs.

In this way, disruptions have been used to systematically push the boundaries of established practices from the inside, by means of an elaborate combination of at the same time participating in technological innovation and its appropriation on basis of existing practice. Since such ideas were introduced into design methodology, there have also been explorations the ways in which such dialectics can become a part of use. Though this moving back and forth between use and reflection is typical to ordinary use (it was after all initially meant to capture certain aspects of how we relate to the things we use and live with),

Social Cups. Kristina Niedderer, 1999.

the idea here has been to explore how design may influence and to some extent cause these disruptions to occur.

One such example of how disruptions in interaction can be used is to be found in Niedderer's (2007, p. 10) concept of mindful interaction: »I argue that a modification of function in the sense of a disruption-of-function can be used to break through patterns of perception and preconception, and to cause mindfulness.« Examples of such disruption-of-function include her own *Social Cups*, drinking vessels not capable of standing on their own but only together. As using them now requires all the participants to synchronise their drinking, the Social Cups puts a new emphasis of the social character of drinking. The Social Cups are interesting in that although they are primarily spatial objects, and not »interactive« in the sense colonized by information technology rhetoric (cf. Aarseth 2003), they still, to a significant extent, explore temporal form.

Though the disruption-of-function in question concerns the ability to stand, what happens is that the acts of *drinking*, including when and for how long, are transformed. Thus, the kind of disruptions we can work with in interaction design are not by default tied to, for instance, computation, machinery or even mechanics.

Investigations of disruption and interaction can, however, also be closely tied to the materiality of technologies. In our work on Slow Technology (Hallnäs and Redström 2001), acts of using computers were, if not entirely disrupted, then at least slowed down to the extent that practical functionality faded into the background instead, leaving room for more subtle explorations of temporal form. In the *Information Deliverer* (Hallnäs et al. 2002), the normally instantaneous moment of delivering a new piece of information was slowed down and re-interpreted. Here, information was delivered by means of thousands of pieces of fabric flying out of large plastic tubes during the course of 28 days. Disruptions are introduced at many different levels ranging from the cutting up of text into small printed fragments printed on pieces of fabric, to the complex non-repetitive patterns of fans turning on and off over the course of several weeks. In this case, interaction becomes reflective in a quite different sense than was the case with Niedderer's Social Cups, but they are both based on the disruption of an established function where time and timing have a central role.

The use of (sudden) disruption and a distance opened up between people and things, have also been used to critique the ideological components of design, for instance by using that alienation to uncover aspects not seen when we become immersed in the situation that is being targeted. Dunne's (1999, p. 30) work on creating a poetic distance between people and electronic objects is one example: »By poeticising the distance between people and electronic objects, sensitive scepticism might be encouraged, rather than unthinking assimilation of the values and conceptual models embedded in electronic objects.« And further that »The apparent unusability of many of these objects creates a heightened sense of ›distance‹ ... It is not enough to look and decode their visual iconography: they must be used.« (ibid, p. 56).

Information Deliverer. Interactive Institute, 2001.

The intentional use of alienation in situations where much work otherwise aims at overcoming alienation may seem like a paradox. There is a basic difference between alienation as an unplanned side-effect and its use as a conscious design tactic. Niedderer (2007, p. 10) argues that »[i]ndeed, in the analysis of examples, it becomes apparent that a second step is needed which provides a content or theme, and which also has the task of compensating for the disruption of action. I have called these two steps the ›disruption‹ and ›thematization‹ of function, which can be linked to the pragmatic and symbolic levels of function, respectively.« Again, this also relates to the discussion about breakdown in design methodology, and the central difference between breakdowns taking place within the domain or practice in focus and (unwanted) breakdowns related to other, external issues. Indeed, detached reflection might happen in both cases, but the issue is to make it happen in relation to that domain which is in focus. There is a basic difference between things hard to use and understand because of unintended side-effects and poor design, and objects that intentionally resist easy appropriation in specific ways and for certain reasons.

We can, however, also work with interferences between domains, with breakdowns outside the original domain of use, as a way of creating connections between issues or domains. In our work on »erratic appliances« we aimed at interrupting normal modes of using electronic appliances by means of connecting their behaviour to issues of energy consumption and awareness. In the *Erratic Radio* (Ernevi et al. 2007), the reception of radio transmissions were controlled by, and thus sometimes also disrupted by, a second (hidden) receiver detecting the amount of electromagnetic radiation in the 50 Hz band in its vicinity, thus connecting the radio's performance to the amount of active electrical devices around it. In this case, something partly outside the domain of using a radio to listen to broadcasts were introduced as to highlight how its operation depends on electricity, and thus in the end also to issues of energy consumption at a systems level.

All the examples above engage in issues of disruption primarily because of an interest in aesthetics and expressiveness. However, there are also examples where design issues more closely related to usability are in focus. Interestingly, also these are often found in the early stages of technology development. One example is the *Canon Cat* developed by Jef Raskin and colleagues in the late 1980s (Alzofon et al. 1987, Raskin 2000). Developed primarily as a word processor, its design was based on a series of innovative ideas and quite of few of them relate to how the machine appears to the user in relation to disruptions. For instance, the Canon Cat continuously saves bitmap images of the screen so that when the user wakes it up, it is able to instantaneously appear exactly as it was when it was shut down by showing the most recent image while loading the rest of the data. To the user, it appears as if the Cat loads the entire disk in a fraction of a second. Certainly, this is more about hiding technological disruptions than exposing them, but nevertheless it deals with the expressions of interruptions in use.

Another interesting feature of the Canon Cat is the lack of a hierarchical file structure: essentially each disk is treated as one »document« or »file.« Instead of navigating file structures, the users have access to specific keyboard buttons and search mechanisms to navigate by content, e.g. by searching for word strings or other characters. This idea also relates to interruptions, Raskin (2000, p. 118) comments: »File names are bothersome when you are about to save work, because you have to stop in the middle of your activity, which is trying to store your work away, and invent a file name.« What is interesting here, given the discussion about the character of digital materials, is how this approach directly addresses (and critiques) the relation between how information is cut up (in this case into files), and how certain disruptions are introduced in use. This relation has also been explored in other innovative information appliances, such as the *Apple Newton* (cf. Apple 1996), where information is not characterised and stored as certain kinds of files or documents, but rather in more general databases known as »soups« accessible by all applications. In some ways, the Newton pushes the idea of getting rid of files even further by removing for instance the save command entirely as it continuously saves whatever changes the user make. Indeed, this idea has some resemblance to the saved screen images of the Canon Cat, in the sense of a detailed design of the effects (and expressions) of turning the device on and off.

FORM OPENINGS

This chapter has primarily been about expressiveness and aesthetics as reasons for redirecting our attention towards disruptions in interaction not as design problems, but as central design elements. To conclude this discussion of examples and approaches to design, however, this is not only about aesthetics; there are also other reasons for considering the role of disruptions in the shaping of the temporal forms of use. Some of them relate to the issue touched upon at the beginning: how we think about the presence of computational things in everyday life.

In many ways, the idea that continuous interaction is the most natural mode of using a certain technology is based on an assumption that disruptions are also a threat to continuity in an existential sense. When seen as a failure, as shortcomings of technology, disruptions might well be such a threat to continuity. But even in the office world that personal computers come from, this is not the whole story (e.g. Harr and Kaptelinin 2007, Mark et al. 2005). While the continuity of work, and life, might be challenged and even disturbed by interruptions, it is also the case that such interruptions are at least as »natural« as is being immersed in the interaction with a computer for hours.

One example illustrating how deep the perspective that uninterrupted interaction is what characterises efficient use of technology runs, is to be found in research on the use of mobile phones when driving. While laboratory experiments may indicate decreased attention to the traffic situation while talking over a mobile phone, their experimental design is in many ways also a representation of the act of talking in mobile phones being understood as a matter of interrupting driving. Interestingly, studies of actual driving suggest much more complex relations between these activities, and that it is not a question of phoning interrupting driving but a matter of people managing several parallel and interwoven processes. Esbjörnsson, Juhlin and Weilenmann (2007, p. 39) report that:

> The ethnographic field study reveals a number of strategies on interactional adaptation used by the drivers to make their phone use fit with driving, which are not previously accounted for in the numerous controlled experiments dealing with phone use in cars. The analysis of the empirical data displays how the drivers adapt their handling of the phone, as well as the conversations, to fit with the traffic situation. They use suitable situations in traffic to retrieve phone-numbers, or to dial. Drivers provide remote conversationalists with awareness of any eventual problems in the traffic situation, which may lead to a demand of more focus on driving. Further, they adapt their driving to fit with the mobile phone use, and with the adjacent road users.

Here, what would typically be considered disruptions in the flow of one activity, are instead openings for engaging more in another, e.g. as in how a stop at a traffic light opens up the opportunity for initiating a phone call as less attention is required towards the traffic situation. Such elaborate interactions must not be reduced to a question about disturbing or interrupting »driving«.

Though the perspective of instrumental rationality seems to suggest it, disruptions are not something to be designed away, but elements of interaction we need to take care in forming. It seems we need to consider disruptions as form elements not only because they are intrinsic to what it is like to use digital technology – its expressiveness and aesthetics – but importantly also because they seem to be points of interaction between acts and activities. In this way, disruptions can be a kind of transition point where temporal form is opened up, also for unexpected interaction and interpretation. While hiding such gaps and glitches away through design might support the development of a human-technological symbiosis, it is far less obvious how this approach can contribute to our basic task of empowering people.

ACKNOWLEDGMENTS

I would like to thank the editors for inspiration and feedback. Thanks also to Anker Helms Jørgensen for providing me with Simon's paper, to Mark Napier for the image of the Shredder and to Kristina Niedderer for the image of the Social Cups. Special thanks to my friends who participated in the online photography experiments.

REFERENCES

Aarseth, E. (2003). We all want to change the world: the ideology of innovation in digital media. In Liestøl, G., Morrison, A., Rasmussen, T. (Eds.) *Digital media revisited: Theoretical and conceptual innovations in digital domains*, pp. 415–442. Cambridge, MA: MIT Press.

Alexander, C. (1984). The state of the art in design methods. In Cross, N. (Ed.) *Developments in design methodology*, pp. 309–316. London: John Wiley and Sons.

Alzofon, D., Caulkins, D., Raskin, J., Winter, J. (1987). Canon Cat Advanced Work Processor Reference Guide. Menlo Park, California: Information Appliance Inc.; Tokyo: Canon Inc.

Apple Computer Inc. (1996). Newton 2.0 User Interface Guidelines. Reading, MA: Addison-Wesley.

Brecht, B. (1957). Short description of a new technique of acting which produces an alienation effect. In Willett, J. (Ed.). *Brecht on theatre: The development of an aesthetic.* New York: Hill and Wang.

Cascone, K. (2000). The aesthetics of failure: »Post-digital« tendencies in contemporary computer music. *Computer Music Journal* 24(4):12–18.

Dunne, A. (1999). *Hertzian tales: Electronic products, aesthetic experience and critical design.* London: RCA:CRD Publications.

Ehn, P. (1988). *Work oriented design of computer artifacts.* Hillsdale, NJ: Lawrence Erlbaum Associates.

Ernevi, A., Palm, S., Redström, J. (2007). Erratic appliances and energy awareness. In Hummels, C., Koskinen, I., Redström, J. (Eds.) *Knowledge, Technology & Policy* 20(1):71–78 (special issue on design research).

Esbjörnsson, M., Juhlin, O., Weilenmann, A. (2007). Drivers using mobile phones in traffic: An ethnographic study of interactional adaptation. *Int. J. Human Computer Interaction* 22(1):39–60 (special issue on In-use, in-situ: Extending field research methods).

Hallnäs, L., Melin, L., Redström, J. (2002). Textile displays: Using textiles to investigate computational technology as design material. Proceedings of NordiCHI 2002, pp. 157–166. New York: ACM Press.

Hallnäs, L. and Redström, J. (2001). Slow technology: Designing for reflection. *Personal and Ubiquitous Computing* 5(3):201–212.

Hallnäs, L. and Redström, J. (2002). From use to presence: On the expressions and aesthetics of everyday computational things. *ACM Trans. Computer-Human Interaction* 9(2):106–124.

Harr, R., Kaptelinin, V. (2007). Unpacking the social dimension of external interruptions. Proceedings of the 2007 international ACM Conference on Supporting Group Work, pp. 399–408. New York, NY: ACM Press.

Heidegger, M. (1927). Sein und Zeit. In von Herrmann, F.-W. (Ed.) *Gesamtausgabe*, Vol. 2, XIV, 1977. Frankfurt am Main: Vittorio Klostermann.

Johansson, T.D. (2007). Notes on failure: Mistakes, errors, and failure in the performative tactics of art and product design. Proceedings of International Association of Socities of Design Research 2007, Emerging Trends in Design Research.

Jones, J.C. (1984). How my thoughts about design methods have changed during the years. In Cross, N. (Ed.) *Developments in design methodology*, pp. 329–336. London: John Wiley and Sons.

Jones,J.C. (1992). *Design Methods*, second edition. New York: John Wiley & Sons.

Kennedy. S. (2001). Material presence. In Kennedy, S., Grunenberg, C. (Eds.) *KVA: Material Misuse*, pp. 4–21. London: AA Publications.

Krippendorff, K. (2006). *The semantic turn: A new foundation for design*. Boca Raton: CRC Press.

Liestøl, G., Morrison, A., Rasmussen, T. (Eds., 2003). *Digital media revisited: Theoretical and conceptual innovations in digital domains*. Cambridge, MA: MIT Press.

Löwgren, J., Stolterman, E. (1998). *Design av informationsteknologi: Materialet utan egenskaper*. Lund: Studentlitteratur. English version as: Löwgren, J., Stolterman, E. (2004).*Thoughtful interaction design*. Cambridge, MA: MIT Press.

Mark, G., Gonzalez, V. M., Harris, J. (2005). No task left behind? Examining the nature of fragmented work. Proceedings of the SIGCHI Conference on Human Factors in Computing Systems, pp. 321–330. New York, NY: ACM Press.

Moholy-Nagy, L. (1923). The new typography. Reprinted in Kolocotroni, V., Goldman, J. and Taxidou, O. (Eds., 1998) *Modernism: An anthology of sources and documents*, pp. 302f. Edinburgh: Edinburgh University Press.

Niedderer, K. (2007). Designing mindful interaction: The category of performative object. *Design Issues* 23(1):3–17.

Norman, D.A. (1993). *Things that make us smart: Defending human attributes in the age of the machine*. Cambridge, MA: Perseus Publishing.

Raskin, J. (2000). *The human interface: New directions for designing interactive systems*. Reading, MA: Addison-Wesley.

Redström, J. (2005). On technology as material in design. In Willis, A-M. (Ed.) *Design Philosophy Papers: Collection Two*, pp. 31–42. Ravensbourne: Team D/E/S Publications.

Simon, H.A. (1966). Reflections on time sharing from a user's point of view. *Computer Science Research Review* 45(31).

Schaeffer, P. (1966). *Le traité des objets musicaux*. Paris: Éditions du Seuil.

Shklovsky, V. (1990). *Theory of prose.* Naperville, IL: Dalkey Archive Press. First published in 1925, translation by B. Sher.

Sparke, P. (1982). *Ettore Sottsass Jnr*. London: The Design Council.

Suchman, L. A. (1987). *Plans and situated actions*. Cambridge: Cambridge University Press.

Udsen, L.E., Jørgensen, A.H. (2005). The aesthetic turn: Unravelling recent aesthetic approaches to human-computer interaction. *Digital Creativity* 16(4):205–216.

Virilio, P. (1995). *The art of the motor*. Minneapolis: University of Minnesota Press. Translation by J. Rose.

SARA ILSTEDT HJELM

ON A SCALE BETWEEN ART AND DESIGN:

ON THE AESTHETICS OF FUNCTION FROM THE BAUHAUS UNTIL TODAY

SARA ILSTEDT HJELM

on a scale between art and design – on the aesthetics of function from the bauhaus until today

One picture from Bauhaus in Dessau has stuck with me. It shows a stairwell with two doors and a radiator. At first glance trivial, grey coloured, boring. Nothing sensational but if you look closer you will find something peculiar. These three parts, the doors and the radiator, are in fact arranged as an abstract composition. The handles at the doors are placed against each other instead of located on the same side, and the radiator is centred above them on the wall. Placing a radiator close to the ceiling is not very functional, as the heat goes upwards to the roof. The composition of the stairwell must be regarded as a provocation, a critical design where stripped functional elements in the building are focussed for their esthetical value. This must be one of the few moments in history when a radiator is allowed a decorative function. It will take almost a century before it happens again and this time by the design group Droog from Netherlands (which I will discuss later).

What Gropius is telling us, in this case, is what the students at Bauhaus learned during the famous basic course—to see objects as variations of abstract components. To see function as an aesthetical quality and show what is usually hidden in walls and basements. But Bauhaus is unique in this aspect. The aesthetical expression in functional parts of the home, such as heating and electricity played an out of sight role during the twentieth century. The motto has been to hide or make invisible. Today, due to environmental issues, these functions are observed, focussed and visualised in our homes. In this chapter I will use the energy issue as a starting-point for exploring different aspects on aesthetics as well as the relation between the foreign and the familiar in design. How can strategies from art help us to notice formerly hidden elements in everyday life?

Turning around the aesthetical ranking in order to present something not seen by everybody is an artistic trick very efficient in visualising norms and context. Marcel Duchamp's »bottle dryer« from 1914 is considered to be the very first in that genre and perhaps the most famous. Duchamp has changed the vision of a bottle dryer to the very extent that we cannot see its function anymore, only what it represents as an artistic milestone. This is efficiently utilised by artist Dan Wolgers in his *Absolut Wolgers*, a duchampian bottle dryer with

Duchamp's bottle dryer was reused in Dan Wolgers' piece for Absolut vodka. An alliance of three strong trademarks that balance of the border between advertising and art. Image by permission of V&S Vin & Sprit AB.

a hanging Absolut vodka bottle and the text Absolut Wolgers beneath it. An alliance with three strong trade marks dancing on the border between art and advertisement.

The difference between art and design can be defined as; design has a function whilst art has not. At the moment Duchamp lifts a totally functional bottle dryer from its position in the kitchen into the gallery, it stops having a function and becomes »art«. The role of the artist today is not to create beautiful objects but to criticize, question and change the way we see things.

When the art academies evolved during the end of the eighteenth century art became more and more secluded from the rest of society. Art philosophy too, primarily with Kant, separates Art from function. The artistic experience, according to Kant, is a subjective assessment based on the art object itself, something he calls »disinterested pleasure«. Kant considers the work of art to have a sublime dimension: »We call that sublime which is absolutely great« (Kant 1790). Kant separates the beauty from the sublime and explains that while aesthetical beauty »is connected with the form of the object«, and has »boundaries«, the sublime is »to be found in a formless object«, and is represented by »boundlessness«. Kant's theory on the sublime as a boundless, aesthetic experience is crucial for the role of art during the subsequent centuries and leads directly to modernism and the German expressionism with Kandinsky and others.

The handicraft movements developing during the nineteenth century aimed to reclaim art back to industry, with associations such as Deutsche Werkbund, Svenska Slöjdföreningen and the Arts and Crafts movement. This was also Gropius' objective with Bauhaus. In the Bauhaus manifesto written in 1923 (Gropius 1935) he criticized the academies claiming that they had created an arts proletariat, merely getting along in their belief that they are creating great art, while the industry needs skilled designers to participate in the construction of the society. The long-term goal for Bauhaus was the spiritual liberation of people:

> As long as the economical life and the machine itself remains the primary purpose instead of being means to liberate the spiritual forces from the constraint of labour—as long will the individual be captured and society in a state of disorder. (Gropius 1935)

Gropius' Bauhaus texts revolve, as for many other thinkers in this time, around the conflict between machine and hand, between spiritual liberation and material blockage. Gropius says that it is not the machine itself that is the problem, but our use of it. The artists must participate in the creation of society where primarily the building was the multi-artwork to be the highest goal with this work. The other wing at Bauhaus, represented by Kandinsky and Itten, says that art should turn away from the common and realistic to the sublime and the boundless, spiritual experience.

New and troublesome technology is often hidden in a familiar form to make us accept it easier. Here is a radio in the shape of a piano from the 1920s.

With the sublime as a supporting concept art becomes, by definition, the non-functional, but also the improper, the alienated and boundless experience.

Everyday objects are on the other side of the scale: well-known, familiar tools that we use without further reflection. Heidegger says that the only way to come close to the objects, to really understand them, is to use them. Everyday objects are suitable, comfortable and secure, to an extent that almost makes them invisible.

The artist can select an object and take it from its context, maybe to a gallery, as a still life or a part of an installation and suddenly the everyday invisible object becomes »art«. A reversed strategy could be making something trouble-

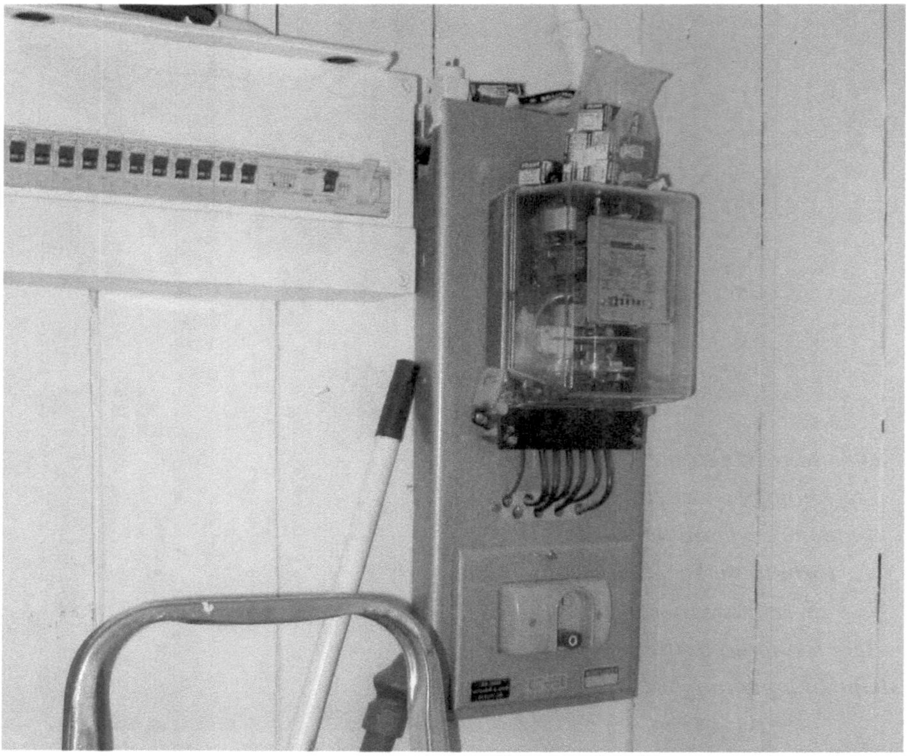

some and provocative more »common« simply by making it invisible, to hide it. This is often what happens to new technology.

In the beginning of the last century people were frightened of technical development. Electricity could start a house fire and radio waves could make us sick. Design became a way to enable the understanding of these unpleasant technologies and the implied changes in the surrounding society.

Adrian Forty describes how many products pass through different phases during their aesthetical evolution (Forty 1986). At first they are technical solutions, in the next phase the product is hidden in more well known objects and, finally, a phase where the product finds its own shape and function in the home. Forty takes the radio as an example, from a simple box with transistors, cords and

Left:
»Not a single human being understands the electricity bill.«
From interview in the Aware project field study.

Right:
the Eva armchair by Bruno Mathsson, 1933. Instead of covering the chair with upholstery, Mathsson shows the structural materials: saddle girth and bent wood.

antennas – to a period of disguise in cupboards or furniture – to the classic round bakelite radio. This is also a negotiation between form, function and importance where the identity of product slowly evolves. What »is« a radio in fact? Is it an object for listening to concerts in the living room? Or is it something for the kitchen table reporting the latest news from the war?

But very little has indeed happened in the evolution of electricity and heating during the 100 years of central heating and electric lighting in our homes. Electricity meters still look as they always have, a little box in a corner near the ceiling in your hallway or in your basement, with figures slowly ticking, showing an incomprehensible interval. Seen as interaction design it is hard to imagine a more secluded and user-hostile object. It is obvious that the electricity meter never passed its first phase in the design development. The electricity bill is no more comprehensive, and still it is the only feedback we have between everyday behaviour and consumption.

But why was electricity never domestified and »designed« in the same way as the radio? One component of the modernistic aesthetic was to be honest in material and function. An ethics taking its motto from Sullivan's famous: »Form follows function.« A typical example, from the Swedish modern design, is the chair *Eva* by Bruno Mathsson. Instead of covering the chair in upholstery, Mathsson shows the supporting structural materials: saddle girth and bent wood.

But electricity was never a »material« in the classic sense; it seems to be regarded as a structural component in the house, like the beam frames or insulation material, hidden behind beautifully white-plastered façades. Radiators, sockets and electricity meters seem, in the same way, more a part of the building's structure than something connected to the inhabitants. The pioneers of modernism have obviously not been consistent in letting form follow function. The white sleek surfaces of modernistic architecture were full of hidden infrastructure and the »honesty of material« became more of an aesthetic position than a practice.

The late modernism during the 1950s and the 1960s by former Bauhaus architects became a style associated with the growth of global capitalism, with airports, bank palaces and skyscrapers. Was that really what Gropius had in mind when he started the Bauhaus?

Centre Pompidou, finished in 1977, and designed by the architects Renzo Piano, Richard Rogers and Sue Rogers, was the start of a penetrating criticism of the modernistic theory and aesthetics. Centre Pompidou is a building turned inside out with all supporting structures and infrastructures as gaudy coloured pipes on the outside of the building and the interior left free and open like a contemporary cathedral. The characteristic piping was colour-coded according to the contents: yellow for electricity, red for transport (elevators), blue for air and green for water. »The Pompidou revolutionized museums, transforming

Centre Pompidou is a building turned inside out, with all supporting structures and infrastructures as gaudy colored pipes on the outside of the building and the inside left free and open like a contemporary cathedral.

what had once been elite monuments into popular places of social and cultural exchange, woven into the heart of the city«, as the Pritzker jury phrased it.

A lot has been written about Centre Pompidou and its revolutionary significance for architecture and design. The building is filled with architectural references and still not quite »finished«. It looks like a building covered with scaffolding, open for change and interpretations.

The Heat Wave radiator by Joris Larman for Droog Design, 2006, has clearly taken the leap from invisible function to decoration. It is as much a sculpture on the wall as a functional heater.

The square in front of Centre Pompidou is one of the most popular in Paris and filled with a swarm of people. The idea is for people to meet, be seen and see each other. Here, people, the users are in the center of the architectural design.

From Centre Pompidou there is a red thread to the various critical experimental design groups during the 1980s and 1990s. One of the most exciting, and even commercially most successful groups is Droog Design from the Netherlands. Their design is conceptual and humorous, using aesthetics to investigate and change conceptions.

Joris Larman's *Heat Wave* radiator from 2006 is a softly bulging, decorative shape in abstract plant forms. It consists of different parts, which can be assembled to an organic growing part of the room. So different from the rigid radiator from Dessau 80 years earlier, but there is still a spiritual connection in

The Element by the Static! project at the Interactive Institute, 2006 is a radiator that emits both light and heat. It consists of 35 lightbulbs and enables us to experience how much warmth that is actually emitted by them.

the grey colour and the Spartan surroundings. This radiator has clearly taken the final leap from invisible function to a decoration, it can serve as well as a sculpture on the wall as a functional heater.

Interactive Institute is a research institute in the borderland of art, design and IT, started in Sweden in 1998 on the initiative by Pelle Ehn and others. At the Institute a critical and experimental attitude is essential in their work and at the beginning the institute was a part of the Digital Bauhaus in Malmö. At the Interactive Institute a number of projects have centred around sustainability and how to visualise energy consumption in everyday life (Backlund et al. 2006). *The Element* is a radiator that emits both light and heat. Candle lights and fires are highly appreciated in Sweden, especially during the winter time, and many informants admit that they leave the lamps on in empty rooms as »they give some warmth in the house, so it is not a waste« (Lundell et.al 2007).

Left: The Aware Laundry Lamp allows people to hang clothes in the home to dry and explores the aesthetic qualities of laundry. The mundane task of drying laundry becomes part of the home decoration and allows user to create their own lamp shade.
Right: The Energy Aware Watch electricity meter takes the familiar kitchen clock as a metaphor in order to make energy consumption part of everyday life, connecting it in a simple way to the daily rhythm of the household.
From the Aware project at the Interactive Institute, 2007.

Instead of making people switch off all their lamps, The Element delivers both light and warmth – preferably on a spot where heating is needed. The Element consists of 35 bulbs, each 60 W; together they radiate heat equivalent to 2100 W. Sensors connected to a thermostat control a dimmer to regulate the light and subsequently also the heating effect of the radiator.

The fact that bulbs give 90% heat and only 10% light is something most of us know in an abstract level but perhaps do not grasp to the full extent. With The Element we are given an opportunity to experience this in a practical sense. The most interesting effect is that the combination of heat and a light slowly changing in intensity gives the impression of an open fire.

The Element is to some extent a critical design aimed to question our preconception about energy and heat. But it is also a functional object used in a chilly office at the Interactive Institute.

In the design of today we find an intention to let people design themselves. This can be expressed as »user driven innovation«, as »participatory design« or as different initiatives to customise the end product.

In Droog's *Lamphanger* (2007) the user is given an opportunity to create a lamp shed from suitable articles of clothing. The *Aware Laundry Lamp* (Interactive Institute 2007) is based on a similar idea – that clothes can be used as decoration for a lamp, but in this case the lamp is a laundry hanger exploiting the heat from the bulbs to dry the laundry. Energy savings is not only a matter of awareness, but also about giving people practical solutions to enable a simpler and more environmental friendly behaviour. People often prefer hanging laundry to dry over using the spin-drier, but there are not many practical solutions for this in modern homes. Laundry has become part of our domestic routines, but why is it not integrated in the interior design of the home? Why not use the aesthetic qualities of the laundry itself as decoration?

Aware Laundry Lamp reminds us, both in shape and concept, of Duchamp's bottle dryer. The idea to have your underwear at public display as a lampshade is both provoking and humorous. It questions our preconception about what is allowed to be shown of your private life and what can be considered decoration – even in your own home.

Research clearly shows that the biggest obstacle for people to save electricity is that they do not know the real consumption for different appliances and functions, or the actual effect from changes in behaviour. The electricity bill, checked once a year against the real consumption, is too far away from all the every day actions to be considered a feedback to daily energy behaviour. There are endless possibilities to visualise energy consumption in an exciting, beautiful and natural way for the end user. One of the challenges is to find and utilise visual metaphors that are received as obvious and meaningful.

Energy Aware watch (Interactive Institute 2008) is an electricity meter that resembles a kitchen clock with a round screen and a circular movement. The idea is that you should glance at the energy watch in much the same way you glance at the clock every now and then. It shows the electricity consumption in real time, at the time it is actually consumed. If the dishwasher is switched on it shows immediately on the display of the energy watch. Yesterday's graphs fade away slowly and today's consumption is drawn on top of it, making it possible to survey the energy consumption for a week.

The electricity meter is made to remind us of the kitchen clock, in form as well as in place and use. This makes energy consumption a part of everyday life and connected in a simple way to the daily rhythm of the household. Therefore the energy watch is not designed to feel strange or break norms but rather to make us accept it.

There is a strong similarity between IT and electricity if we regard them as materials. They are both media where the aesthetics of the products they »occupy« are designed according to traditional material such as wood, textile, plastic. They can both adopt a number of expressions but still have latent specific possibilities and limitations. They are immaterial, physical phenomena that have found concrete expressions in everyday items. The energy projects agenda was to explore energy as a design material and to create critical design prototypes aiming to encourage awareness on energy consumption. Here lies an ambition both to create objects raising questions and thoughts in a critical artistic tradition, but also to give examples on items that are really used and have a practical function. Therefore the research projects cross the borders of art and design and the design prototypes can be seen as borderline objects aiming in several different directions; energy research, consumer market and culture.

In his manifesto for Bauhaus, Gropius dwells on the relation between hand and machine, a topic that is no longer of immediate interest. Something still of great interest, however, is his vision that different professional groups should cooperate to bridge over divisions and create buildings with high artistic quality. Today we talk about society building as an objective for our collective creativity and problem solving capacity, but the aim to bring design, art, technology and social science together still exists and is a supporting theme for the Interactive Institute. The purpose of the energy project was to enhance the awareness regarding energy issues. In order to create design prototypes stimulating critical thinking and raising questions, you need a cup of artistic strategy for visibility and alienation. At the same time we expect the products to be attractive and to function in the everyday environment. Is this utopia? Will art and design ever meet or will they eternally be two poles on a scale between function and non-function?

ACKNOWLEDGMENTS

The Interactive Institute prototypes shown here are from Static! and Aware. They were financed by the Swedish Energy Agency as a part of a long-term objective to make households more efficient in their energy consumption.

REFERENCES

Backlund, S. et al. (2006). Static! The aesthetics of energy in everyday things. Proc. Wonderground (Design Research Society Int. Conf.), Lisbon, Portugal.

Forty, A. (1986). *Objects of desire: Design and society from 1750–1980*. London: Thames & Hudson.

Gropius, W. (1935). *The Bauhaus*. London: Faber and Faber.

Kant, I. (1790). *Critique of judgment*. Dover Philosophical Classics, this edition published in 2003.

Lundell et al. (2007). Om energianvändning och uppfattningar kring elektricitet och konsumtion. Aware field study report, Interactive Institute.

More information on topics of this chapter is found at www.bauhaus.org, www. tii.se/static, www.tii.se/aware and www.droogdesign.nl

JOAN GREENBAUM

APPROPRIATING DIGITAL ENVIRONMENTS

– (RE-)CONSTRUCTING THE PHYSICAL THROUGH THE DIGITAL

JOAN GREENBAUM
– (RE-)CONSTRUCTING THE PHYSICAL THROUGH THE DIGITAL
APPROPRIATING DIGITAL ENVIRONMENTS

INTRODUCTION

This century's transition to social networked interaction is *not* one that interaction designers can take much credit for. On the web, social, political, entertainment and economic interactions grew out of the extensive use of sites such as ebay, Facebook, YouTube, Amazon, and many others. Certainly good algorithms, good interface design, sensible database structure and solid infrastructure were key elements in making these sites successful. But the main ingredients of course were people – those we used to call end-users – finding a need and a desire to use them, and use them in new ways. Likewise, mobile phones, digital cameras, music devices and personal digital assistants, have taken on new dimensions as software engineers and designers scramble to latch on to creative practices in-use.

While traditional computer systems design took for granted that design was about future use, interaction designers have begun instead to focus on the *now*. This raises an interesting set of questions; indeed throwing the traumatic tension of tradition and transcendence into new light (Ehn 1988). In consumer and public-oriented software and interface design it appears that we are designing for now – the immediate experience of people in their daily situated actions and their experience with the blurry boundaries of the evolving future. Indeed even work-oriented systems increasingly build upon the current use of social networking sites and communication devices. All acknowledge the blend of work and home, work and travel, work and play, although some large corporate systems try to build firewalls against it (often to no avail).

This chapter looks at interaction design from the standpoint of user experience, starting with people's political and pragmatic problems in daily environments. An important starting point for understanding political and pragmatic problems is to look at the ways that people's embodied actions flow through the in-between places, between the physical world and their daily encounters with digital environments. In examining and designing *from use* a key element is understanding and accepting the embodied and situated nature of our interactions and building that into research and design practice (Suchman 2007, Dourish 2001). This chapter uses examples from ongoing research and design projects in New York where the political and practical experiences of people become the starting point for new design. And where people's appropriation of their experience, opens up new possibilities, through collective participatory experiences.

Over the last 20 years we have learned a lot about designing digital environments. We have also overcome some of the obstacles inherent in our work with digital designs' predecessor – computer information systems. But now it is time to go back to basics: reintegrating design concepts from the physical world with those from digital and mediated environments. Drawing inspiration from activities in our daily lives and returning to view some of the political questions tackled by Bauhaus designers, among other sources of inspiration. This chapter analyzes some of the ways that others outside our immediate digital design world have understood how we *appropriate* spaces and get a feeling of belonging to them as experienced *places*.

Appropriating our environment is something that comes naturally to us in the physical world and which we seem to adapt quickly to in our digital encounters, particularly through social networking technologies. A common way of appropriating physical environments is to *inhabit* the spaces we are in – building piles of papers by our work area; nesting in our waiting room seats with laptop on our knees; drinking coffee while rifling through the newspaper with headphones and PDAs ready-at-hand. Similarly we appropriate digital environments by inhabiting them and adopting them to lived experience in the physical world. While stories about the intersection of physical and digital experiences through Facebook and MySpace and, of course, Second Life, abound, this chapter will address examples that grow specifically out of problems in the physical world using digital tools to confront them. Interaction designers are beginning to understand how we experience the physical and the mediated, particularly in relation to museum exhibitions and urban landscapes, but we have much further to go (see for example Ciolfi and Bannon 2005).

The chapter is rooted in three assumptions: firstly that *place* is an important concept for understanding our embodied interactions in digital, as well as physical, environments; secondly that *participation* in the situated and lived experience of mixed digital and physical environments is essential to ongoing design; and thirdly that *political and economic roots* lie within and beneath considerations for design.

An important point of departure here stems from these assumptions and grows further from the realization that embodied experience in the physical world is being acted on through digital social networking facilities. Thus embodied digital interactions are being designed by people experienced in their use. This is useful information for interaction designers and is critical for acknowledging people's digital, as well as, physical lived experiences.

THE HERE AND NOW

In the 1980s Pelle Ehn's *Work-Oriented Design of Computer Artifacts* was immensely useful in helping software designers look at the practicalities of tools that would help people traverse the terrain from how they were currently working (usually without computer support) to future practices (with computer tools). One of his contributions to the mix of practices was his descriptions of the difficulties inherent on the road from traditional work tools to transcendent work practices. This dilemma is an important one, for in all walks of life we have difficulty imagining the future with the tools and techniques that are at hand. Yet now, with rapid prototyping, beta testing and intense production schedules new devices and their software support are in use seemingly as fast as they can be designed; making current use, often through social networking, jump-start the process of future use. I would argue that our focus is not so much one of how do we transcend current practice, but rather how we experience, examine and participate in it and thus design from and along with current practices through lived-experience.

In a sense this change is as profound as those the Bauhaus designers (architects, furniture, etc.), had to confront in the rapidly mass-produced world of the early twentieth century. For them the questions they chose revolved around how to blend craft practices with practical mass production and how to do so for consumption by the emerging (pre-depression) middle and working classes. Their goals were rooted in the ideal that art and design should be harnessed into practical everyday design that could be more inexpensively produced in factories, making good art and design accessible for more people, and of course creating jobs.† My goals in this chapter are not as lofty but I believe that the political and economic origins of what we attempt to do must be made visible in our work. And, as the following examples and sources illustrate, our engagement, through participation in the lived-experience of the present, help us define and pinpoint future interaction design scenarios.

LIVING IN PHYSICAL PLACE

In his discipline-bending 1977 book, *Space and Place, the perspective of experience*, Yi-Fu Tuan turned geography toward the everyday experiences of people in places. Place, he argued, is the experienced physical world that we remember through our senses. And this memory of place – say a specific home or hill – is a way we organize our thoughts about our history and our social situations. His often cited work has many implications for design (see for example Ciolfi and Bannon 2005, Harrison and Dourish 1996, Dourish 2006). My intent here is to show how the concept of place is equally appropriate to digital and mixed environments and to offer examples of how the importance of place as a concept, can influence design *from* use through participatory, situated involvement.

Understanding how we live in a physical place involves an understanding, of course, of our sensual experiences. These sensual experiences can be understood through phenomenology, which approaches our joined mind-body experiences as an integral aspect of our acting through our situated and embodied practices. Ehn's early work understood this as part of his analysis of Heidegger's contributions to philosophy; namely that we gain meaning through our being-in-the-world (Ehn 1988). Dourish uses Heidegger to invoke his principles of interaction, explaining that »We uncover meaning in the world through our interactions with it« (Dourish 2001, p. 129).

† It is of course difficult and dangerous to summarize the entire Bauhaus movement into brief passages. More of the ideology was indeed socialist in nature and while the results actually were appreciated by the professional middle class, the intent was one of furthering socialist economics and politics through practical design.

This chapter assumes that there is a tight coupling between Tuan's concept of place and Dourish's use of embodied interaction. Dourish uses the concept of embodiment as a jumping off point for design. He argues that »The embodied interaction perspective begins to illuminate not just how we act *on* technology, but how we act *through* it« (ibid., p. 154.) As the following examples illustrate, our political actions flow from our embodied interactions in physical place(s), and from these sensual understandings of place we then can appropriate digital environments for real world problem-solving.

Maurico Leandro is a professor of Psychology at the Universidad de Costa Rica, in San Jose, Costa Rica. His studies are concerned with road deaths in his country caused by speeding. His focus is *not* on building better roads but rather on understanding the social and political roots of his country's problem. Initially he had decided to import a speed control device used in Sweden that visualizes to drivers their speed and impedes their speed by controlling the gas pedal.† But the study revealed that such an individual/private control would not be effective in his country. His approach then turned to the question of public and collective visualization of travel and what effect public sharing of information would have on individual private behavior. He initiated a mini project using an inexpensive GPS device and offering his own private travel data for public and participatory viewing. He carried the device with him for a period of five weeks and asked a group of eight people to view his posted results each week. The act of making private data public and the response of people to his movements was at first disconcerting to him. But the participants asked questions and Leandro refined his approaches to presenting the data, moving from simple data lists (the device's default) to putting his movements on Google Maps (from different perspectives) to adding photographs of himself and his family at various points along his routes.

† The device is called an ISA (Intelligent Speed Adaptor) and includes an onboard GPS device, a database of roads and their speed limits, an LED warning light and a control for the gas pedal.

The results of his preliminary study have led him to prepare a proposal for funding of a study in Costa Rica that will involve groups of teenagers sharing their travel information with others on the web. The concept takes his research about the importance of social networks in physical and net-based environments into the arena of making public the normally private and individual behavior of driving. Blogs will be used to report and record movement among groups of young males and the study will utilize photographs and other artifacts to personalize and politicize mapping and story telling. Group meetings will also be part of the action-based study.

Leandro's approach illustrates, among other points, that place matters. Shared photographs of where and when people are, or have been, make imprints of experience available. By making personal and private behavior public, through forums, blogs, photos and maps that are commonly in use, reminds us that the personal is political. Designing from use with a specific political problem in mind, highlights this. Leandro's use of shared mapping bridges the physical world of movement through places, with public digital experience—a useful illustration of the in-between hybrid worlds we live in.[‡] It also appropriates available technologies in the intersection between life in a car and life on the web.

His approach also relies heavily on Lucy Suchman's (2007) in that the importance of moving computational design beyond the cognitive into the situated actions of social interaction is paramount. His analysis and action also build on Dourish's (2001) understanding of embodied interaction, in that his interpretation is closely rooted in a cultural and visceral »being-in-the world« – his experience of the places where he lives and works. Unfortunately in the discipline he is working from, psychology, as in computer systems development, a cognitive approach lies at the root of other ways of viewing the world. Suchman calls our attention to the problems inherent in this cognitive approach:

---

‡ See Acknowledgements for a list of the names and affiliations of project participants.

> The cognitivist strategy is to interject a mental operation between environmental stimulus and behavioral response: in essence, to relocate the causes of action from environment that impinges on the actor to processes, abstractable as computation, in the actor's head (Suchman 2007, p. 37).

Clearly it is not the thought of speeding, nor is it the individual's cognitive processes that need to be captured in preventing accidents. Rather Leandro's approach moves the design focus to the social and interaction activities that people engage in, that can be better captured and represented through maps and narratives. The technologies he chooses to work with are those that encourage people's active engagement with, and reflection of, the act of speeding – emotional and place-based interaction that go to the heart of the issue, not the usual Western approach of building wider roads.

EXPERIENCE OF PLACE

In another small-scale project with wide implications a teacher from an overcrowded, under-funded public school in a poor immigrant neighborhood in New York decided to reframe the boring (and tests show, unsuccessful) task of teaching basic mathematics in the classroom. Instead he took his students out into communities and had them price »market baskets« of foods in different stores in different neighborhoods. They then mapped their findings using readily available mapping programs and presented their results to other students.† He also used a modified community-asset mapping approach that is generally used by adult community organizers and social workers, in order to make the tasks collaborative and more oriented towards community-building. His work was based on John Dewey, the well-known American pragmatist and educational reformer from the first half of the twentieth century who argued that action-based and experiential learning would be more effective than traditional

† The software that he, his colleagues and students used was Mapple (see mapple.com) which was easily adapted by the students to make interactive pictoral maps of their communities. It is important to note that in the US prices in poor neighborhood stores have steeply marked-up profit margins resulting in poor residents paying far more for their basic groceries.

approaches (Dewey 1938). By starting the action in the places that the students knew, rather than in the classroom, the project moved the thought and action to connect with the students' experience of their world.

The project was also inspired by Tuan's ideas, and his understanding of the ways that experience and place are deeply intertwined. By bringing students out into the world and having them explore the difference in prices between neighborhoods, they were able to get an understanding of how supermarket prices in poor neighborhoods are markedly higher than those in middle-class and wealthy neighborhoods. By illustrating these differences through the social networking tools they know, they were able to tackle both mathematical problems as well as explore the political and economic roots. The digital medium allowed students to asynchronously annotate, collaborate and overlay their maps, all with the purpose of identifying common grounds and intersections amidst the great diversity within New York City. In a strong sense the political economy of New Yorkers drove the purpose of the project, and once that purpose was identified by teachers in poor neighborhoods, the social interaction of software was appropriated to build bridges between thought and action, as well as between physical reality and abstract mathematical reasoning.

An important study and design-in-progress is that of an artist from the multinational neighborhood of Flushing, Queens. Flushing has become the major immigrant hub of New York City, and is known as a place where Indian, Korean, Chinese, Pakistani, Greeks, Salvadorians, among 120 national groups, bump and blend with the ethnic feasts of prior immigrants such as Puerto Ricans and Irish. The Flushing project is a collaborative, community-based challenge to conventional notions of New York City's immigrant populations and multi-ethnic neighborhoods. The interactive map, which will be generated by community members, will explore individual experiences of life in a global city and the connections between local groups across cultural and religious lines. The project takes neighborhood participants through their daily activities and enables them to map, photograph and make oral histories and sound stories to show their multi-layered experiences within the community.

A starting point for this study is Dolores Hayden's work (1995). Hayden examines how communities reshape their environment through their actions, leaving traces of personal and political lives in their path. The Flushing study is, and will continue to be, based in community group activities and utilizes web-based tools to involve and show the overlapping interaction of the various national and culturally diverse peoples. It brings the physical and the virtual into a tangible reality for the multiple language groups who live in this community.

POLITICS OF THE HERE AND NOW

The Costa Rican project on speeding, the community-based learning project in New York and the immigrant project for Flushing have deep political roots. David Harvey, a political geographer, tackles similar issues from a theoretical framework in his classic 1990 work, *The Condition of Postmodernity*. Like Lefebvre (1991) his arguments highlight the political and economic nature of the social construction of places. Behind each piece of property – behind the places that we live and work in– lie the legal and transactional rules about how commodities are made and sold. Writing from a Marxist perspective, like most of the Bauhaus originators, Harvey explains that:

> Places are constructed and experienced as material ecological artefacts and intricate networks of social relations. They are the focus of the imaginary, of beliefs, longings, and desires (most particularly with respect to the psychological pull and push of the idea of »home«). They are an intense focus of discursive activity, filled with symbolic and representational meanings and they are a distinctive product of institutionalized social and political-economic power. (Harvey 1996, p. 316)

One example that Harvey offers of this phenomenon is the »Disneyfication« of Times Square in New York. Under New York's Mayor Guiliani in the 1990s the »reformation« of Times Square was completed by bringing in theme-park industries to buy up properties at publicly supported prices in order to rid the area of »low rent« stores turning the area into a magnet for tourists. It was successful within the framework of commodifying Times Square and its activities, but it left a hole in the infrastructure of city life for people who live there.

The popular press is given to reporting on stories about the freedom of the Internet and the lack of capitalist exploitation on the web. But now, as mega-monopolies like Google buy up mere monopolies like YouTube, the fallacy at the center of this fairy tale is being exposed. As in the physical world, virtual environments are built by human labor. The human labor involved in building websites, interfaces, software and the other intangible pieces of digital environments, in turn relies on wages for living in the physical world. Indeed software and computer chips are made out of the tangible existence of our work. The way they get standardized and simplified to be channeled into chips is an old story with some new twists (see Greenbaum 2004).

The labor involved in building both the physical and digital world reflects, supports and changes the world we live in. This was at the heart of the issue that the Bauhaus artists tackled when they sought to design for the pre-depression growing masses of consumers, using craft-inspired design choices. And a similar wave of actions appears to be what is occurring now as teachers, students community organizers, social planners, traffic experts and others appropriate social networking software and open source tools to feed back into their influencing physical environments.

Ehn's 1988 book *Work-oriented design of computer artifacts*, originated in empirical projects that grew out of studies of the political economy of the way work is organized. The political concern of projects like the UTOPIA project that Ehn worked with, was to help skilled workers, such as printers, keep their jobs and their skills with the introduction of computer technology. But the task of helping one group of workers retain their skills and jobs in a complex global exchange is no longer viable, if indeed it ever was so. Today, the world-wide division of labor continues along with a global redistribution of labor into specialized work being done in different parts of the globe. This global redistribution, in turn is based on the »freedom« of capital sources to flee higher-waged areas and relocate in countries where labor costs less. And the global capital flow is knitted together by the intangible labor of internet-based tools and communication devices.

Manuel Castells, a geographer with a long history of work in urban design explains some of the consequences of capital flows. His interest is on helping us understand the place of cities amidst the »space of flows« that digital technology supports. He tells us that:

> Advanced telecommunications, Internet, and fast computerized transportation systems allow for simultaneous spatial concentration and decentralization, ushering in a new geography of networks and urban nodes throughout the world, throughout countries, between and within metropolitan areas. (Castells 2003, p. 83)

Thus, Castells explains, cities still gain importance as a »space of places«, while interactions flow through the fiber optics of what he calls a »space of flows«. Castells and others, like Harvey, who move from analysis that grows out of political economy offer us design suggestions for the built environment of physical places like cities and neighborhoods – suggestions that I believe can be used and supplemented by those of us studying interaction design. It is well worth reading these critical authors to see ways in which participatory actions of neighbors and residents combined with analysis by researchers can lead to viable design suggestions.

DESIGNING IN THE HERE AND NOW

Such are the practical political problems facing a new generation of interaction designers. But the solutions cannot be found in grand ideology or prescriptive design practices. Rather, as this chapter hopefully illustrates, politically situating problems in the intersection of the digital and physical world is a reasonable starting place. And insuring that the focus is on current use – what is actually happening in the world around us – can be a better guide for participatory design from praxis.

In explaining the need for embodied interaction design Dourish reminds us that we can change systems in two ways; first »by giving users more direct control over how activity is managed«, and, very importantly to the projects described here, »the second response is to help support the process of improvised, situated action by making the immediate circumstances of the work more visible«

(Dourish 2001, p. 160) My use of these concepts goes well beyond what the designed system can and should do. Rather the approach taken through these examples illustrates, I believe, that improvised actions by users in their physical experience in the world, coupled with appropriation of interactive software can produce answers to questions that are begging to be asked – questions like those Ehn raised in his early work, as well as those hammered out in the Bauhaus school.

Bauhaus designers used their political perspective to join art and design into practical physical products. Today, interaction designers are already on the road where art and design are blending in new media environments. Yet the political groundedness of how we merge art and design, and the specific situations we choose in which to apply our knowledge, is a wide open territory. And of equal importance are the ways we choose to involve, engage and actively participate in the process of designing from place-based use.

ACKNOWLEDGEMENTS

I would like to deeply thank the following people at the Graduate Center of City University in New York for sharing their extremely careful research and design projects for this article. Listed in order of the descriptions in this chapter, they are the following: Mauricio Leandro, a professor from Costa Rica, currently at City University, who is engaged in a study of speeding accidents; Haiwen Chu is a teacher in New York City who actively works with immigrant students and is currently working toward his doctorate in Urban Education; Meral Agish, an artist who lives in Flushing Queens is engaged in the interactive study of that place. Design and implementation is also being done in conjunction with the New Media Lab of City University of New York. I have worked with all the people and projects discussed in this chapter.

REFERENCES

Castells, M. (2003). Space of flows, space of places: Materials for a theory of urbanism in the information age. In Graham, S. (Ed.) *The Cybercities Reader*. Routledge.

Ciolfi, L., Bannon, L. (2005). Space, place and the design of technologically enhanced physical environments. In Turner, P. , Davenport, E. (Eds.) *Space, spatiality and technology*. Springer.

Dewey, J. (1938). *Experience and education.* Touchstone.

Dourish, P. (2001). *Where the action is: The foundations of embodied interaction.* Cambridge, MA: MIT Press.

Dourish, P. (2006). Re-space-ing place: Place and space ten years on. Proc. ACM Conf. Computer-Supported Cooperative Work (CSCW 2006), Banff, Alberta.

Ehn, P. (1988). *Work-oriented design of computer artifacts.* Swedish Center for Working Life and Lawrence Erlbaum.

Ehn, P. (1998). Manifesto for a Digital Bauhaus. *Digital Creativity*, 9(4):207–216.

Greenbaum, J. (2004). *Windows on the workplace: Technology, jobs and the organization of office work.* Monthly Review Press.

Greenbaum, J., Kyng, M. (Eds., 1991). *Design at work.* Hillsdale, NJ: Lawrence Erlbaum.

Harrison, S., Dourish. P. (1996). Re-place-ing space: The role of place and space in collaborative systems. Proceedings of the 1996 ACM Conference on Computer supported cooperative work, pp. 67–76. New York, NY: ACM Press.

Hayden, D. (1995). *The power of place: Urban landscapes as public history.* Cambridge, MA: MIT Press.

Harvey, D. (1990). *The condition of postmodernity.* Blackwell.

Harvey, D. (1996). From space to place and back again. In *Justice, nature and the geography of difference.* Blackwell.

Lefebvre, H. (1991). *The production of space.* Oxford: Blackwell. (Translation by D. Nicholson-Smith, original work published in 1974.)

Suchman, L. (2007). *Human-machine reconfigurations: Plans and situated actions, second edition.* Cambridge: Cambridge University Press.

Tuan, Y. (1977). *Space and place: The perspective of experience.* University of Minnesota Press.

BRENDA LAUREL

DESIGNED ANIMISM

BRENDA
DESIGNED ANIMISM
LAUREL

My interest in the relationship between pervasive computing and animism has been brewing for some time – an anthropological bent and an engagement with poetics are old friends. I followed Mark Weiser's work on ubiquitous computing at Xerox PARC and witnessed other early developments in the domain at Interval Research. During my time as chair of the graduate Media Design Program at Art Center, I was drawn to thinking about ambient and pervasive computing from new perspectives within the world of art and design. When I also joined Sun Labs in 2005, I got to see the development of the SunSPOTS up close and personal. Of course, it didn't hurt to be married to one of the principal researchers on the SPOTS team, who continued his work with sensor networks at the NASA Ames Research Center. I'm now heading up a new transdisciplinary grad design program at California College of the Arts, where pervasive computing and sensor networks will play a significant role in many of our studios as well as in collaboration with other institutions. I see pervasive computing as an extremely important phase shift in our capabilities, opening up huge new vistas of possibility for design, discovery, experience and human agency.

What does pervasive computing have to do with animism? Essentially, it can become a tool in manifesting what I call »designed animism«. The goal is fundamentally experiential, but the conequences are profound: designed animism forms the basis of a *poetics for a new world.*

Animism as a spiritual belief system attributes in-dwelling spirits to natural objects like trees and rocks (Bali), places (as in the Greek notion of the *genius loci*), or architectural or made objects. These spirits may be ancestral or local, protective or representative of a kind of agency within the object or the natural world. What's lovely to me about animism is not so much its philosophical or religious dimensions but the *behaviors* and *artifacts* that are created by people in response to animistic beliefs. In Shinto practice, natural objects are worshipped as sacred spirits. One of the four principal affirmations of Shinto practice is the honor given to the Kami – divine spirits that may be found in sacred places such as mountains or springs. You may know them from *Princess Mononoke*. Again, these beliefs order life for the believer in terms of the behaviors and constructions they inspire. In both Balinese and Shinto examples, these include shrines, prayers, and dances.

But animism points at a kind of truth that is consistent with science as well. There are in the natural world many entities within entities – like mitochondria or chloroplasts within cells – each with its own individual perception-representation-action loop. This is a trope to which I will return. All entities that have such a loop may be seen as having purpose – teleology – distinct from the questions of self-awareness or spiritual nature.

In biology, there is a strong trend toward the theory that Earth's enormously diverse and interrelated array of beings, with its numberless feedback loops, functions itself as a kind of organism, where individual entities – including ourselves – are parts of a larger organic whole. This idea can be traced from the Lovelock hypothesis and on through the work of contemporary scientists like Lyn Margulis and Dorian Sagan, but it is also hinted at in several of the works of Aristotle. In a Gaian sense, focusing on the experience of animism in terms of the behaviors it might engender, a healthy dose could do us a lot of good just about now. Designed animism may help us make crucial changes in how we frame the world and how we behave in the face of enormous environmental challenges.

The behaviors and constructions associated with animism are, of course, *designed* (or emerge through cultural evolution) within a context of beliefs, ethical values, and aesthetics. Less formally, animistic beliefs and ritual behaviors act as »co-designers« of everyday life. Because animism is seated in nature, the design of an animistic life encourages the imagination to construct beauty through projection onto the natural world, just as it invites nature in as an active participant. This is also a theme to which I will return.

Designed animism calls for a marriage of the notion of animism with a sense of poetics. Poetics, although most often associated with Aristotle, refers in general to literary theory that deals with the nature, forms and laws of poetry. Aristotle's *Poetics* looked at the various forms of poetry and their attributes, at the ways in which each kind of poetry might produce pleasurable experience, and how the form of poetry – a drama, for example – has value or serves its purpose; that is, the notion of virtue.

Nearly twenty years ago, in a book called *Computers as Theatre* (which is, strangely enough, still in print), I explored principles from Aristotle's works, primarily the *Poetics*, to discover whether and how they might apply to interactive drama or what you and I might now call a computer game. I revisited some of that work to think about how we might design systems that incorporate sensor networks and other distributed computational devices. How might we design new sources of pleasurable experience with the new affordances of ubiquitous or ambient computing? The Stoics and the Epicureans had some thoughts on the use of pleasure that can be revisited in light of modern affordances – and in the context of new conversations with mitochondria, rain forests, and our own selves.

The goal of pleasure seems somewhat at odds with the prevailing ethos of ubiquitous computing, which is still most often seen as having an essentially utilitarian or productive purpose. The discourse of ubiquitous computing emphasizes its value as a kind of human-computer interface coupled with software technologies that can make accurate inferences about the human need or desire to create an automagically convenient world. It also looks at the complementary problem of how a human can make needs or desires explicit. In terms of efficiency, a centralized computing model is often envisioned as the machine behind the curtain. Of course, this is the idea of Central Services that Terry Gilliam maligned in his classic film, *Brazil*. But in fantasy as well as in the reality of research labs – from smart houses to well-monitored cities – the tidy, efficient notion of ubiquitous computing is suspect. Over all hangs a cloud of social concerns: trust, privacy, erosion of human agency, reification of classism, and so on.

I don't mean to diminish the importance of the ideas and concerns I just sampled. I am simply exercising a particular design tactic, which is to look for the less populated area of the landscape, or what a designer might call the »opportunity space.« I'm hung up on pleasure because it seems a bit underserved in the discourse, because, well, I *like* it, because pleasure is good for getting people to notice things that they might not otherwise care about and because technology continues to offers new capabilities for creating it.

Water striders position themselves on the basis of wave patterns created by their fellows' movements.

In several domains we can observe something that my husband, Rob Tow, and I have been chewing on for a while: that is, the difference between a model of unitary central control versus a model that invites emergence from the summed actions of many actors, each with its own perception-representation-action loop. Rob characterizes this contrast variously: »clockwork and windmills«, or »Apollo and the rain forest«. The contrast might be delineated as a closed versus open system design, point versus field, or indeed »Central Services« versus a rain-forest *ecology of relationships*. In a rain forest ecology you can knock out any one species and the system still functions, other species slide into vacant niches. Central Services just doesn't work like that.

This contrast is apparent in many realms, and it can obviously inform our design practice. Let me give you an example. In 1976 in his book *Computer Lib*, Ted Nelson envisioned a system that would make all of the world's knowledge available and traversable through hyperlinks. He called his system »Xanadu.« The idea was glorious and massively inspirational, but the system concept was »closed« and proprietary – even quite secretive. Central Services again. As a closed world, this vision was too big to get one's arms around. And then along comes a noisy, crowded *field* of individual agencies and cockeyed affordances that ended up making Ted's dream a reality: the Web. You see what I mean.

Here's another example from the world of computer games. Back in the 1980s, about the time that Chris Crawford, myself and several others founded the Game Developers' Conference, the central issue in the game design community was the design of non-player characters and the kinds of »artificial intelligence« that could be used to animate them well enough to entertain, challenge and surprise human players. I took a similar tack in *Computer as Theatre*, attempting to figure out what aspects of Aristotelean poetics might be useful in designing interactive fantasy worlds – worlds that would provide robust, dramatic experiences for players or participants by incorporating some Aristotelean intelligence into the ways a computational system might generate actions of non-player characters and situational variables in a fantasy world.

Near the end of the 1980s, most likely inspired by Vernor Vinge's canonical tale, *True Names*, guys like Chip Morningstar started fooling around with the idea of graphical MUDs (standing for Multi-User Dungeons, in honor of the D&D community). Chip and his colleagues developed a system at Lucasfilm called *Habitat*. Although online multiplayer games had existed since the days of *Spacewar* and later in the domain of MUDs and MOOs, I think it was primarily the avatar-based graphical UI of Habitat that pushed multiplayer games over the »tipping point«. The change in design was profound, based upon the simple observation that, in contrast to AI-driven non-player characters, the source of the most interesting and lifelike actions might actually be *other human beings*. What a concept!

With the advent of this sort of space (and it progeny, such as *Everquest*, *Ultima Online*, and today's panoply of massively multiplayer online games and social spaces like *Second Life* and *Myspace*), designers had to *give up some authorial control*. In these cases, they give it up to other human beings. As you might imagine, many of the old lone-wolf designers just couldn't cope, where designers like Will Wright, who always seemed to understand that his players were his co-authors, jumped in with both feet. Computer game designers had to step back from *formal* control of the *shape* of a game and focus instead on the manipulation of *material causality* – that is, designing materials and environments that would predispose players to take actions that would yield dramatically satisfying outcomes.

Because computer games bear a striking resemblance to theatrical representations, with the addition of interactivity, it makes sense to look at dramatic form and experience and how interactivity changes it, not only for the interactor, but also for the author or designer. From there we may begin to look at how experience and design morph again when we introduce distributed sensing and computing devices and begin to incorporate their inputs into designed platforms for experience. This analytical exercise brings us back to Aristotle.

In the *Poetics*, Aristotle wrote about three different kinds of poetry. The *Epic* is a story or chain of stories describing events that may unfold over long periods of time, meant to be recited (or read), in the first or third person. It relies upon *extensification* – stretching time, as James Joyce did so well, so that a second can take minutes or hours to unfold. *Drama* is an imitation of an action with a beginning, middle, and end, and of a certain magnitude that can be taken in during the course of a day, enacted by players. Dramatic form relies upon *intensification*. So while the stand-alone computer game tends to take a more or less dramatic form (intensification), persistent multiplayer online games or worlds are more epic in nature (extensification).The *Lyric* form was more mysterious to Aristotle – he referred to »flute-playing and lyre-playing« as forms that incorporated music and rhythm. He also included in this category a form which, with the addition of language, still had »no name« in his day – this would be what we now think of as lyric poetry, spoken word, or even narrative music – that is, songs that tell stories.

Aristotle believed that any instance of poetry – a play, for example – was the result of four distinct but interrelated causes:
END – what a thing is intended to do
FORMAL – how the thing is influenced by a notion of form
EFFICIENT – how it is influenced by its maker(s)
MATERIAL – how it is shaped by what it is made of.

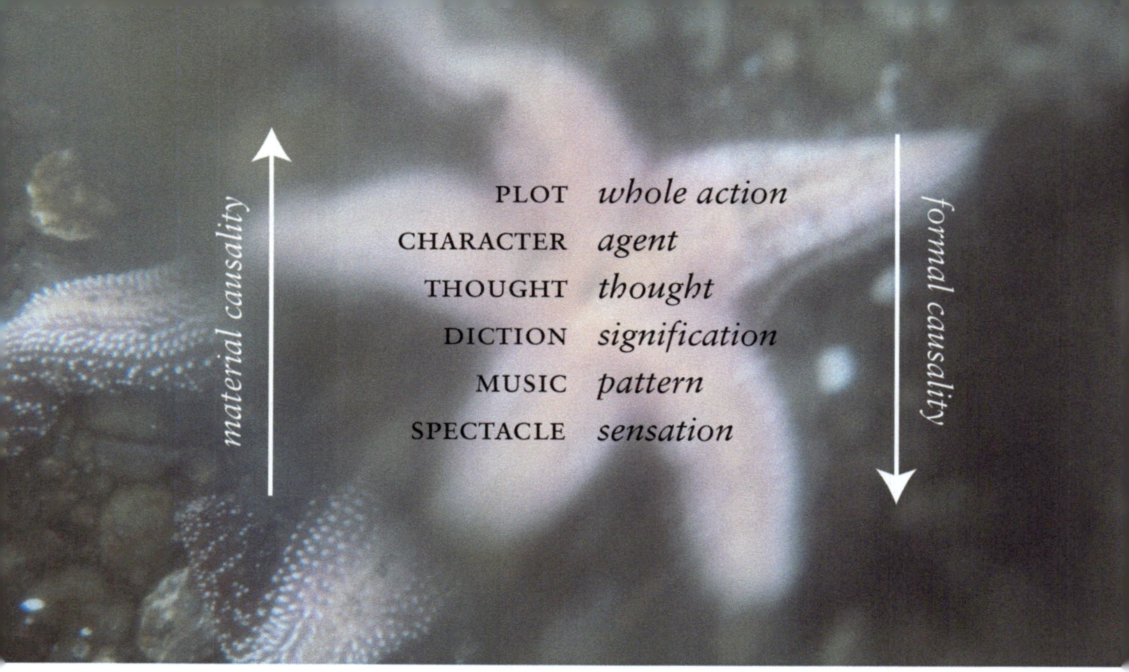

Moreover, Aristotle saw that a drama had six fundamental structural elements: plot, character, thought, diction, music, and spectacle. A nifty thing here is that each element could be seen to exist in causal relation to those above and below it, so in terms of material causality, sensation in the material from which pattern is constructed, thought is the material for character, etc. while character is the formal shaper of thought, thought of meaning, and so on.

Designing from the direction of the material cause is like reasoning or creating inductively. Formal causality begins with a notion of form and works more or less deductively to fill it out. In reality, most artists and designers work both ways at once.

Aristotle saw the action of a play as a progression from a wide range of possibilities, narrowed down through the choices and actions of characters and changes in situation to a smaller set of probabilities, which eventuate in a necessary end. Because the playwright controlled all of these choices and actions, he could also control the *shape* of the overall plot by *structural* means.

Left: Aristotle's elements of dramatic structure.
Action of play progresses from wide possibilities to narrow necessity (above), but what if the author loses control (below)?

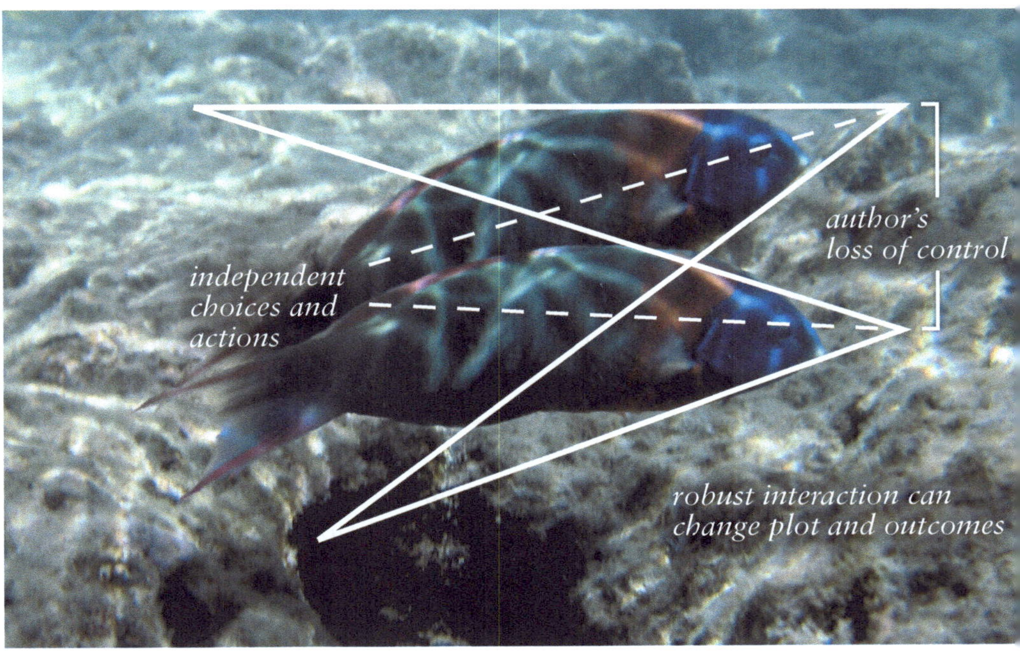

But what if the playwright is not the only fish in the sea? What if there is another agent – a character with free will, so to speak – making choices and performing actions that the playwright might not have foreseen? Then the trajectory of the plot will likely have a different end point – a different ending to the story. The interactor joins the playwright as the efficient cause of the whole action. What's an author to do with this loss of control?

Making a drama interactive means that the author has less and less influence from the direction of *formal* causality (that is, direct manipulation of plot, character, and thought). As we discovered in the days when interactive plays were in vogue, a way to compensate is to work more strongly from the direction of *material* causality, manipulating the environment and the materials out of which a »free agent« will construct thoughts, choices, and actions. The playwright's influence on the shape of the plot becomes indirect; he must *predispose* the interactor to make choices and take actions so that the interactor's *experience* has a pleasing shape.

How do we judge whether the action of a play has a pleasing shape? Aristotle described the metrics in terms of kinds of actions and emotions, as well as other structural elements. A big leap in our understanding of a pleasing shape for a plot came in 1863 from a fellow named Gustav Freytag, who created a visualization of dramatic action that was essentially a simple triangle labeled with Aristotle's anatomical terms, showing complication and resolution over time.

The triangle was refined by succeeding critics to show the relative duration and slope of these anatomical parts, giving us a more finely articulated vision of dramatic »shape.« The slope of each segment shows the relative level of complication, tension, stress, or suspense for that part of the play.

If you think of complication as asking a question and resolution as answering a question, you can see the shape as a kind of information analysis. Suddenly you're not looking at a picture of dramatic structure or even a picture of an

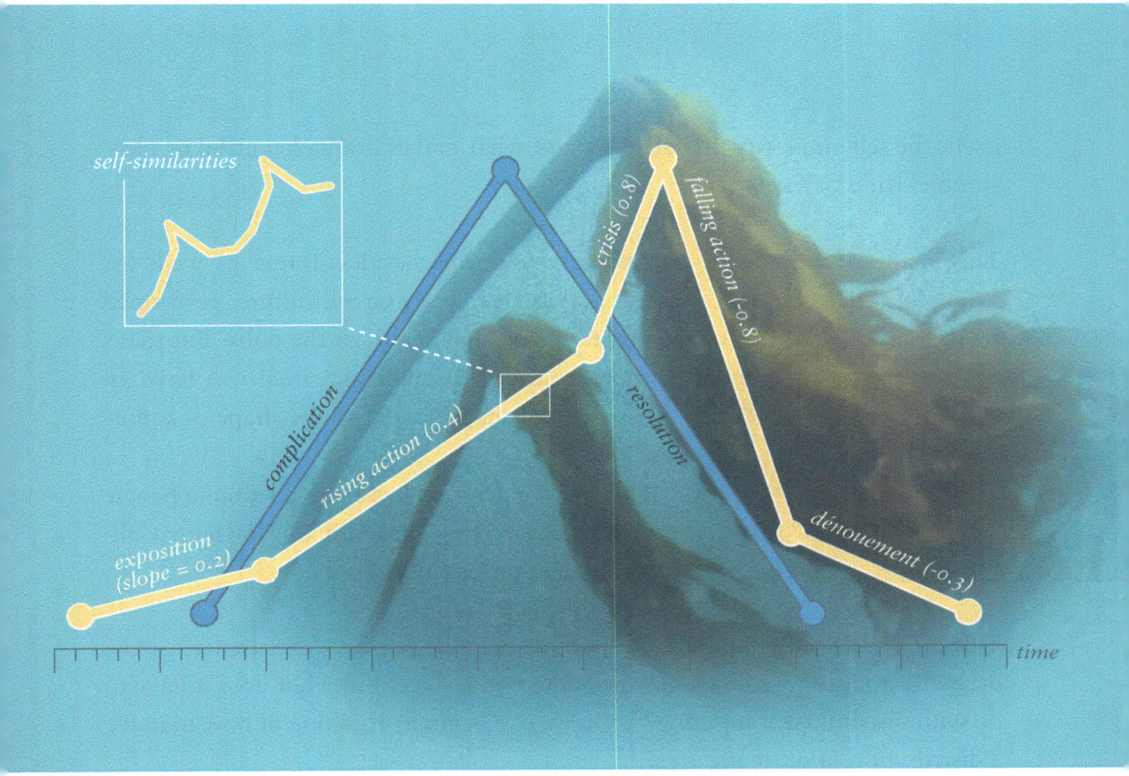

Basic Freytag graph of dramatic action (blue) and elaborated (yellow).

emotional progression, but simply a picture of information dynamics. But this a pretty grainy picture.

If you were to do a scene-by-scene or even line-by-line analysis of the play, you would find roughly self-similar curves at a smaller scale. Thanks, in part, to the invention of soap operas, episodic drama shows that sub-plots within episodes exhibit similar shapes, as well as overarching plot developments that arc across several episodes, encouraging the viewer to tune in again and again.

You are probably wondering what this analysis is good for in the context of this topic. What I've tried to show here is that there is a characteristic shape of dramatic experience that exists at various scales of time and granularities of information. I find this provocative. I suspect that, beyond the canonical shape itself, the self-similarity at scale is part of what makes drama beautiful or pleasurable. Kind of *fractal.*

This shape of experience might apply to forms besides drama as well; for example, rituals. Dramas were in fact rituals in early Greek culture, performed by priests of Dionysus for the greater emotional health of the polis. But that's another story. An animistic ritual can have an experiential shape similar to the shape of a plot.

This particular ritual has emerged among people of the Midwestern diaspora in Northern California. Yeah, tree-hugging.

This analysis is all well and good for the arc one person's experience, or the dramatic arc proposed by a play presented on a stage. But what does it have to do with distributed computing? Well, we can begin by thinking of how to make a distribution of dramatic arcs.

We move from a point source to a field.

A play is a kind of point source. Thinking along the trajectory of material causality, we can turn this point into a field by creating an environment that predisposes people to have different, but dramatically satisfying, experiences within a shared »field« of materials, patterns and so on. Here's an example from my own experience: the Renaissance Faire.

Trolls, royals, lepers, washer-women and the obligatory Spaniards vie for participants' attention. From the enormous spectacle of the joust to in-your-face excoriations of Protestants and whores, the participants' experiences seem to be somewhat »self-similar at scale«. Participants dress as wenches, pirates, faeries, trolls – even Samurai out here on the Pacific Rim. The Renaissance Faire is a field of materials for myriad dramatic experiences. The environment – the material causality of the Faire – predisposes those experiences to be pleasurable in similar ways. The miracle of the fishes.

Master storyteller David Ponkey (»Jack«) pictured above at the Northern California Renaissance Faire.

So there are two central, related ideas that I hope I've communicated by this look at drama: that there's *pleasure in the pattern of action* (which may exhibit self-similarity at different scales), and that *moving toward material causality* in authorship or making is a good strategy for collaborating gracefully with free agents to achieve experiences with pleasurable shapes.

Here's a bonus. Just as *Habitat* and multiplayer games demonstrated that a designer or author might have to do less rather than more to accommodate shared authorship, so the designer may have to do less rather than more by inviting nature into the collaboration. *Materials derived from the natural world usually come with »pleasing shapes« already embedded in them – shapes that please in ways that are different from the pleasure of a dramatic arc.* This is the third movement in our allegory: from the point source of drama, to the field of interactive media (which, although greatly more complex and inviting of emergence is still essentially *human-centric*), to the notion of inviting the *natural world* into our work as a collaborator.

Take the example of a windchime. It works on several relevant levels. It is what most would describe as a pleasing pattern of sounds. This pattern brings the invisible (wind) into the realm of the senses. The qualities of both the wind and the chimes exhibit chaotic patterns of a fractal nature, and these patterns may be rendered to address various sensory modalities. The windchime maker invites nature into collaboration. The maker crafts the materials and structures of the chimes and then lets the wind have it.

Sensors that gather information about wind, or solar flares, or neutrino showers, or bird migrations, or tides, or processes inside a living being, or dynamics of an ecosystem are means by which designers can invite nature into collaboration, and the invisible patterns they capture can be brought into the realm of the senses in myriad new ways.

As you undoubtedly know, Pythagoras, Copernicus and Kepler explored music as a representation of some of nature's deepest principles. Some musical compositions, like Holst's *Planets*, take the narratives of astrology as their core rather than any actual natural object or process.

Kepler's work in mathematics and astronomy is better known than his influence on musical theory of the time. »The Music of the Spheres« was to him much more than a metaphor. In his book on the history of music and science, Jamie James reports that »Kepler's most marvelous revelation came when he began to make ratios by pairing off the planets.« Kepler said, »...in the extreme movements of two planets compared with one another, the radiant sun of celestial harmony immediately breaks in all its clarity through the clouds.« James continues, »Using these extreme values, Kepler was able to construe the entire musical scale. Furthermore he discovered that each of the planets had its own scale, which is also determined by its speed at perihelion and aphelion.« For example, Saturn, the deepest, and Mercury, the highest pitched were notated this way.

That is not to gloss over mathematics and science. The twin inventions of the telescope and microscope changed fundamentally how we could see and think; real entities from the natural world that *were* invisible became visible. Kepler can be seen as a transitional figure between the solid geometry that reigned from Ptolemy and Euclid through Galileo – a span of over 20 centuries – and the new world of Newton's calculus. There was a pause of another 150 years, give or take, before mature chaotic dynamics, fractal math and emergent phenomena showed up as breathtaking new ways of understanding the world in the later twentieth century. It's worth noting here that these three domains were enabled by a new affordance: the computer.

Contemporary composers use information from the natural world by different means in their work. The controversial composer John Cage used probability and chance in some of his compositions, embedding chance events correlated to the I Ching or to computer-generated random numbers. Physics PH.D. Fiorella Terenzi used optical and radio data from galaxy UGC 6697 as the basis for a composition she called *Music from the Galaxies*. Composers like Stravinsky, Debussy, and Ravel attempted to express natural processes as music based upon a fusion of phenomenological observation and musical style. Debussy's *Voile* – French for »sail« – attempts to capture complex layers and dynamic shapes of wind and water, and the motion of a boat as the wind rises and falls. This piece of music is almost like a movie. In it, Debussy has approximated in a non- or pre-scientific way a kind of beauty that will later be amenable to exacting mathematical description.

Beginning with Turner, many painters in and around the impressionist period worked from an explicit desire to find artistic styles that more accurately represented human vision. Monet is an intriguing example: from his paintings, scientists were later able to derive his astigmatism, functioning as a kind of proof of the accuracy of his phenomenological observation. From his paintings of the Rouen cathedral, later scientists could also derive information about air pollution, something that Monet probably didn't think he was looking at.

A truly stunning example of the pre-scientific expression of a kind of pattern in nature that was not well understood by science at the time is the work of painter Jackson Pollock. In an article entitled »Fractal Expressionism« published in *Physics World* in 1999, Richard Taylor, Adam Micloich and David Jonas were able to demonstrate that Pollock's painting accurately represented fractal patterns. The authors observe that »experimental observations of the paintings of Jackson Pollock reveal that the artist was exploring ideas in fractals and chaos before these topics entered the scientific mainstream.« Pollock's motion around the canvas and his application of paint by dripping are natural causes for the fractal nature of the work. He literally invited physics in as a collaborator. Pollock saw beauty in forms that could not even be named when he painted them.

Mandelbrot brought the work of the centuries-long explorations in the realm of chaos theory to mathematical fruition. Fractal geometry, created principally by Mandelbrot, has been dubbed »the true Geometry of Nature.« The impact of fractal geometry and new tools for generating fractals on art and popular culture has been huge, from feature film effects to computer games.

The purpose of this part of my rant is to observe that in areas such as music and visual arts, artists have captured patterns in nature based purely on phenomenological evidence that were later reified by mathematics. Computational tools have allowed contemporary artists to collaborate directly with the natural world in novel ways through the use of mathematical and computational representations of nature. Surely there is more to come.

Here's another discovery that just blows my socks off. In 1976, Richard Voss and John Clarke identified the temporal manifestation of fractals in the mathematical expression of 1 over f noise, commonly called »pink noise.« Mandelbrot and Frame tell the story of this discovery in the course notes for »A Panorama of Fractals and Their Uses« taught in the Mathematics department at Yale:

> As a graduate student at Berkeley, Richard Voss was studying this problem, using signal-processing equipment and computers to produce the power spectrum of the signal from a semiconductor sample. When one sample had burned out and another was being prepared, Voss plugged his signal-analyzing equipment into a radio and computed the power spectrum. Amazingly, a 1/f spectrum appeared. Voss changed radio stations and repeated the experiment – another 1/f distribution. Classical, jazz, blues, and rock all exhibited 1/f distributions. Even radio news and talk shows gave (approximate) 1/f distributions.

Mandelbrot and Frame have documented 1/f noise in Western music as well as African, Japanese, Indian, and Russian, and through a range of times, from the Medieval period through the Beatles. They conclude that:

> Voss uses these observations eloquently to bring closure to one of the classical Greek theories of art. The Greeks believed art imitates nature, and how this happens is relatively clear for painting, sculpture, and drama. Music, though, was a puzzle. Except for rare phenomena such as aeolian harps, few processes in Nature seem musical. Voss uses the ubiquity of 1/f noise to assert [that] music mimics *the way the world changes with time.*

I'm hearing windchimes again. Here may also be the definition of Aristotle's elusive Lyric form. We live in a time in which many new forms of »windchimes« reveal previously invisible patterns and forces in the natural world.

1/f noise is not just a characteristic of music. Mandelbrot and others have explored in depth how chaos works in economic systems – 1/f noise is present there as well. For me, this is a clue that human behavior – even in a pinstripe suit – is much more closely related to the natural world than we generally acknowledge.

I want to turn to a different kind of pattern: the pattern of emergence based upon the interaction of entities with perception-representation-action loops. Water striders are a gorgeous example of emergence in the natural world (see the picture on p. 255). Rob calls them little state machines. They have fairly simple rule sets that respond to characteristics of water, light and proximity to other mass-y things. By operating independently, they dynamically arrange themselves evenly over the surface of a pool to optimize each individual's feeding area. There is no Water-Strider Central trying to manage this distribution. It is emergent from the local rules of each individual in interaction with its environment.

I won't attempt to catalog all of the wonderful examples of emergence in natural, social, and computational systems. I want to simply call your attention to emergence as a design resource that can be tapped by networks of sensor-enabled devices working on local rules to create both beauty and knowledge.

So here's a funny thing. In 2005, Sun Labs sponsored a transdisciplinary studio hosted by the Media Design Program at Art Center. Bruce Sterling, who was in residence in our studio that year, co-taught the course, along with Nik Hafermas and Phil Van Allen. The idea was to lob a bunch of SunSPOTS – networked devices that are capable of producing emergent behavior – at a bunch of design students and let them have it. Jed Berk and Nikhil Mittner, both Media Design students, designed a flock of blimps that they called ALAVs – »autonomous lighter-than-air vehicles«. The blimps could be »fed« through an array of fiberoptic tubes. When they were »hungry« they descended, and when they were nourished, they lifted off. When they were close to one another, they flocked and cooed. I have to say, it was totally trippy. When I last spoke with Jed, he was attaching video cameras to them and let them create a kind of ambient video BLOG. Cool.

ALAVs 1.0. Wind Tunnel, Art Center College of Design. Project by Jed Berk and Nikhil Mittner. Photo courtesy of Theo Alexopolous.

Cool. So what? This chapter was about pleasure, poetics and designed animism. I guess I'd better give you some examples of what I mean by designed animism in a technological context before I conclude. As I said earlier, with animism I am not so concerned with the attribution of spiritual powers to beings and processes in the natural world as I am concerned with what those attributions induce in us. When we see the world as deeply alive and beautiful, how does it change us? How does it change what we decide and do in the world?

My good friend Sean White has been working on a system called an Electronic Field Guide. The vision for the project is to explore new forms of field guides that enhance cognition and memory. The project's explicit purpose is to serve botanists and other scientists in identifying plants and observing or visualizing some of the relationships at work in their ecosystems. The project is a large-scale collaboration between Columbia, the Smithsonian and the University of Maryland. A prototype system has been deployed on Plummers Island and will soon be mounted again at a science station on Barro Colorado Island in Panama. Sean says:

> Biologists of all stripes go down there for research and most of them have their own specialty. We are exploring the possibility of providing the EFG to aid researchers in quick identification of flora relevant to their own ecosystem research. If a botanist is studying a caterpillar, they may not be able to identify the species of plants that it eats. The system will help them create an ecological web of relationships and perhaps even help build a semantic web in the field for further eco-informatic study.

Sean has experimented with multiple cameras and sensors as inputs and with hardened tablets, augmented reality displays and mobile phones as UI devices. He believes that a distributed system without centralized control will eventually be an optimal form. He describes his goals this way: »We do this to support being *in* the world and *part* of the world.« He reports that when people experience these realtime streams of data in combination, a holistic sense of delight often emerges. In other words, emergence happens *inside the person*, and this is true even when one brain could not possibly sort the specific information content of each of the streams of information that are available to them. He's had botanists tell him that they have felt the boundaries of their bodies dissolve. But, he cautions, this transcendental awareness is fragile and must be approached with a spirit of lightness.

As Sean's system demonstrates, the process that I described in the context of pre-scientific representations in art and music is has its inverse. In the first case, the creation of a representation that delights the artist reveals a deeper intuition of some of the unseen shapes of nature. In the inverse case, the fusion of inputs from distributed sensors delivered in delightful ways creates the same sort of joyous intuition.

When discussing this phenomenon at the 2006 Ubicomp conference, Bruce Sterling asserted in his usual acerbic way that »there is no magic.« Sean's project combines sensor data with machine learning techniques to look at covariance in an n-dimensional space and find the eigenvectors or most meaningful axes in that space. Those reveal interesting patterns that a person can experience in sensory ways. They look at frequency patterns with Fourier transforms and the

Augmented reality image of matching virtual leaves overlaid on physical scene as viewed through Sony LDI-D100B color, optical see-through, head-worn display. The image of the user's view was captured directly from inside the head-worn display, using a Toshiba remote lipstick camera and digitized at 720 x 480 resolution. Courtesy of Sean White.

texture of irises with gabor jets. With semantic zooming they are able to move in and out of the pattern space. Now *that's* magic!

In my garden, there are faeries.

One of my faeries watches the lavender. This one has a history of the flowers and knowledge of how sun and shade move over the garden as the day passes. The lavender faerie brings the scent of warm flowers into my room just at the sunniest hour. It also whispers with the bee faerie, who knows that when the lavender is just so, the bees will come. The water faeries taste the soil around my plants and drip when they are too dry. The lizard faeries dance around the top of my desk when they see the lizards scurry from the Oregon grapes to the woodpile.

We see faeries, or make them up, but now we can also *make* them. We have, for the first time, the capacity to create entities that can sense and act autonomously, or with one another, or with living beings. They can learn and evolve. They can reveal new patterns, extend our senses, enhance our agency and change our minds.

My fairies watch the sun set with me. They dance the changes in light and temperature, in the closing of certain flowers, in the quieting of songbirds and the wakening of owls. And I have this perfectly joyful sense that my body is my home, my garden, my canyon, my trees. If I had more sensors, my body could be the earth. With matching effectors, I become a »Gaian Gardener«, responsible for and enacting the health of the living planet.

Scientists and artists know that patterns drawn from nature tickle our nervous systems at a deep, preconscious level. Designed animism is a healing system for our disconnect with our planet. But as our history so vividly shows, we are not likely to come to new awareness though fear, or even through information. We may, however, come to it through delight.

ACKNOWLEDGEMENT

My thanks to Rob Tow for his invaluable conversations and contributions. Thanks also to Sean White for his inspirational work.

REFERENCES

Clarke, J., Voss, R. (1978). 1/f noise in music: Music from 1/f noise. *Journal of the Acoustical Society of America* 63(1):258–263.

Freytag, G. (1897). *Die technik des dramas*. Leipzig: S. Hirzel.

James, J. (1993). *The music of the spheres: Music, science and the natural order of the universe*. Springer.

Lovelock, J. (1979). *Gaia: A new look at life on earth*. Cambridge: Cambridge University Press.

Mandelbrot, B., Frame, M. (2002). Panorama of fractals and their uses in fractals. In *Fractals, graphics, and mathematics education*. Cambridge: Cambridge University Press.

Margulis, L., Sagan, D. (1999). *Symbiotic planet: A new look at evolution*. New York: Basic Books.

Nelson, T. (1974). *Computer lib: You can and must understand computers now.* Nelson.

Taylor, R., Micloich, A., Jonas, D. (1999). Fractal expressionism. *Physics World* 12:25.

Vinge, V. (1987). True names. In *True names and other dangers.* Baen Books.

White, S., Feiner, S., Jopylec, J. (2006). Virtual vouchers: Prototyping a mobile augmented reality user interface for botanical species identification. Proceedings of IEEE symposium on 3D user interfaces (3DUI 2006).

ERIK STOLTERMAN

IN SEARCH OF A CRITICAL STANCE

ERIK
STOLTERMAN
IN SEARCH OF A CRITICAL STANCE

FINDING POTENTIALITY IN TECHNOLOGY

Technology in general, and digital technology in particular, shapes and influences our individual and common lifeworlds in ways that cannot fully be grasped. As a society we are facing a design challenge when it comes to the interaction between technology and people of a complexity and magnitude never experienced before. One of the questions that arise about the future of our digital and interactive environments is if we are using the new technology in a way that supports a »good life.« Does the environment with its interactive artifacts and systems promote a desired way of living? It is obvious that we, as a society, truly believe that it is. Technology is commonly seen as a provider of solutions that will bring about the »good life« and move us all in a desired direction. However, this view is problematic and needs to be explored. In this chapter I will discuss how an individual researcher in the field of digital and interactive technology can reflect on the purpose of research and how to go about doing research if she wants to do »good.«

Many believe that the *potentiality* inherent in digital technology is enormous. It is not uncommon to hear statements arguing that the use of this technology is only limited by our own imagination. This idea of potentiality can however be interpreted in different ways. The idea of the unexplored potentiality of interactive technology is also the idea that this text is based upon.

One of my underlying assumptions is that, despite all the attention and attempts to explore new uses of digital technology, there is still *a need for theoretical ideas suitable for a critical and positive exploration of the potentiality of digital technology*. This need is not only for purely philosophical purposes, instead, there is a need for real practical approaches on how to conduct research in a field where technology and use are under constant evolution.

I will argue that the field of human-computer interaction design research must seriously take on the challenge and responsibility to develop new ways for people to interact with interactive technology that will, and can, support the »good life« or maybe with a better concept: the human wellbeing. This chapter is an attempt to respond to that challenge, by arguing that it is possible to take on this responsibility if we devote more time to *critical reflective thinking*. This is, of course, not a unique argument. Many have argued that complex problems and complex situations have to be approached with some kind of *reflective mode* of thinking. In most cases, though, those arguments are meant to support a designer doing design work. As such, it is about the development of individual competence and skill, for instance in the tradition of Donald Schön (1983). I will not deal with that kind of reflective thinking in this context; instead I will approach critical and reflective thinking on the level of a *research discipline*, which in my case is human-computer interaction.

I will argue that the field of human-computer interaction (HCI) has a broader responsibility than what is commonly recognized. HCI research is not only about finding new ways to improve the interaction design process, or new insights on how individuals interact with artifacts, or how new technological findings can change the way we interact with technology, it also has to address broader issues. There is, of course, research that does take on broader issues, such as the study of social and psychological consequences of use of digital artifacts and studies of how the technology influences learning, communication, collaboration, etc. All this is good. I am not arguing that such research is not important or not responsible research, but I am arguing that there are other perspectives or aspects of research that are not well developed in HCI.

I am advocating research that takes a fundamental critical perspective with the aim to reveal the »one-dimensionality« underlying the present mainstream research in the meaning that Marcuse put forward in his well-known book *The one-dimensional man* (1964). The Marcusian way of thinking is critical to its nature, but it differs from the existing research in our field that advocates critical research aimed at, for instance, unfolding and revealing power or gender structures inscribed in the use of contemporary technology. The Marcuse approach is critical in a similar sense, but the aspect of his approach that I will focus on is his goal of exploring undeveloped potentiality. Marcuse does not address in particular the undeveloped potentiality of modern technology, but in this context that is the focus.

I will argue that one way to develop a critical reflective approach aimed at potentiality is through a theoretical examination of the meaning of being *close* to the *material* at hand (as inspired by the work of James Hillman) and *distant* to the technology (as inspired by the work of Herbert Marcuse). I will argue that such a double examination might help us form an understanding of what reflective thinking could mean in practice. I will also argue that the notion of an *aesthetic sensibility* is a possible and inevitable intellectual tool needed in this endeavor.

WHAT'S SO SPECIAL ABOUT INTERACTIVE TECHNOLOGY

One quality of information technology, and in this case, interactive technology, that separates it from many other and earlier technologies is that its manifestations influence almost all aspects of our everyday lives. There are, of course, specialized applications of information technology in science and industry, but the technology is well suited for use in our homes and workplaces in ways that few earlier technologies have been. It is a technology that lends itself to pervasive and ubiquitous use. This is causing both problems and some confusion, and there are signs that we do not really know how to relate to this possibility and challenge. It is even possible to describe our relation to digital technology as paradoxical and perplexing, as embodied, or as subjective experience, or as »living with« (McCarthy and Wright 2004, Croon 2006, Dourish 2001). This diverse understanding of a technology and its use is in itself fascinating and a sign that there is something important going on that seems difficult to comprehend.

It is apparent that people relate to and understand digital technology in numerous and varied ways. Maybe the most common way is the »traditional« understanding of technology as an unstoppable force that evolves due to some intrinsic and almost inevitable logic. Such a view evokes questions like »Where will technology take us?« What is interesting is that if we fully accept this view, there is no potentiality in technology to be explored or reflected upon. Instead, technological development becomes more or less inevitable and we can only be part of, or »passengers« of, that development. Another and opposing view is based on an understanding of technology as a »material« completely open for our desires and wishes. A typical statement based on this view is: »Only our imagination sets the limits for what we can do with this technology.« This view is based on the idea that digital technology itself is open for design – hence a carrier of endless potentiality. Given such potentiality, there is a strong need for critical reflection. With *potentiality comes responsibility.* When it is possible to explore potentiality, we need critical reflection to make meaning and judgments.

These two opposing views are of course idealized conceptualizations of what, in each of our minds, is a complex and often messy reality. One fascinating aspect of these two views is that they seem to have such strong presence in peoples everyday lives, and also that they seem to exist side-by-side, sometimes even within one person. Each of us can probably recognize that contradiction. We can easily be lured into a defensive and conservative mode of thinking about technology caused by deterministic tendencies in our thinking or into an either energetic or tiring feeling caused by the infinite possibilities presented to us. The need for reflective thinking is obvious. The basic premise of my argument is that the way we understand technology as a bearer of potentiality, or not, forms and shapes our minds and our creativity and thereby how we try and find it possible to design our reality.

All this has to do with how we understand digital technology. What is its potentiality? Human-computer interaction design is, as all kinds of design and as a basic human activity, based on the very idea of potentiality. There is no possibility for design if we cannot see potentiality in our materials, activities and ideas. Design is about seeing and creating something not-yet-existing based on what is potential in the world around us (Nelson and Stolterman 2003). Potentiality is therefore at the core of design of new technology. Focusing on potentiality is first of all a question of creating an appropriate *mindset*, but could, of course, be further developed into both knowledge, skill and tool sets. So, the question becomes how do we understand potentiality when it comes to a technology, and how it can be explored?

BEING CLOSE AND DISTANT

In this context, technology is seen as the *material* by which our designs are realized. Technology in all its richness and with its multifaceted properties is what the designer uses in imaging a potential interactive artifact, application, or system. This potentiality in technology can be approached on different levels. These levels can be understood in a similar way as a skilled crafts person, for instance a carpenter, relates to their material. There is the *abstract discourse*, which is the level where the overall understanding of technology and material is played out in the reflective thinking of the crafts person. For a carpenter this is shown in the way they talk about their material in general terms, for instance about how they can treat their material, what constitute good raw materials, how it can be used and to what purposes. Sometimes this discourse, or these reflections, is almost poetic and filled with respect and even love towards the material and the tools used to handle the material. To someone who is not closely acquainted with the specific material, this kind of discourse is usually difficult to understand, since it is too abstract and »philosophical« and has no »practical« meaning to a layperson.

At another level the carpenter has the really *close and tangible relation to their material.* They can determine quality with their hands and other senses. They might not be able to describe these qualities in words, only show it in action. »This is what it should feel like when the material is right!« To an amateur it can be almost impossible to »feel« the difference; trying to describe it in words usually doesn't help since you need a *well trained »hands-on« sensitivity* to be able to recognize subtle differences in quality.

These two ways to approach a material or a technology are extremely important, that is, to have a *distant* »theoretical« or abstract *understanding* of the technology and to have a *close* and hands-on *sensitivity.* My suspicion is that much academic work on technology and its potentiality is not grounded in any of these two levels. What seems to be more common is something in between, where the understanding becomes neither abstract nor »hands-on« enough, and very seldom both. The carpenter has no problem mixing his poetic abstract notions about his material with his hands-on sensibility of the qualities in the material.

The combination of these two seemingly disparate approaches to a material is needed if the *purpose is to explore the full potentiality* of any material. It is an approach that we need to develop in order to find the potentiality of digital material. To be able to combine these two ways, reflection is needed. Reflective thinking is when we integrate and compose our understanding by using our intellectual capacity not only in a strict logical or rational way, but also in an intentional and intuitive or integrative way.

It is possible to find theoretical arguments for such an approach in earlier work. I will mention two thinkers that can help us, first Herbert Marcuse can help us reflect upon the notion of *distant understanding*, and secondly James Hillman can help us with the notion of *hands-on sensibility*.

DISTANT UNDERSTANDING. One possible way to approach potentiality in technology at the level of abstract discourse is found in the writings of Herbert Marcuse. Marcuse argues that our modern society, in all its domains, fosters and even enforces one-dimensionality in the way we understand progress and development (Marcuse, 1964). One-dimensional thinking emerges, according to Marcuse, partly as a result of a technological development that supports the dominating way of life without questioning its basic assumptions. Technology, viewed that way, even creates a form of unfreedom. The ironic twist is that we do not necessary experience this »unfreedom« as something bad. »For this unfreedom appears neither as irrational nor as political, but rather as submission to the technical apparatus which enlarges the comforts of life and increases the productivity of labor« (Marcuse 1964, p. 158).

If we take Marcuse's ideas seriously we have a tough methodological problem at hand. We are »trapped« in a mindset in relation to what technology is doing to us (giving us) and maybe more seriously, trapped in our imagination of what it *could* be like. Marcuse argues that our *imagination* has to be trained to be able to see the »real« potentiality in our technologies. This might be compared to the way the carpenter with a *poetic understanding* of their material opens up for a full appreciation and use of the material qualities. To Marcuse this is an approach that has to *step away* from an empirical approach since such an approach »confirms« our preconceptions and makes it extremely difficult to imagine other ways to use technology.

One practical example of this could be the way *metaphors* have played a crucial part in the history of interaction design. It has not been easy or maybe not even possible to create new interactive designs solely based on a careful study of earlier designs and solutions. Instead, the surprising new designs in the field have, in many cases, been based on a radical new way of conceptualizing or theoretically thinking about interaction, for instance, in the form of new and sometimes strange metaphors. These new ideas have opened up the possibility of *imagining design spaces* that were not visible earlier. In many cases, these new ideas have been a result of someone's reflective and critical investigation of the underlying theoretical concept or metaphor of existing solutions and not a result of careful analysis of its implementations. So, metaphors and other abstract notions can increase our ability to see and imagine the potentiality of the technology. Therefore we need *critical theoretical thinking*, since it can challenge and relive us from the one-dimensionality in our empirically formed assumptions about reality. So, stay distant, use imagination, think theoretically and be critical.

HANDS-ON SENSIBILITY. On the other level discussed above (that of being hands-on and close) it is possible to relate to the works of James Hillman (1996). Hillman does not address technology at all in his book, instead his topic is how to understand and raise children (even though he discusses technology in the form of the ensouled world, »anima mundi« in some of his other books). Hillman argues that it is possible, and useful, to assume that people have a soul and that the soul has a calling. With the risk of misinterpreting his idea, I think it is possible to make the same assumption when it comes to technology and especially digital technology. Hillman is very careful in not getting drawn into the delicate questions of whether people actually have a soul or what a soul really might be. Instead he is pragmatic in his approach. The basic idea is that parents have to listen closely to their children, with the purpose of finding out who they are and who they »want« to become. If parents don't listen carefully and closely enough they might try to »form« their child into something that goes against the child's soul and that will lead to tensions that later on might lead to disastrous consequences.

We could make the same assumption about digital technology, namely that every technology has a »soul« and a calling. If we try to develop the technology into something that is at odds with it's calling, we will create great tension, which might lead to some kind of »disaster«. Similarly to what can happen if we push a child to become what he does not have a calling for, there could be a strong and unpredictable reaction. The key notion that Hillman presents to overcome this, is the *careful listening*. It means, »to get close«, to pay attention, to listen. Hillman uses the concept of *notitia*. Notitia means paying attention to *details*, to the *real thing*, not in the first place as interpretation, but actually getting so close that you fully *»feel« the qualities* of that you are approaching. It means being careful and caring. It means a closeness that is similar to the carpenter's hands-on feeling and touching. With digital technology, this means that it is not possible to fully understand the technology without getting close, without getting a »feel« for it, without notitia. To fully understand the »calling« of the technology you have to get close.

An example of this might be the way good programmers relate to their »material«. It is commonly known that really good programmers, in most cases, want to use tools for programming that makes it possible for them to get as close as possible to the material. They want to be able to »touch« the bits, to feel the material, in its genuine form of logic and procedures. Amateurs are usually fine with using tools that make things easy to do and keep them far away from the bits, for instance with the help of drag-and-drop techniques. The amateur cannot come close to the technology as a material and therefore can't build a sensibility for what is possible, that is, its potentiality, while the programmer with a close, almost hands-on, feeling of the bits, can explore and imagine a virtually unlimited space of potentiality.

This relation between the material, the tool and potentiality is intriguing. The tool manifests how close a designer can come to the material, which is true for the carpenter too. The skilled carpenter does not want to use multipurpose »hobby« machines that can do anything, but nothing of really good quality. Instead, the carpenter, as the programmer, likes tools that make it possible to, in a non-prescribed way and in detail, manipulate the material. Strangely enough, being hands-on, in control of the material, has to do with imagination and the possibility to explore potentiality. So, feel and touch the material, care for details and quality, stay close.

TWO APPROACHES – ONE MIND

To some extent it is possible to see the two approaches, as illustrated respectively by Marcuse and Hillman, as opposed and maybe even an example of the clash between how social science (*distant*) and engineering (*close*) approaches technology. However, the point here is *not* to separate the two. The idea is that the two are needed and should be *integrated and internalized within the same intellect*. In the same way as the skilled carpenter can deal with two ways of understanding his material.

Any »approach« or new way of thinking needs some tools for evaluation and guidance. It is obvious that the ideas of *potentiality*, *notitia*, *distant* and *close* are so abstract and ephemeral that we need some kind of practical »tool« or guidance in how to actually do this. So, what would constitute as a »tool« for such guidance? One suggestion is that it is all a matter of *judgments*.

In the writings of both Marcuse and Hillman we can find a similarity in that they both stress a form of judgment that could be labeled *aesthetic sensibility*. They both argue that we can develop an aesthetic sensibility as a *skill* if we pay enough attention and have the courage to do it. This means that good interaction designers can, and do, develop an aesthetic sensibility in their relationship towards technology. They develop a way of working where they can, by exercising their aesthetic sensibility, explore, imagine and value the potential worth of undiscovered possible design spaces.

Design is always an *act of judgment* (Nelson and Stolterman 2003). It is through judgment that we can bring together the distant understanding with the hands-on sensibility. And if we, as designers or researchers, want to expand the overall design space and create new arenas for the use of digital technology, we have to open our minds and exercise our judgment. The act of judgment is the only way to bring the two forms of technology awareness together and to escape the overwhelming one-dimensional thinking that comes with the existing discourse around new technology.

There are, of course, enemies of this kind of thinking. One of the strongest opponents to this approach is the firm belief in the outstanding value of narrow and specialized competence. This belief has, as I see it, two roots. One is in the tradition of the industrialized society where production is seen as becoming more efficient if division of labor is employed. The other tradition comes from science, where the specialization is a key to the success of the ongoing knowledge production. The number of disciplines is growing, and the specialization is a natural development within the traditional scientific approach. This means that these two traditions, division of labor and specialization, are naturally opposing the notion of bringing things together, or involving judgment as a tool to handle design complexity (Stolterman 2008). When it comes to design, division of labor and specialization, are not suitable. Design is about bringing things together with the purpose to understand and see emerging qualities, to be able to explore and connect things that seem unrelated, to explicitly work with particular instances of things and not with abstractions and generalizations. Design is all about the »whole«, it is about the composition of the design and its situation. This means that there are many »enemies« to the approach suggested here, not the least organizational and administrative.

This *critical stance* towards technology, resting on the hands-on sensibility and the distant understanding, can influence (i) the individual designer, (ii) the education of interaction designers, and (iii) the societal discourse around digital technology. When it comes to the influence on the individual design, it is the responsibility of that individual designer to make it happen. When it comes to education, it is of course the educator that has to make sure that the critical stance is implemented in curricula and courses. For the societal discourse, it is the interaction researcher who has the responsibility to advance the discourse and influence the broader understanding of the technology. I will briefly discuss what kind of implications this critical stance could lead to for these three groups.

IMPLICATIONS FOR THE DESIGNER. Designers of interactive artifacts and systems create new realities. The position advocated here, the critical stance, argues that these designers have to stay *distant* and *close* to the technology at the same time. They have to be able to get close to the material, the technology, in the way Hillman talks about *notitia*, the careful listening, while they, as Marcuse argues, have to stay distant with a philosophical eye, to be able to grasp the overall potentiality of the technology. This is not easily done, and in many cases this goes against the way division of labor works in the professional field. It is not uncommon that division of labor leads to a split right between the two aspects, since it is assumed that some people should envision and design, and others implement and build. This distinction, as is argued in this chapter, leads to a situation where neither side will build the competence needed to be able to fully explore the true potentiality of technology. Design is about the hand *and* mind. One of the practical consequences is that interaction designers have to *insist* on being involved in the design and development process from the beginning to the end.

IMPLICATIONS FOR EDUCATION. The critical stance advocated here, can be implemented in the education of interaction designers. This means that a curriculum should include courses that make it possible for the students to approach technology in the two ways described above. They should have courses where they are expected to work, in a concrete and close way, with technology and other materials. The important part is that these courses should not be seen as »practical« in the sense that they are only about application and training of needed skills and tools. Instead, they should be seen as a way for students to build a deeper understanding of technology and what can be done with it. The skills and tools will vary over time, but the deep understanding of the technology is valuable for a long time.

It is also important that a curriculum includes courses where technology and interaction is approached from a critical discursive perspective. This means that students need to be challenged with advanced theoretical materials by classic and contemporary scholars. It is crucial that students are made aware that theoretical and critical thinking is not only a way to understand the field, it is not »just« theory, but a way to challenge it and to explore new possible ways of utilizing the technology. It is a way of thinking that will expand their design capabilities.

IMPLICATIONS FOR THE RESEARCHER. There are, of course, researchers in the field that already have this dual competence, this eye for the potentiality of technology that is lacking in the general public. In the same sense as architects and other designers feel it is their responsibility to »educate« the general public by being involved in the public discourse about city planning and architecture, the interaction designer should take the same responsibility for their field. There are a never ending stream of topics that relate to interaction in media and other venues where design researchers could, and should, be involved with their expertise and by bringing a perspective that makes it possible for people to at least experience a broader understanding of the potentiality of technology and not be caught up in a simplistic one-dimensional perspective dominating the general public discourse.

These three areas are places where it is possible to find a starting point in how to find, develop and exercise a critical stance to the development of interactive technology. There are probably other ways of doing this, and maybe some more efficient ones. But, these three are at least possible to do, and are in the hands of us, as researchers in the field. There are also a number of places where this is already happening, especially when it comes to educations that have curricula that resonates with these ideas. And there are companies where there is a new understanding of design that has led to different ways of organizing the process and there are a few (but very few) researchers who try to influence the public discourse by being active outside the internal venues of academia.

CONCLUSION

As interaction design researchers, we are responsible for the education of those who will be the future designers of interactive artifacts, systems and environments, and there is a need for a more critical examination of the direction of this development as it unfolds through the design of these artifacts and systems. In order to find new directions, there is a need to develop the competence that will make it possible for designers to explore and examine the full potentiality of the technology. There is a chance that we can find potentiality in this technology that will lead to fundamentally different systems and designs, for instance designs that will support people in their strive for physical and mental well-being, for relaxation, for contemplation, for deep communication, for democratization, etc. And all this, with the overall goal, not of making life easier and faster, but richer and more desirable from a long-term individual well-being perspective.

How all this can be practically done is not easy to see, even though I have given a few examples. Nevertheless, the challenge is still there and cannot be escaped. If human-computer interaction wants to be active and have an impact in the exploration and development of human centered use of digital technology, we have to be intentionally reflective and critical when we examine the way technology can be understood and designed.

We have to accept that there is an infinite potentiality hidden in the technology that researchers has the responsibility to reveal, since this is not the premier goal for the industry who is primarily looking for solutions that fit the existing one-dimensionality. Both Marcuse and Hillman shows us that we cannot expect anyone else to find the potentiality, except for those who with engagement devote time and energy to both being distant and staying close, with the aim of improving the human well-being.

REFERENCES

Croon Fors, A. (2006). Living with technology. PHD thesis at the Department of Informatics, Umeå University, Sweden.

Dourish, P. (2001). *Where the action is: The foundations of embodied interaction.* Cambridge, MA: MIT Press.

Hillman, J. (1996). *The soul's code: In search of character and calling.* New York, NY: Random House.

Marcuse, H. (1964). *One-dimensional man.* Boston, MA: Beacon Press.

McCarthy, J., Wright, P. (2004). *Technology as experience.* Cambridge, MA: MIT Press.

Nelson, H., Stolterman, E. (2003). *The design way: Intentional change in an unpredictable world.* Educational Technology Publications.

Schön, D. (1983). *The reflective practitioner: How professionals think in action.* New York, NY: Basic Books.

Stolterman, E. (2008). The nature of design practice and implications for interaction design research. *International Journal of Design* 2(1).

PETER ULLMARK

A SCIENCE OF THE POSSIBLE

– A NEW PRACTICE IN THE SPIRIT OF BAUHAUS

A SCIENCE OF THE POSSIBLE
PETER ULLMARK
– A NEW PRACTICE IN THE SPIRIT OF BAUHAUS

Walter Gropius and the rest of the Bauhaus faculty had a strong belief that both Art and Science can make meaningful contributions to a better future. However, these two practices were subsequently kept apart and even though scientific thinking was highly respected, science was regarded as something fundamentally different from art and design. Although this dualistic view is still prevalent, it *is* being questioned more often. Why then do we separate these two ways of approaching knowledge and reality, when we usually integrate them in most other situations?

Design research has experienced steady growth during the last 20 years. Can this evolving practice help to integrate the artistic approach and the scientific approach and at the same time widen the understanding of research? Or will design research remain a traditional and somewhat marginal discipline which concentrates on investigations of design work as actual or historical phenomena? Other approaches, where future-oriented design work and the creation of artefacts play an active part in the research work, seem to make researchers from other disciplines confused. But is this only because they are not familiar with these new approaches or are there more fundamental problems when Arts and Science are integrated?

In this chapter I will look into different research practices and their views on »what is to come« and relate that understanding to design and design research. Finally, I will try to outline a new research approach that not only makes use of the ability of design to develop new ideas but also goes beyond the traditional focus of design on the artefact itself. Moreover, this approach will emphasise the impact of different cultural contexts and values on how we conceive and try to change our circumstances. Let us call this approach »A Science of the Possible«.

DESIGN RESEARCH AND DESIGN

The understanding and development of design research depends on how we set the agenda and frame the issues for subsequent thought. If we just look at the »knowledge problems« within the specific design practices, our focus would be clear. However, many designers are sceptical of the benefits of research. They believe that practice itself can take care of the »knowledge problems«

and that the designers just need more time for reflection and rethinking. Their main argument is that design problems are so situation-specific and complex, that there are no general solutions. Furthermore, design is rarely a question of optimising given factors. The way designers work and the results they get are dependent on perspective and on the specific context, whereby the possibilities of getting generally usable results and learning from exemplary design projects are restricted. It has also been found difficult to apply research-based methodological knowledge, since the articulated concrete operations appear too abstract and are not able to represent the complex design practice in a productive way.

In order to make a difference, designers believe that design research has to come closer to practice – a practice that is characterised by a high degree of condensation of information and intricate values systems. It is therefore necessary to give up the narrow framing of issues that is the norm in most kinds of research and focus more on the experiences of the whole rather than the analytical understanding of the parts. In this way, research-based design processes may then make interesting contributions to practice, which will, in turn result in new methods and/or in development within specific fields of design. How can these kinds of studies be related to research agendas that are already established?

DESIGN, REALITY AND SCIENCE

The basic difficulty is that designers live in imaginary worlds that are impossible to logically deduce from observations of their practice. When scientists refer to what they are able to investigate, they usually mean that there must be discernable objects and systems that exist independently of human values and attitudes. When this is the case, the investigation is only a question of finding a method. Yet to produce a complete understanding can be difficult. Complexity is often the major problem and the problem then has to be reduced to those few variables that seem most important. However, whatever the complexity, truth continues to be a goal even if it is unattainable. Truth has become a symbol for the ambition to come as close as possible to. Researchers are expected to continue doing their research until no more objections come up or until other researchers present a critique that makes rethinking and new studies necessary.

One approach to make design research more »scientific« has been to concentrate on the artefacts that are created during the course of the creative process, such as drawings, models and prototypes. However, these kinds of studies have difficulty in embracing the creative ideas and the considerations and deliberations behind the consecutive choices, even when they are combined with interviews with designers and users. Furthermore, they are a very unreliable source when it comes to a more general understanding of the genesis of new ideas and concepts. Creative processes do not merely appear by means of descriptions. It may, therefore, be difficult to use the results in a generative way; they may be useful only in very similar design situations.

Does this mean that design processes cannot be based on a scientific understanding? Or are there other ways to grasp that which does not yet exist? Is our intuitive way of working as designers actually an effect of our lack of knowledge of what is actually going on? Would the process be more rational and transparent if an adequate knowledge about processes and the play of forces could be produced? The traditional scientific approach to »what is to come« is to look for components that are constant and regulatory laws that decide the space of action. Searching for elementary particles and models that describe the relations between them is still the basic approach in physics and chemistry, even if the understanding of the particles as phenomena has become more intricate. A large number of regularities, which have been found useful and coherent, have also been established by means of experiments and mathematics. The models have successively become more complex and difficult to explain by using ordinary concepts and language. Even scientists have to use metaphors in order to maintain an overall understanding of their basic ideas, where they originated from and what they once opposed. Sometimes these simplifications even influence forthcoming work and presume qualities that are not based on any evidence.

Furthermore, results are not always coherent and contradictory facts show up sooner or later. Yet major changes of the basic models are unusual. As Thomas Kuhn and many others have shown, most scientists are deeply committed to one basic model and try to include the new in the old (Kuhn 1970). Bruno

Latour has shown that research carried through with the help of complex and expensive instruments show considerable continuity (Latour and Woolgar 1986). If scientific equipment has been invested in, it has to be used. Consequently, contradictory results risk being omitted as a matter of routine. Most new paradigms, however, have been accepted only after the objections against old paradigms have been repeated and worked through over and over again.

Consequently, no one is prepared to predict the end of this search process: the finding of the final particles and their interplay arranged in solid models. Scientists of today admit a genuine and never-ending uncertainty, even when their results seem unequivocal. Lately, many scientists have pointed at the risk of only having one line of search at a time and have argued for the acceptance of several, parallel and fundamentally different models that can compete with each other on equal terms. Unfortunately, however, this liberal attitude does not always direct the distribution of funds.

We have to accept that all theories and models have their specific qualities and dead angles and, even if there are general laws at the basic level, aggregated levels may show up a complexity that cannot be handled in an easy way. All conceivable states and changes cannot be set up. In contrast to the very »big« and the very `small«, which we cannot have a concrete perception of and therefore have to rely on models in order to be able to apprehend them, the reality we meet every day cannot always be reduced into its abstract parts but remains complex and confusing.

MODELS AND PARADIGMS

However, if an incontestable understanding is impossible to reach, what is the role of basic models and how can they be related to designers' ways of working with the whole in relation to the parts? Much of our present day thinking goes back to Immanuel Kant who regarded basic understandings as necessary »a priori postulates« – something that is different from knowledge and truth. According to Kant, we cannot form a connected whole out of the single experiences or act in an ethically consistent way without these postulates. Values are also involved and Kant talks about »regulative ideas«. We cannot either reach »das Ding an Sich« since we are trapped by a specific way of apprehending and interpreting experiences. However, the advantage of us having these prerequisites is that we are able to share knowledge.

Later philosophers do not differentiate belief and certainty in such a strict way (Wittgenstein 1969) as Kant. Kant's idea of given »categories« has also been rejected and language has become the key to mutual understanding. The concepts we use control our lives, even if meanings can change and even if we can move smoothly between different meanings. All knowledge has become regarded as situated. »Episteme«, which was understood as the real knowledge, has become obsolete and »doxa«, which Plato despised, has undergone a revival.

What kinds of models are used in science? For centuries, the Newtonian mechanical world view has been the basic model for the natural sciences. However, the understanding of biology has been of a different nature and has also influenced other parts of science in recent years. The perspective of evolutionary biology and qualitative changes has been actively introduced as an alternative to variation within determined frames. Differences rather than similarities are looked for. The notion of entropy has become more interesting than the notion of emergence. Previously, the problem has been to describe evolutionary processes in other ways than what has already happened. However, new computer systems have made simulations and the generation of more or less probable outcomes possible. One tool is »genetic algorithms« by which both risks and potentials in complex, natural and artificial systems have been put forward at a new level of accuracy. However, simulations of less regular and multi-dimensional systems are still out of reach.

Why do these kinds of very basic paradigmatic changes appear at a specific moment? These changes are often regarded as sudden breakthroughs but when the processes that led to the changes are traced backwards, a long succession of precise, comprehensive and critical questions and less satisfactory answers can often be found. Consequently, most scientists believe that the process of rethinking is a clear result of the persistent work involved in the systematic testing of the ability of alternative models to include already established relations and to present answers to upcoming questions. Still, many scientists, when asked explicitly, admit a certain lack of control. The resulting models also seem, at least sometimes, to be a result of an independent, intuitive thinking of another kind, which is not always so easy to grasp. The simplicity and elegance of the model that is finally chosen is such a factor. This choice often follows the principle of Occam's razor (Hawking 1988).

This may also be a reason why scientists are so reluctant to talk about these processes. Another reason may be that such evolutionary processes are so difficult to differentiate since there are so many steps that need to be taken in order to reach this new understanding. At the beginning of the process, no one is aware of the importance of what is happening and then, when the process has been completed, everyone has difficulty in remembering how the critical process proceeded and developed into a creative one. Another reason for this is that scientists focus on the result. Attempts with models that did not lead to any progress are left behind and forgotten. Only on rare occasions are old models actualised again.

However, parallel to basic research in the natural sciences, there is obviously a lot of applied research that works differently and more constructively with future possibilities, especially within medicine and technology. What are their points of departure? Their practices are usually described as downright applications and combinations of single scientific results. In reality, they actually have most of the characteristics of a design project, other than the fact that educated scientists are in charge. The starting-point is often some kind of model with presumed causes and effects that is developed by trial-and-error. However, an important difference, compared with most design practices, is the much stronger focus on the security of the results, especially in medicine. The results are not only examined by experimental studies in laboratories but also by clinical testing in real life situations in order to embrace all possible problems. This kind of scrupulous follow-up could be a prototype for developing practice guidelines for design research that includes creative work.

SOCIAL SCIENCES AND HUMANITIES

Even in the social sciences and the humanities, a deterministic understanding of reality and of the future has been predominant. Universal principles and consistent systems based on observations of behaviour, social systems and values were what were looked for. This was not, however, very successful (Winch 1958). Contradictions could not be eliminated and it was impossible to generate consistent models and more constructive political discussions.

Nowadays, these deterministic ideas have few supporters. Most social scientists and researchers within the humanities share the understanding of human and social conditions as historically developed phenomena that undergo continuous change as a result of interventions and interaction. Even if nature is principally an independent force, most of our context is artificial and cannot be understood without considering purposes and values (Simon 1969). It has also become obvious that all the »parts« of human conditions cannot be understood by a single set of theories. There are strata that are unique and separate, e.g. nature, man and society (Deleuze and Guattari 1988). Understanding phenomena related to several strata becomes a difficult matter. However, even evolutionary perspectives from the natural sciences have been influential (Grosz 2004) and the notion of equilibrium, which was so important earlier, has also lost its significance. Moreover, coincidence, where even one single person, under specific conditions, may change the whole course of history, is understood in a new way.

Yet, social scientists still talk about solid conclusions. Their argument is that people and institutions change very slowly. Relations and values are fairly constant, at least seen on a comprehensive level. Some understandings prevail to such an extent that they have even become a self-fulfilling power. Giles Deleuze and Felix Guattari talk about abstract machines (Deleuze and Guattari 1984). Social scientists believe that this stability makes it possible to discover even radical changes. Theories can be established and confirmed by the collection of data and substantial predictions can be generated. The problem is to discover and follow up the qualitative changes that appear self-evidently. There is a strong belief in the assumption that if we focus attention on the divergences from »the expected« and have a long historical perspective, this makes it possible to see

»the new« when it appears. However, there are many examples of social and economic changes of great importance that have been missed and also of conclusions that have been drawn too quickly from ill-founded assumptions. These mistakes are mostly related to bad methods by the researchers themselves. The impact of too rigid an understanding of the phenomena and the social context is very seldom mentioned as the explanation. Political interests to maintain a specific understanding, since the latter underpins certain institutions and political initiatives, are other suppressed reasons.

Paradoxically, these new relativistic perspectives seem to have reduced, instead of increased, the interest in discussions about different basic understandings of behaviour, society and economy. This tendency is strengthened by the well-meant ambition to maintain the autonomy of both science and politics. When debates involve people from universities, a neutral language that hides the ideological content is used. Even value-impressed statements appear as objective truths, which is confusing for the general public.

At the same time, political parties are also less eager to talk about long-term goals and to take part in ideological discussions. They have, in fact, become profoundly pragmatic. The result is that obvious problems instead of possible prospects dominate the public debate and the assigned measures are, for the most part, reactive and repressive. When people try to present new perspectives, they are asked to keep to the agenda. This deterministic and discouraging discussion makes people in general less interested to take part. They tend to regard the public debate as only something for the initiated.

The effect of this attitude is that already established theories have become even more established. To genuinely doubt or criticise notions such as »the economic man«, »the market economy« and »the western understanding of parliamentary democracy« is regarded as odd and pointless. This development of »normality« can be an obstacle in the discovery of profound qualitative changes.

UNDERSTANDING CHANGE AND CREATIVITY

Is this lack of thinking about future possibilities in relation to research practice a cultural phenomenon, or is it an effect of a genuine belief in the benefit of keeping knowledge production and ideas for the future apart? Could the split between analytical and creative work actually be a rational one because it results in a reasonable balance between old and new understanding? Should we leave the future in the hands of politicians and designers and keep to descriptions and analytical work in research – and also accept the limitations this imposes, e.g. the difficulties for new understandings to be accepted? If so, how can we make politicians and designers take their responsibility?

What do we know about the relation between analytical and creative work? Are some people perhaps even more suited for one or the other? In spite of a lot of research, neurologists and psychologists still cannot say much about creativity in relation to analytical capability and personal values. We know that each individual's ability to relate to reality and develop a strategic thinking differs. The reasons for this are explained in different ways depending on the basic theoretical understanding that is accepted. Biology-based theories emphasise organic and genetic reasons and regard environmental factors as secondary. Psychoanalytical-based theories concentrate on personal experiences (which are sometimes of a traumatic nature) that may leave the individual with long-lasting difficulties to cope. However, these biases can be controlled by a reconstruction of important parts of our history. New possibilities appear and we are, in a way, able to design ourselves.

We also know that our brain is more or less constantly scanning our context to find appropriate ways to combine internal urges with external conditions. The mechanisms in the region of the single brain are presently being elucidated (Damasio 2003). It has, for example, been shown that the whole memory of an episode is not stored at one and the same location in our brains but that the brain identifies different categories of elements, for example, memories of colours, which are then transferred to specific zones. So when we remember something, it does not appear as a whole from the start. An extremely effective communication network that reconstructs what has happened, which is, moreover, a mechanism that we never notice, is activated. This network is probably able to connect memory elements in other ways, e.g. when a number of quite loosely-connected memories emerge at the same time and create new patterns. The analytical and creative functions may be physically separated but are, at the same time, obviously closely connected. There seems to be no reason to make a principal split between the understanding of »the actual« and »the creation of the possible«. Neither does this mean that the two always have to be integrated but that they represent different phases in a development process and use different methods. Still, there is much to gain by continuity.

A SCIENCE OF THE POSSIBLE

How can a future-oriented research practice that is able to integrate analytical and creative human faculties be created? How can we combine the design-based way of solving concrete problems with a comprehensive critical reflection that opens up for new perspectives on the overall situation and initiates completely new ways of approaching more specific problems? In order to keep in touch with both a complex situated reality and the underlying basic understanding, we have to develop a way of working with recurrent shifts of focus. The methodology should be similar to the methodology used in case studies that use subsequent empirical investigations to question and develop a preliminary understanding into a well-founded theory (Yin 2003). Here, the difference is the focus on a) the variety of ways the context can be framed and b) the ambition to develop a more comprehensive overall understanding.

How can we find problematic situations that are generative enough for the development of this new research practice? The segment of reality and the kind of problems we use as a setting are probably not so important. A certain complexity, however, which prevents us from getting an immediate overview of alternative approaches and possible solutions, is crucial for progress. In the longer run, a broader discussion about different agendas is also necessary in order to really find the critical parts of the process and explore the potential. Themes such as »after the car«, »sustainable consumption« and »flexible cities« could be starting points for many projects and programmes.

The most rewarding situations to start with will probably be the ones where there is no obvious problem but just a feeling of dysfunction and imperfection and where there is no, or at least delimited, understanding of the character and the causes. No self-evident point of departure appears. »To get going«, we have to be open-minded and try different road maps. If we ask other people about their experiences, the difficulty is to find adequate questions that are emancipated enough from established perspectives and our own prejudices. Here, framing these questions and understanding the context is of special interest.

It is also important to find ways to describe and compare the different understandings of the actual situation and to relate them to the more general perspectives. This is a critical moment, since the ways we use will play a major role for our subsequent work. We can easily become captives of our own representations. At the same time we have to find recognisable patterns. However, those patterns do not have to be closely associated to the actual situation in order to be generative. Even very different patterns may be used analogically or metaphorically, if they show up. The difficulty is that the initiation of this scanning process may be a conscious one but the search process itself is not. In this process, our brain works without any active thinking and the result will then depend on our training and experience and on the situation-bound inspiration.

What is the difference between this process and what traditional scientists do in the early and inductive stages of their research work and what designers do? Scientists mostly concentrate on one idea at a time and focus on validation rather than on generation. If scientists document the generative process, which is not at all self-evident, they mostly avoid an articulation of the intuitive moments within the black box. Moreover, they do not take much interest in the potential of different kinds of representations.

Designers, in contrast, do not restrain their creative efforts by an immediate search for evidence and are not worried about the black box. The ideas that come up are evolved as far as possible out of their inherent logic before the result is critically examined in a more detailed way. If all ideas are adequate or not is less important, as long as the process contributes to the understanding. Designers seldom find any reason for controlling the generation of ideas; even very unorthodox ways to discover new possibilities and even very odd perspectives are welcome. Impulsive and intuitive thinking often play a major role in the designer's progress. Finally, designers are generally very conscious of the importance of different means of representation and communication.

It is important to note that, in this process, there is no clear demarcation between what is new and what already exists. Not only what comes, but also what exists, is created. In order to validate those constructions, we have to find ways to connect them to a shared knowledge of reality. However, this cannot be done before the idea is sufficiently articulated. Since we cannot control the generation of our ideas, we therefore have to scrutinise the result. Even if this result only consists of theories or models, the latter are »artefacts« that can be investigated like other artefacts or phenomena in nature – an investigation that can not only be accomplished in a systematic way but that may also cover many different aspects. It is not so much a search for evidence but more like the process of falsification that Karl Popper talked about (Popper 1945). In this process we look for imperfections that make us continue our search to come closer to the real problems and really interesting solutions. Unfortunately, we cannot give all our ideas the same attention but have to finally decide which of the promising models are worth considerable empirical effort.

However, the kind of scientific work Popper is aiming at is different from the one we discuss here. He talks about situations where a complete verification is principally possible. This usually means that the understanding has to be compressed to just a few very clear statements and that this understanding is not able to represent the complex whole we just discussed. The purpose of the verification process is also fundamentally different; a possibility that is not a real possibility, in the meaning that no one or very few are in favour of it, is not of much interest in our kind of research process. The verification process has to consider different contexts and values of the people involved or in other ways concerned and look at different time perspectives. The choice of references is, of course, also of great importance for the assessment and therefore has to be thoroughly motivated. To really find the effects, advanced simulations may have to be used as tools in the Science of the Possible and be presented in an imaginative way.

Finally, can a Science of the Possible represent a new approach that is able to follow up Bauhausian ideas in an interesting way? As we have already noted, a kind of a Science of the Possible exists close to the natural sciences i.e. in technical and medical research. However, only parts of the full innovative potential of this practice are made use of. A more open process, especially in the initial phases, could result, in many cases, in quite a variety of different approaches and even approaches that use completely different means, which we could build on and qualify. Within the fields of the social sciences and the humanities there is no such corresponding practice. A new practice has to be created from the very outset, which is difficult to do in established institutions and within existing fund systems. Artistic research may become an arena for part of the development of this practice, if the right conditions are realised.

However, there is still need for basic research that concentrates on specific causes and effects even if it has to retreat from its position as a producer of superior knowledge. The research practices of Art and Science can also learn from each other even if their goals are different. In basic research, the critique of paradigms and the creation of new ones must not be regarded as something exceptional but as a natural and recurrent part of the practice. Basic research may also be inspired by practical applications, for example, as in the case of the steam-engine where most of the theoretical understanding came after the first realisation. Finally, if a Science of the Possible is compared with design practice, the introductory and validation processes have to be much more ambitious and can learn a lot from established research practices.

ART AND THE SCIENCE OF THE POSSIBLE

For the Bauhaus faculty, Art and Science were two necessary and complementary practices in society to create a better future. However, within Bauhaus, science was mostly used rhetorically to turn away industrial products that imitated an old handicraft-based style. The idea of a Science of the Possible is to make use of both Art and Science in an equal way. But what do we mean by art in this context? The kind of art that was recognised by Bauhaus was primarily oriented towards form and materials. In the art of today, underlying concepts are more emphasised, which makes this practice easier to connect to the development of new understandings in a Science of the Possible.

However, it is not the ability of art to create new ideas that is the most important quality in this context, it is the way art manifests ideas by representing them as entireties that consider the context in a comprehensive way and that get beyond the sum of the parts. The ideas become an artefact that can be perceived, interpreted and judged in the same way as an actual reality. After an artistic experience, we cannot account for the elements that created it. We either appropriate or reject it as a whole. A kind of condensation is achieved that not only communicates a clear and specific content but also maintains the complexity. Nothing is taken away and other people feel welcome to make their own, unique interpretations, whereby completely new concepts may arise.

What has this to do with aesthetics? What do people mean when they talk about beauty in relation to artefacts? For a long time in history, eternal principles for beauty have been looked for. Nature has been a dominant source of inspiration and it is easy to verify the importance of such experiences for aesthetic judgments. Still, the impact of actual cultural expressions is also obvious. Robert Scruton comes close to a usable understanding of aesthetic judgments of artefacts when he talks about »appropriateness« (Scruton 1979), where he emphasises that criteria are contextual and can be changed. Designers often say, "That´s it!" when they are satisfied with a solution as a whole but do not mean that there are no other solutions that others could possibly regard as superior.

This ability to grasp and judge entireties differs fundamentally from the one in science, since the latter neither builds up an understanding by combining single elements to make a whole nor is acknowledged in the epistemological discussion. Consequently, both the ability, per se, and the results are difficult to communicate by means of statements that are constructed by the subsequent adding of symbols. In a Science of the Possible, we are in need of more associative representations such as the ones used in art, e.g. pictures and literary texts. To use this kind of knowledge in a research context may seem adventurous considering the inherited reverence for clearness and transparency that has previously been the basic norm.

To develop a Science of the Possible without acknowledging and using it would be impossible. However, cultural references often have to be presented to get people on track. Methods and critical procedures also have to be discussed, but not only with the aim of finding a standard.

»Open endings« cannot be reached without »open beginnings.«

ACKNOWLEDGMENTS

I am grateful to Lynn Preston for linguistic and stylistic revision.

REFERENCES

Damasio, A. (2003). *Looking for Spinoza: Joy, sorrow and the feeling brain.* New York: Harcourt.

Deleuze, G., Guattari, P.-F. (1984). *Anti-Oedipus.* London: Athlone Press.

Deleuze, G., Guattari, P.-F. (1988). *A thousand plateaus.* London: Athlone Press.

Grosz, E. (2004). *Becomings: Explorations in time, memory and futures*. New York: Cornell University Press.

Hawking, S. (1988). *A brief history of time*. New York: Bantham Books.

Kuhn, T. (1970). *The structure of scientific revolutions*. Chicago: University of Chicago.

Latour, B., Woolgar, S. (1986). *Laboratory life*. New Jersey: Princeton University Press.

Popper, K. (1945). *The logic of scientific discovery*. London: Hutchinson.

Simon, H. (1969). *The sciences of the artificial*. Cambridge, MA: MIT Press.

Scruton, R. (1979). *The aesthetics of architecture*. Princeton University Press.

Winch, P. (1958). *The idea of a social science and its relation to philosophy*. London: Routledge & Kegan Paul.

Wittgenstein, L. (1969). *Über Gewissheit/On certainty*. Oxford: Basil Blackwell.

Yin, R. (2003). *Case study research: Design and methods*. Thousand Oaks, CA: Sage Publications.

FRIEDER NAKE

WORK, DESIGN, COMPUTERS, ARTIFACTS

FRIEDER NAKE
WORK, DESIGN, COMPUTERS, ARTIFACTS

Nokia produces mobile phones, out of Finland. They are a *Scandinavian* company and, therefore, in the rest of Europe some believe Nokia must be different. Different in their products, their designs, in relations with their workers. Scandinavian! That has a good sound, a good reputation in design, in product quality, in industrial relations.

But why should they produce differently, and why for different goals than others? Why should they treat their workers differently? Why should a global player be capable of putting quality over quantity or, better, use-value over exchange-value? By this switch in terminology, more experienced readers may be thinking – ah, what's this, some old Marxist writing? But don't be afraid, relax, and in particular, don't be afraid if you are young. If you continue reading, you will *not* be indoctrinated. You may rather discover that for global playing to be comprehended we need a bit of the theoretical insight of Marx.

So, returning to Nokia, it is wise to accept that wishful thinking cannot change the iron laws of capitalist production. Any capital, as long as it is supposed to function as capital, must grow, and it can grow only as long as it produces *surplus-value*, and as long as it realizes the surplus-value in form of profit.

A short tutorial on the principles of our societal environment would be in place here. But that will not happen. It is enough to say that economic growth is the driving force behind everything, and that surplus-value is that portion of the value of a product that originates in the worker's work but does not get paid for.

What sort of an introduction have you got yourself into, you may wonder. The current writer has no real excuse for his aberration from the common style of this sort of chapter. He invites you to follow him on his path, and discover how he is taking apart the title of a famous Scandinavian book, *Work-oriented design of computer artifacts*. It will be dissolved into four tiles dealt with in separation. He does so because he likes taking things apart, a typical rationalist. But before he actually does so, he really wants to provide some background leading up to the chapter's question.

QUANTITY

On the European continent, people ask heavy questions and expect answers of an essential kind. Elsewhere, pragmatism and analytic philosphy are preferred. Don't be dogmatic for a moment: in a capitalist society, everyone can become rich, don't you think? But what about the others?

Quantity is the soul of capital. The capitalist who mainly praises the commodities his workers are producing for their *quality*, can in the long run do so only by hiding his real intentions behind a wall of fog and false beliefs.

People in the street still raise accusations of blatant moral ugliness against a capital whose owners are doing nothing but pursuing their best interests as capitalists. So why fuss about this? Isn't it immoral to accuse someone for doing nothing but what the continuation of his existence forces him to do? Why should a capital deny its innate drive to grow, and thus do nothing but grow? If it doesn't grow, it dies. Capital has no choice. Pure quantity can only grow or die.

At the time I was preparing this chapter, the tremendously successful Finnish company of electronic consumer products, Nokia, had announced the intention to shut down their German factory at Bochum. Several thousand workers were going to be fired even though the European Union and the German state had spent millions of Euros to lure the Northern capital into the poor area of the once mighty Ruhrgebiet. The Northern capital had happily accepted the money. It was, of course, later forced to move on to the next, better, place as soon as conditions allowed, and the natural laws of making profit required it. Romanian labor turned out to be as skilled but much cheaper than German labor. The Finnish management had no choice but to move on, playing globally. The same story is repeated over and over again.

Ordinary people claimed they were apalled by the decision, and some German government representatives put on dreary faces to express disgust or despair. They should have known better. Nobody is surprised when a rock falls down the hill instead of up.

The collected knowledge of the world, we have repeatedly been told since around 1980, has arrived at your fingertips. Only very seldom do those fingers type lines like the following by Karl Marx who, in the famous chapter 15 of his *Capital*, says this:

> John Stuart Mill says in his *Principles of Political Economy*: »It is questionable if all the mechanical inventions yet made have lightened the day's toil of any human being.« That is, however, by no means the aim of the application of machinery under capitalism. Like every other instrument for increasing the productivity of labour, machinery is intended to cheapen commodities and, by shortening the part of the working day in which the worker works for himself, to lengthen the other part, the part he gives to the capitalist for nothing. The machine is a means for producing surplus-value. (Marx 1976, p. 492)

Repeat: »The machine is a means for producing surplus-value«, and for emphasis add: »and nothing else.« The knowledge of the world tells you, that production of surplus-value is identifying capitalist production. So don't get excited on moral grounds about the eternal chase of capital around the globe for ever better conditions of valorization. Economic logic always wins over existential ethics.

The machine we are here concerned with – the computer, or calculating machine – is a late-comer in comparison. It appeared only 70 or 80 years after the first volume of *Capital* had been published in 1867. In chapter 15, the book talks about the history of machinery and large-scale industry. If we read it carefully, we may detect a hidden, yet revealing remark. From a far distance the remark announces the task that the machinery of planning, controlling, and applying human labor must solve about 100 years later.

When I read it in 1973, we were engaged in a discourse about a new academic discipline. How could it be justified to take computing machinery as the reason for that discipline? Europeans had started to establish it in the mid 1960s, and the end of that decade saw a flood of new university departments spreading up everywhere. In continental Europe, they called it *informatics* instead of computer science although it revolved around computing machinery. A few years later, the University of Bremen thought they should also offer such a programme. How could we possibly do this, given the fact that informatics was about improving capitalist production? Was it possible to identify an emancipatory component in all that?

So here is the thrilling observation of Marx's announced above. In the year 1851, Marx tells us, the engineers in the cotton and spinning industry in Great Britain had waged a wide-spread and long-lasting strike. Breaking such a strike, and thereby reducing the great harm strikes meant for capital, something had to be done so that the machinery itself could better be used. Machinery is the means to get more surplus-value out of the workers; it can also force workers into a situation where no chance is left for them to escape the factory toil. Nasmyth, the inventor of the steam-hammer, had this to say »before the Commission on Trade Unions, with regard to the improvements in machinery he himself introduced as a result« of those strikes:

> The characteristic feature of our modern mechanical improvements, is the introduction of self-acting tool machinery. What every mechanical workman has now to do, and what every boy can do, is not to work himself but to superintend the beautiful labour of the machine. The whole class of workmen that depend exclusively on their skill, is now done away with. (Marx 1976, p. 563)

In the middle of the nineteenth century, at the height of mechanical machinery in large-scale industry, skilled labor starts to become superfluous whereas superintendence of machinery appears as a new kind of separate work. Control of what the hand was doing had, of course, always been an integral part of manual labor. But now, when the machinery took over large parts of skilled *manual* labor, the portion of work that depended on the worker's senses and mind – sensory-based mental work of control – was singled out from the labor process. It became that part of labor that remained with the worker. Young boys could take over this sort of work, reducing cost of labor.

The work of the senses does not require manual skills. It requires only to be alert, to listen to the steady noise generated by a hall full of smoothly running machines. It also requires watching the gentle flow of material moving through those mechanical machines. Even a young person can easily detect an irregular sound or movement – in which case he has to stop the machine and call some other person to repair it, or otherwise put it back to normal condition.

So at exactly the historic moment when manual labor had reached its peak in advanced machine work, the quest for the next type of machine development appeared. The *mechanical* machine, unknowingly and deep inside its inner functions, carries the *cybernetic* machine as part of itself. Only when the mechanical operation has matured to a point where further improvement appears not to be possible, hidden aspects of work – as, e.g., control – may emerge and require the right of taking on their own specialized form. Manual labor at its peak calls for the machinization of mental labor. Computing machinery is mechanical machinery's logical consequence under capitalist rule. The work of control must itself be automated to control the rest of work.

This lengthy remark may be viewed as an invitation to re-read parts of *Capital*. Whenever something is about work and computers, like this chapter, to read *Capital* is a good advice. Unfortunately, this famous text has come to be thought of as being dogmatic. It is the opposite: a clear, scientific, exciting text. A text, by the way, that praises capital like no other text does.

INTERLUDE

I hope I don't annoy readers by reminding them of this long-gone story. But is it not true that we may understand current states of affairs only if we gain a rudimentary insight of history?

Hasn't work been the starting point and end point of all our attempts to understand computers, algorithms and programs? We never liked the computer just for itself. We often rather wanted to do without it, until it became clear that the economic thrust was against us. The computer was here to stay. It has become an integral part of culture that nobody can deny. If some still resist on principle, in splendid isolation, all the worse for them.

Once the technical basis of society's infrastructure had been totally reversed, it had become dangerous to ignore this as a fact. The fact was that nothing could exist anymore without existing twice, in duplication: first, as that that it is, in a *material* sense of the word. Second, as that that it is, in a *semiotic* sense of the word.

Insight in this state of affairs started to spread in the 1980s, and two books approached the situation from different but related positions. Winograd and Flores (1986) wrote about understanding computers and cognition by laying out a new foundation for design. A bit later, Ehn (1988) also put design at the center of his book but with an orientation on work. Both of these seminal books rely on three inspirations, partially different ones. Heidegger's philosophy of Sein and Dasein (being and being-in-the-world) is one discourse that both Ehn and Winograd and Flores rely on. Both also draw from language philosophy. Winograd and Flores prefer speech act theory (with Austin and Searle as their sources), whereas Ehn favors the alternative of language games (Wittgenstein). Their third sources, however, differ. Cognitive science is referred to by Winograd and Flores in theit approach to individual cognition (Maturana and Varela). Economics is the basis for any theory of work and labor; therefore, Marx is Ehn's author of choice.

These great traditions build the foundation, in both cases, of a critique of rationalism. Rationalism was at the center of the immense success of Western science, technology, and philosophy. It had come under heavy attack after World War II, especially with computer technology, and with new insight in epistemology. Modernity was so successful and strong that it could, from the inside, generate a serious critique of its own results and methods.

The success of science, art, technology and philosophy of Western modern thinking and acting shows best in its horrendous destructions. It is literally devastating the world. In all its destructive furor it is so successful that the newly emerging hyper-powers are still following its logic without questioning the principle.

The harsh but friendly critique of rationalism in Ehn and Winograd and Flores was a necessity during the 1980s. Putting together the pillars of their books to establish a theoretical basis for a newly understood academic discipline of computing, students would start by discussing Marx, Heidegger, Wittgenstein, Searle, Maturana, Varela, and others. They would thus become acquainted with some of the strongest insights of modernism on its way to becoming obsolete. Two streams would be missing from this and would become the second and major focus of study: algorithmics and aesthetics.

But work! Work was the European left's focus in all its critique of the computer. The European critics intended to defend work against capital's grip. The technologically often more advanced American progressives – with a few admirable exceptions like David Noble and Joan Greenbaum – had it easier. When the European critique lead to the position of rejecting information technology altogether, the American critique was to contend with friendly surface phenomena that they turned into slogans like, »Empowering people«.

Work became design, computer tools turned into digital media, art took over in games. The bourgeois style of life and capitalist economy seemed to be unbeatable, and we all took to design of media. Was this a necessary and consequential development? The following four sections are on work, design, computers and artifacts. The reader will easily discover in this sequence, the title of Pelle Ehn's thesis, *Work-oriented design of computer artifacts.*

Very briefly, I would like to indicate why such a title expressed – for those who knew – a very important message. The key lies in the attribute *work-oriented.* Everybody could design computer artifacts. In fact, many did. Nothing was special about this. But precisely because of the seeming neutrality of design of computer artifacts, such design was implicitly profit-oriented, or capital-oriented. Ehn, by the choice of his title, expressed his intention to study design work from the point of view of the work, of the workers, of the working class.

Ehn's book appeared in 1988, years after André Gorz had started his critique of the classic Marxist position on labor and the working class (Gorz 1980). On the continent, in Bremen, we had formulated a position to justify study programmes in computer science. From the observation above it followed that the age of mechanization would be followed by an age of automation of manual labor which would, in turn, not stop before it reached mental labor. Rather, computer science turned out to be the science of *machinizing* mental labor. The historic-materialist analysis clearly showed this. A critical position towards the computer must start from here. The position was internally written up in 1974, and published in accessible form in Nake (1984, 1992).

Our hopes had been put on the alliance of workers and intellectuals through trade unions and progressive projects. We put up the banners of use-value against profit, quality of work and product against quantity of output, democracy at the workplace against the silent pressure of social conditions. These were reformist hopes. We were allowed to run some nice projects. We had some moderate success. We grew older, young generations appeared, and globalization raged around the world.

Have we betrayed our origins? Have we cut our own roots?

What kind of silly questions, a younger person might ask today. And they are right in some way. The technological turnover of society's infrastucture has been so tremendous and so successful that nobody would even think to question the ubiquitous presence of information technology. »When the computer reached me as a kid,« a student tells me, »it had become the home computer, and the personal computer.« And he continues: »We always liked the computer for itself.« The medium had become the message.

And yet, there were those beautiful kids in Sweden who appeared in books by Astrid Lindgren all around the world.

> Discussion with Hanna! – about technology (according to Hanna) as the knack of so arranging the world that we need not experience it. Mania of the engineer of turning God's Creation into something usable because he cannot stand it as partner, and doesn't know how to use it for anything. Technology as the knack to eliminate from the world the world as resistant matter ... (Frisch 1977, p. 169, my translation)

Homo faber is active man. To be active, to be engaged in activity, is our predicament and eternal fate. The human race has no choice, by their very nature, but to be active and working. »Labour is, first of all, a process between man and nature, a process by which man, through his own actions, mediates, regulates and controls the metabolism between himself and nature« (Marx 1976, p. 283).

If we accept Marx's position on the labor process as the eternal general condition the human race is forced into, before that process takes on particular form under certain social conditions, and if we further accept that during the course of history the eternal *conditio humana* creates technology (as part of the means of production) and develops it to incredible heights, then Hanna's observation must come as a real shock. According to her, the engineer Faber writes in his diary, technology is »the knack of so arranging the world that we [engineers?] need not experience it.«

The engineer appears as a sort of artist. They are, first, human beings like anybody else. But, other than ordinary humans, they experience the world in a way that makes them suffer. The world to the engineers, Frisch seems to tell us, is there for them to make use of. If such a state of affairs could successfully be achieved, we wouldn't need to experience the world anymore. All experience dissolves into use. Technology is the knack helping us attain that state, and the engineer is in charge of developing technology. Their place in the world is clear and of utmost importance in this analysis.

In their grand achievement, the engineer would show up as the true and ultimate artist saving humankind from the drudgery of experience (and painful learning?), which is replaced by pure use. Use would in itself take on the quality of a value. No other, external value criterion would be needed. The act of use justifies the decision for use. In consequence, use justifies itself. A state of pure aesthetics would be the consequence of such a state of the world. The utmost and final creator, the engineer-artist, would occupy the top of the social pyramid. Dream of a totally stable and static society. Pure reason taking command. In fact, no reason anymore.

But the engineer Faber in Frisch's novel is also always threatened by random events. They just happen. Whatever he is doing, something may happen or appear that he had not foreseen, and such events may take on extremely dangerous forms. We see active man as the great hope and the great achiever. But at the end of this hope is the hopelessness of lost control.

We are bound to work. In all our work we hope to gain control. The more we strive, the more dangerous random interruptions become. In a class society, control is only with a minority.

DESIGN

Paul Watzlawick et al. (1967) has told us that we cannot *not* communicate. Some have extended this to: we cannot *not* design. This is questionable, but also correct. How come?

When I sit at my desk doing nothing but sitting there, breathing, and staring at the wall, or looking out of the window, I am really doing nothing but *then* being *there*. Someone comes along. Even if they don't say anything, and I say nothing, I am unintentionally communicating to them that I am *now* sitting *here*. I am not interested in communicating this to them, and they may not be interested in this being communicated to them, but it is happening anyhow.

This absurd fact seemingly defies our basic logical assumptions: A statement, if it can be stated at all (like, »I am communicating« or »You are working«), can be negated. I can say: »You are *not* working«, and this may be true or false. But it may not be true *or* false to say, »I am not communicating«, for this statement is always false.

Design work consists of communicative as well as productive work. Communicative action happens in the *semiotic* realm. Productive action happens in the *material* realm. The two are, of course, related. In modern times, all work has taken on at least some of this kind. A given activity, we might venture to say, is modern to the extent that it has grown a semiotic layer or a protecting cover to wrap in, and hide the actual skilled manual labor.

But then something new showed up. The semiotic cover grew stranger and expanded at the expense of the corporeal core. Whenever software was introduced, some core activity was semioticized and algorithmicized. In digital media design, this process has reached a state where we may rightfully say that design work essentially happens in the semiotic sphere. It is interesting, however, to observe how performative work is now appearing at the periphery of digital media. As if the swallowing of the corporeal core by the semiotic cover had dialectically created a new corporeal skin to cover the core, which now has turned semiotic.

Even though I allow myself, in a highly speculative way, to claim that in the digital age this was generally happening to work, I am pretty sure that in many cases of design work it is actually true. It is definitely true for software design, for which Winograd et al. (1996) explicitly requested broad design practice to become a source of knowledge.

Design is the act and result of creative behavior or activity. So is art, and many other areas of human activity. Every once in a while, someone raises the question of what defines creativity, and what distinguishes a creative person from others. Terry Winograd, in the concluding »reflection« of the anthology, *Bringing design to software*, writes of »the magic of creativity« (Winograd et al. 1996, p. 296). He continues to talk about identifiable processes in education and professional work that generate a general background and pass on the experience and work habits of successful practitioners so that the dialectics of *tradition and transcendence* (Ehn's term) may gain a form of dynamics needed for invention to happen.

Creativity – a magic. That is probably as close as you can get in describing the phenomenon of creativity. Instead of solving the puzzle of what makes a person create something new – in art, design, technology, science, or even politics – the effort of generating situations and contexts favorable for creative processes seems to be work better spent.

The Bauhaus in Weimar, Dessau, and Berlin was probably one of those rare cases, where for several years (from 1919 to 1933) a situation prevailed that fostered creativity, or creative behavior, or only products that the public considered to be outcomes of creativity. The Bauhaus went through problems of many sorts, internal and external, but its legacy remains a story of success in design. Many schools and programmes up to our times have studied the Bauhaus approach to design education in their attempts to help students become personalities of whom you could expect extraordinary designs.

An important aspect of the Bauhaus education was the cross-over of practical skills in the workshops and theoretical insights. Although the original idea of two masters meeting – one from art, the other from a craft – was soon abandoned almost entirely, the reason for this idea was the best you could give: skill and invention, repetitive excercise and creative expression must unite. A great idea seeking a new form of expression needs the security of a hundredfold experience in order to appear.

So over-powering is the fame of the Bauhaus that artists and critics keep combining it with features of current times as, e.g., Jürgen Claus (1987) in his book on the Electronic Bauhaus. About a decade later, Pelle Ehn (1998) chose the ambitious form of a manifesto to express the ideas he and his colleagues had been discussing as the basis for an exciting new programme and institution at Malmö University, the art and communication study programme.

In the manifesto, Ehn develops three main points:

1. The historic Bauhaus of 1919 to 1933 was the attempt, after the catastrophe of World War I, to regain the intellectual height of Enlightenment, and to reconcile industrial mass production with the art and craft of masters.

2. The Bauhaus was strongly influenced by progressive tendencies from revolutionary social movements, but also by individual search for aesthetics. It mirrored the contradictions of its time.

3. The Digital Bauhaus must seek a »practical way to unite the ›hard‹ scientific and technological sides of the Enlightenment project with the ›soft‹ ethical and aesthetic sides.« It must become »an arena, a meeting place, a school, and a research centre for creative and socially useful meetings between ›art‹ and ›technology‹.«

Design is by no means only digital design, not even today. Even though digitality has become extremely important for all aspects of current culture, the revolution that has taken place is better identified as the »algorithmic revolution« (Peter Weibel). Algorithmic thinking reduces the world to computable processes. Algorithmic design would be design allowing only for means of an algorithmic nature. Nobody would seriously suggest that. But large parts of design can be, and are actually, done algorithmically.

The other side of the contradictory task of design is aesthetics. In spite of heroic attempts in the 1960s to establish information aesthetics as a pseudo-computable form of aesthetics, value judgment remains an act of subjectivity and thus outside the reach of computability. The grand challenge for the Digital Bauhaus is to give shape to the dynamics of the algorithmics/aesthetics contradiction.

A contradiction – I hasten to add – in dialectics is not necessarily an antagonistic polarization. It is a pair of two forces driving a process of development by pulling or pushing in different direction. The actual movements of the process and the power of the driving forces influence each other in a recursive manner. They need conditions for their configuration to evolve.

COMPUTER

Each generation of students could be characterized by the percentage of believers in an incessant progress caused by computers. Proponents of the belief in computer progress expect that sooner or later those artifacts will reach our level of intelligence (to say the least). More even, they will surely surpass us in thinking power, precision, and creativity, and will one day be those which (who?) rule the world. It doesn't matter much to ask such a believer whether he may be ignoring the fact that computers are about computing, and thus about computable functions. From here it follows as a corollary that computers are confined to a quantitative world. The true believer rejects the idea that the world is mainly not computable.

The belief has created generations of scientists, hundreds of books, entire institutions and huge projects. If the money that was spent on artificial intelligence research was used differently, humankind might well be better off and not have some of the pressing needs of today.

The crux with the new religion of computationalism is that the useful distinction between data, information and knowledge is blurred over and over again. Connected to this is a misunderstanding of one of the most basic dialectics: the dialectics of quantity and quality. Dahlbom and Mathiassen (1993) take it as the starting point for their book, *Computers in context*. It has the simple subtitle, *The philosophy and practice of systems design*, which turns out not to be that simple at all.

We should never study a machine in isolation with the only exception of purely functional analysis and synthesis. The computer is a particularly interesting case of machinery. Many software engineers believe they can totally (completely and without contradiction) specify the functionality of a software package yet to be developed. Such a position possessed some justification at a time when software complexity was low. It was still possible then for an individual human being to stay in control of the software, in specification, static function, as well as dynamic execution.

This state of paradise innocence has changed dramatically. Starting with time-sharing operating systems, and certainly gaining tremendous momentum with the enormous, densely interconnected, and dynamically growing operating systems of current times, nobody is still capable of telling exactly what the functionality of a given software system is, or how to describe the state of a hardware system at a given point in time.

The first paradigm of computing science, i.e. *computability*, has, since the early 1980s, been accompanied by a second paradigm: *interactivity*. Computability focuses on the computer machine as an automaton. Interactivity looks at the computer as if it was a tool or, better, a carrier of dozens and hundreds of tools. The metaphorical way of talking about the computer became extremely successful and important in the context of interactivity.

It may well be that the computer, now often taken as medium, will spin off a third paradigm of the algorithmic world: *performativity*.

One characterization of the computer has remained stable over these developments even though it is not particularly popular and, indeed, is more or less hidden in a corner far from the mainstream. I am, nevertheless, convinced of its versatility, explanatory power and validity: the understanding of the computer as the *semiotic machine* (Nöth 2002).

ARTIFACT

All works of art are artifacts. But not all artifacts are works of art. Each artifact is a work. It is literally a result of work. Without work, there are no works. No artifacts. No art.

The artificially made is an *artefactum*, an artifact. The artist is a special sort of worker. Like any other worker he generates works. That's all! The artists, to re-iterate this triviality, do not create works of art. They create works. This is difficult enough.

Only the social group – the community, the cultural setting, and situation – can generate the work of art. Whether the artists like it or not, they are by principle only the source of a *possible* work of art. The artists definitely and desperately want their work to be accepted as a work of art. But unless they start and finish generating the work, there is no chance of it becoming a work of art.

So the work of art is not just a thing. Ontologically, it is more like a complex relation. In traditional terms, we probably think of a work of art as a mounted canvas covered with paint. You can grab it, carry it around, put it up on the wall. However, what the nail keeps in its position on the wall, is the work, not the art. Insofar it would be correct to say the artist creates a work for the nail. Society then transforms the artist's work into a work of art.

Society cannot be observed when doing its work in the same way artists can be observed when doing their work. The reason for this is trivial. The artist is a concrete living being; society is an abstract unity of living beings. Society's actions are actions by individuals who, when acting for society, transcend their individuality. Their actions require justification and recognition by others, including other institutions.

The art critic is such a case. So is the author of a book. The teacher is. When teachers decide to let a work by some artist become the subject matter of their lesson, they become one miniscule organ of the societal total worker whose action is needed to transform the work into the celebrated work of art.

The *work* belongs to the world of *things* or events that are what they are, and that are nothing else. The *work of art*, however, belongs to the world of *signs* or semioses. Signs are more than what they appear to be. The perceivable component of a sign – necessary as it is for the sign to become, and be perceived as, a sign – is the only reason for the sign to happen.

Signs are not here nor there before we arrive, or after we have gone. They happen through conscious acts of interpretation. They are constituted right here and now, by the individual, or individuals, involved. When the individuals leave, the sign leaves with them. They may say that they take the sign with them, in their hearts or minds. It's okay if they say so, because they believe it. But they cannot really take the sign with them. Asked what it is that they took, they must re-construct the sign. They will establish a new sign which may be tied to what they remember from before. But it is newly established, here and now and thus, as well as then and there and otherwise.

Marcel Duchamp is our best witness for all these paraphrases of a simple insight. »The creative act,« he tells us, »takes another aspect when the spectator experiences the phenomenon of transmutation; through the change from inert matter into a work of art, an actual transubstantiation has taken place, and the role of the spectator is to determine the weight of the work on the aesthetic scale« (Duchamp 1975, p. 139f).

Even though Duchamp singles out an individual spectator who does the task of transmutating the work into a work of art, thus shying away from the step of abstractly taking society responsible for the art, the double work on the material thing and the immaterial sign is clearly stated. The champion of art in the twentieth century continues thus:

> All in all, the creative act is not performed by the artist alone; the spectator brings the work in contact with the external world by deciphering and interpreting its inner qualifications and thus adds his contribution to the creative act. This becomes even more obvious when posterity gives the final verdict and sometimes rehabilitates forgotten artists. (Duchamp 1975, p. 140)

Posterity – in the words usually used here, is nothing but society. We find it nice and friendly, human-like, to think of Duchamp's spectator as an individual structure of bones and flesh and nerves, of desires and interests. But the spectator really is a collective, the collective of all those who, through some more or less uncoordinated activity that nobody can really observe and describe or separate from all other activity, create the art in the work of art by so calling the work.

CONCLUSION

Have we betrayed our origins, have we cut our roots? This is the question announced for the deliberations of this chapter. Have I given an answer? Does the question allow for the Christian type of answer, the famously required yes-or-no and nothing in between?

Does the question make sense, or is it pure rhetoric that no-one could be interested in? Any plant, or most of them at least, grows out of its root. It grows and changes in an intricate process between water and nutritious elements from the ground and the sunlight up in the air. The root and the leaves are the organs to collect those components for the biochemical processes to take place that result in the growth of the plant.

The root at the same time keeps the plant at its place, firmly and steadily. When the root is cut, the plant usually dies. Metaphorically, the root stands for the origin. It is where we come from. Our identity derives from our origins and from the process that happens over time.

Our strongest root as human beings is our capability and necessity to work, to be active. All humans are capable, and are forced to work. In the long millenia of evolution of the race, tremendous differentiation has taken place: the race has created society so that today no individual could survive without society. We are human only in relation to other humans, and together with them.

Some are forced to work and do nothing else, even today when the development of technology and division of labor have taken on incredibly complex form. Work must still be done, and even though large parts of it have been handed over to machine systems, to the semiotic machines in particular, capital is constantly looking for cheap labor. Triumphantly it now looks and acts globally. The extension of the search area has brought glorious conditions for capital's inherent longing for valorization.

We have become tired. We may be even more active than before, if we are lucky, we love what we are doing. But what we are doing may not always, or not immediately, withstand a thorough critique from a humanist perspective. It may psychologically not be so easy to admit – but, yes: I have betrayed my own convictions. I have given up the emphatic reference to the worker, to the working class, to work as the synthesis of society (Sohn-Rethel 1970). I am guilty, such self-accusation would perhaps continue, of taking any kind of excuse only to be able to further pursue what I like to do. And what I foremost like to do, it would end, is playing around with computers in which ever way seems fashionable or feasible.

Such an answer would be clear and simple. It would open up for heavy attacks from moralists. The answer would be brave. It would not try to hide behind excuses. It would be honest, but it would be attacked as having given up principles, having cut the roots.

The indicated position may, however, be more serious and politically aware than a quick moralist condemnation may detect. Under the transformations of what was called »work« and »labor« into »activity«, certain positions may appear outdated and not reaching the people in their best interest. André Gorz (1980, 2000) was the first to shake up much of the stable and static concept of labor that we all took as the starting point of our attempts at understanding computing. Richard Sennett (1998) told us a lot about the postmodern way of capital's attacks on labor, before Richard Florida (2004) used the obvious changes for the flashy term of the »creative class«. Critical thinking can never prevent that a concept – that of class – is used in a trivial manner.

The intellectual's place is never only the laboratory, the seminar room, or the studio. The intellectual's place is, at the same time, the public in whichever form available to him. His most prominent duty is the steady, continued, and repeated *radical critique*. The state of technology and of societal power in exploiting labor and suppressing people has risen to such heights and abominable arrogance that a humane scientist or artist, in order to remain what they stand for, must on all occasions, and under all circumstances, stand up for radical critique.

What, then, is a radical critique? A critique is radical if it is firmly rooted in the observation of facts, in studying the phenomena, in staying away from speculation. A critique is radical if its method is dialectics, and its start and end is humanism. A radical critique is asking questions more often than giving answers. Without a maximum of skepticism, a critical position cannot be radical. Nor is a critical position radical without a great deal of optimism.

The radical critic is a person who loves being surprised and being amazed. They marvel at phenomena because otherwise they cannot study them. They allow themselves to be astonished. Before jumping on a quick answer or reply, they sigh in awe because they did not expect what they observe, and they do not pretend that they had expected this anyhow.

A radical critique requires us to take a phenomenon for what it is and for nothing else. As such, the phenomenon is admirable even if terrible. However, the radical critique is not a critique of superficial phenomena, and the critic must always go beyond the surface. Critique must try to reach the deeper and hidden levels of a process. Therefore, it takes time.

Radical critique is not fighting for words. It is about concepts. A concept may be expressed in various words and still remain the same concept. At the same time, we know that words powerfully influence our thinking or even shape it.

Yes, work became design and game. This happened when they all turned out to be subcases of the more general concept of *activity* and when work started to disappear from the society grounded in, and held together by, work. *Virtual reality* is not the enemy of reality. It rather is the brother of actuality. What was reality before, now appears in two modes: as actuality and virtuality. The two occasionally change place. This is the dialectics of the situation and of context.

Things are always to stay with us, no doubt. But the streams of things are now accompanied by streams of signs. Existence has become semioticized to such an extent that it would be dogmatic to ignore semiosis as the emerging synthesis of society. Work in the semiotic domain is to a large extent determined by matters of perception and interpretation, and thus by aesthetics more than by logics. Discrepancies? Dialectics!

ACKNOWLEDGEMENTS

Jörn Ketelsen, Katja Langeland and Özlem Sulak have read an earlier version of this chapter. Their critical remarks have helped me to spot some of the most blatant shortcomings. The remaining ones are solely my responsibility. The editors have extended the most marvellous patience to me.

REFERENCES

Claus, J. (1987). *Das elektronische Bauhaus*. Reinbek: Rowohlt.

Dahlbom, B., Mathiassen, L. (1993). *Computers in context: The philosophy and practice of systems design*. Cambridge, MA, Oxford: NCC Blackwell.

Duchamp, M. (1975). The creative act. In Sanouillet, M., Peterson, E. (Eds.) *The essential writings of Marcel Duchamp*, pp.138–140. London: Thames and Hudson. (First published in 1957.)

Ehn, P. (1988). *Work-oriented design of computer artifacts*. Stockholm: Arbetslivscentrum.

Ehn, P. (1998). Manifesto for a Digital Bauhaus. *Digital Creativity*, 9(4):207–216.

Florida, R. (2004). *The rise of the creative class: And how it's transforming work, leisure, community and everyday life*. New York: Basic Books.

Frisch, M. (1977). *Homo faber: Ein Bericht*. Frankfurt a.M.: Suhrkamp. (First published in 1957.)

Gorz, A. (1980). *Abschied vom Proletariat*. Frankfurt: Europäische Verlagsanstalt.

Gorz, A. (2000). *Arbeit zwischen Misere und Utopie*. Frankfurt: Suhrkamp.

Marx, K. (1976). *Capital: A critique of political economy*. Vol. I. London: Penguin Books.

Nake, F. (1984). *Schnittstelle Mensch–Computer*. Kursbuch 75, pp. 109–118. Berlin: Rotbuch-Verlag.

Nake, F. (1992). Informatik und die Maschinisierung von Kopfarbeit. In Coy, W. et al. (Eds.): *Sichtweisen der Informatik*, pp. 181–201. Braunschweig: Vieweg.

Nöth, W. (2002). Semiotic machines. *Cybernetics and Human Knowing* 9(1):5–21.

Sennett, R. (1998). *The corrosion of character*. New York: W.W. Norton.

Sohn-Rethel, A. (1970). *Geistige und körperliche Arbeit*. Frankfurt: Suhrkamp.

Watzlawick, P., Beavin, J.E., Jackson, D.D. (1967). *Pragmatics of human communication: A study of interactional patterns, pathologies, and paradoxes*. New York: W.W. Norton.

Winograd, T., Flores, F. (1986). *Understanding computers and cognition: A new foundation for design*. Norwood, NJ: Ablex Publ. Corp.

Winograd, T. et al. (Eds., 1996). *Bringing design to software*. Reading, MA: Addison-Wesley.

YLVA GISLÉN, ÅSA HARVARD, MARIA HELLSTRÖM REIMER

THE EVERYDAY POETICS OF A DIGITAL BAUHAUS

YLVA GISLÉN, ÅSA HARVARD, MARIA HELLSTRÖM REIMER
THE EVERYDAY POETICS OF A DIGITAL BAUHAUS

Throughout the history of research, a certain type of building has developed, an edifice of sort, at the same time a vision or utopian idea and a physical structure for everyday practices. The Digital Bauhaus is in this sense no different. It constitutes an example of a kind of building that we choose to call the *Manifesto Building*, a striking formation appearing under many names – from the Wiener Werkstätte to Warhol's Factory.

As a typical example of a manifesto building, it is the kind of house that aspires to edification, a house aiming to program both its own future scenarios and those of the world as such. Yet, as we know, the program is one thing, the everyday poetics something else. In the following, we will therefore confront the Manifesto Building with one of its physical counterparts, realized and lived. The environment in question is K3, The School of Arts and Communication at Malmö University, Sweden, for which the *Manifesto for a Digital Bauhaus* was originally put on paper. Appearing on the following pages is an attempt to compare the arguments of the Digital Bauhaus Manifesto with its physical manifestation over time.

What we are asking is – what did the manifesto suggest? And what did its manifestation bring into being? How well did the everyday praxis answer to the initial visions? And are there still manifesto morsels to be found in the nooks and corners of the actual building?

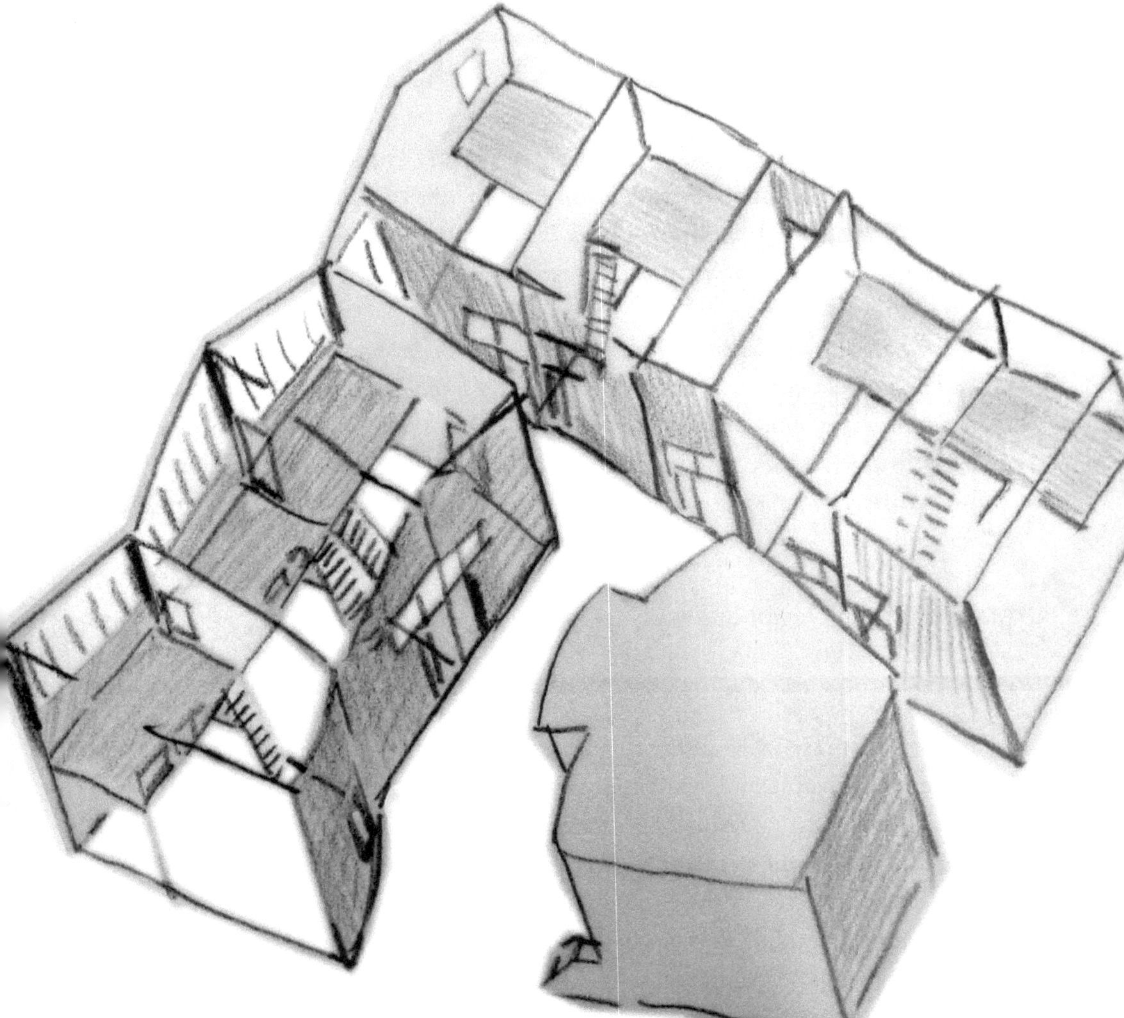

CORNERSTONES

» *A »reflective practicum«: We are strongly convinced that close interaction with research is a corner stone in an environment for creative studies. Research, inspired by the early Bauhaus schools, will be carried out in studios/workshops through close co-operation between researchers, artists and students.*

Members of this nerd generation, laboriously designing new tools to explore virtual as well as material »new worlds«, may have the potential to transcend the inability of communication that »the two cultures« of modern society has repeatedly demonstrated throughout history and, through a practical amalgamation of »art« and »technology«, the soft and the hard, shape the emerging »third culture«.

Manifesto for a Digital Bauhaus

– The two cultures? Most of the time, the Space studio was the austere one, the grave and responsible one, wallpapered with ethnographic snapshots from sewage plants and plastic factories, posters of lorries and industrial control rooms; in short, a studio whose members were always busy mapping out and verbalizing of large fields of knowledge with equally large surfaces of post-it-notes. The Narrativity Studio on the other hand, a permanent drama with kings and queens, toys and musical flowers. Also the food habits diverged: while the Narrativity Studio explored the storytelling dimensions of ethnic and cross-over nutrients, including the mixture of soja milk and coca-cola, the space studio tried hard to live up to its Bauhaus heritage, »Essen wie bei Muttern«, most often going for a decent German carnivorous meal at the little Bavarian restaurant.

– Remember how we all used to log on to the main server, Gropius, every morning, if not to pay tribute to him only to remind him of his multiple personality and non-characteristic materiality. Remember also the design students furiously questioning the radicality of the Bauhaus heritage, draping K3 in huge posters of the masters' serious faces – Mies, Itten, Kandinsky.

– Carnevalesque workshops: Initially two weeks for all students and faculty every semester, then once a year and now disappearing from the curriculum, maybe only to reinvent itself like a Phoenix somewhere in the future. Intense and sometimes strange activities all over the building, workshops on voice, dance, dramaturgy, 3D-modeling and Wittgensteinian philosophy. Light design workshops, critical design ones, mobile design, electronic toy hacking. A workshop on wireless networking – war biking – later on posted on Youtube, used by activists all around the world when announcing their own workshops on wireless technologies.

– The (im)possibilities of »a reflective practicum« in Scandinavian design, where the loud tributes to dialogue and active user-participation sometimes veil a rigid view on the desired outcomes of such a process. Like the interior architect, visiting the premises every 6 months or so in the beginning, to make sure nobody violated the design guidelines by introducing soft furniture, patterned textiles, non-Scandinavian colours etc. Or the army of Arne Jacobsen »Syveren« chairs in black, lining up in the café, later on equipped with anti-theft stickers of the type also used for digital equipment and technology, which turns design into a functionalist wireless networking operating upon environments as well as minds. At the same time there were counter strategies, forms of »creative allocation«, like making a tour of the building late in the evening, dragging all soft furniture found, couches, armchairs, into the studios. Or students creating temporary anarchist spaces, using walls and corners in ways they were not supposed for, adding layers of concept development, new strata of work in progress. Evolution withering away, creatively redesigning itself, just like life itself: an incomplete manifesto for growth.

– Mechatronics squatting the building. The first soldering sessions of Physical Prototyping. No classroom available, no lab-space, no budget, and 40-something students. The course took over part of the cafeteria space and stayed there during two consecutive academic years, constantly generating conflicts over security issues and messiness. But the results were amazing; passionate students working overtime, exhibiting at Malmö Museum, and at Ars Electronica.

– Odd traces of projects, remnants of devices in different stages of finalization, like Device H – a fascinating architectonic project no-one ever understood – a gigantic industrial intruder cutting through the building, from one floor to the other, connecting any level of existence with any other. A kind of brand for the wild-grown creativity of the very first Digital Bauhaus students.

– Rather than only writing or programming stories, the narrativity studio developed into a breeding ground for impersonating new kinds of plots, including researchers in colourful wigs practicing being avatars, or theatrical Wizard-of-Oz performances in order to convey a new kind of programming structure.

– The K-tree. Commissioned by artist Jan Cardell and an early breed of the physical computing that later became one of the trademarks of K3. Sturdy-growing, hammering out its beats over the harbour at the entrance.

THE ART-EDIFICE

A manifesto from the first Bauhaus school written for the first Bauhaus exhibition in Weimer in 1923 envisioned how an idealism of activity that embraces, penetrates and unites art, science, and technology and that influences research, study, and work, will construct the art-edifice of Man (Oskar Schlemmer).

This is, however, just as with the Bauhaus, a project full of contradictions which stands the risk of degenerating into an adolescent doctrine of boundless individualism and technophile hubris.

This emerging »third culture« of nerds and digerati is promising, but still most immature.

[W]e can observe a new set of aesthetic principles emerging. The boundaries between artists and audiences become blurred and the significance of the individual artistic fingerprint grows less important, as in sampling and hybridisation. «

OPEN DOORS AND UN-LAID TABLES

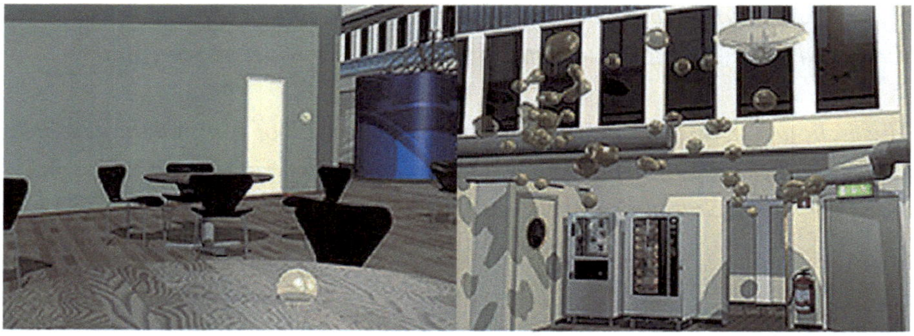

However, this vision of a digital Bauhaus can never grow strong isolated in a corner in the far north of Europe. It has to develop in cross-cultural and international dialogue. [...] What is needed is an international network [...] that embraces, penetrates and unites art, science, and technology [...] — a third culture in the digital age at the door to the twenty-first century and a new millennium.

Hence, this is also our vision of an arena, a meeting place, a school, and a research centre for creative and socially useful meetings between »art« and »technology«.

– Memories of laborious workshops, spaces within spaces emerging, temporary spaces, nomadic structures, tents. Large, demanding pieces of fabric running through rooms, cutting through spaces. A researcher by a sewing machine, draped in cloth, trying to handle a non-participatory material, struggling to deal with a wicked design problem.

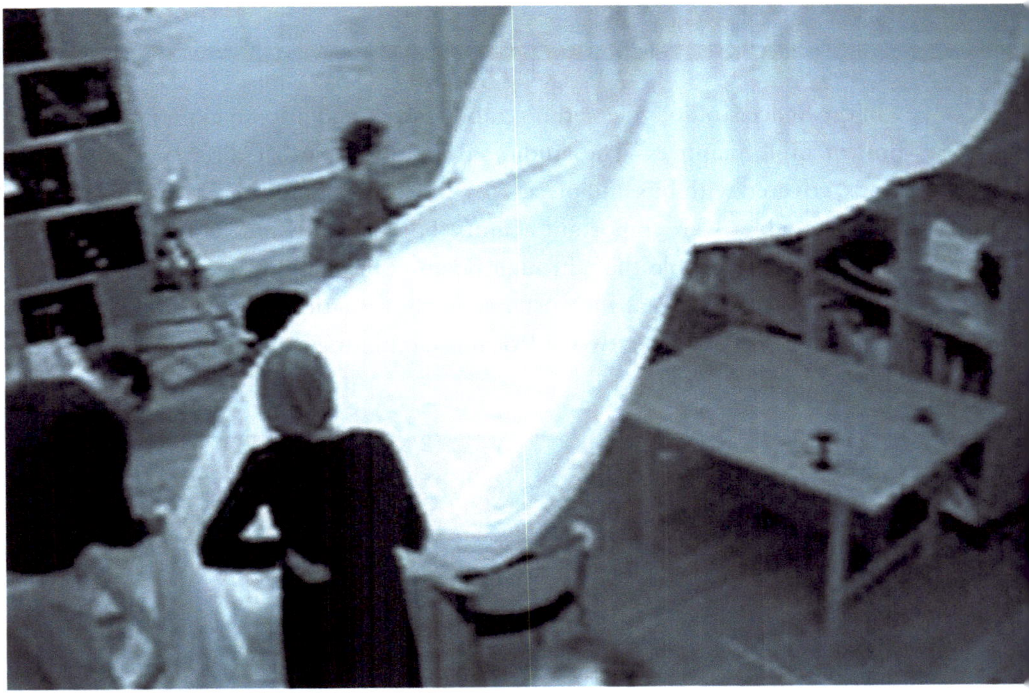

– It was at the mezzanine in Studio 1; a handful of researchers met with one of the most influential intellectuals of our time. With a background in theatre and Fine Arts, we were naively unaware of the importance of the moment, presenting our ideas of movement and location in the form of a role play including mobile phones. Quite improvised and conceptually blurred, the play still inspired the famous philosopher, who enthusiastically started to develop an entire theory about »drama, design and democracy«; a mezzanine studio theory of the intermediary, non-finalized, and in-between.

– The interactive rocking chair was developed over the net. Through an intense collaborative process, the chair grew out of an oscillation of questions, illustrations and ideas back and forth between Malmö and Madrid. Some nights, the concept of the chair would swing back and forth for hours, still more or less malfunctioning. Finally, the furniture was produced in our 12 square meter laboratory space, new circuits etched and tried out every day.

– In the Space studio, video ethnography developed into an experimental question of table manners. The studio saw many tables of different shapes and kinds, covered with bits and pieces, toy-like objects, tagged playing cards or the like. The tables were important actants, both socially and spatially influential, surrounded by people that through posture and comments, despite the playful setting, would signal the austerity of the situation. As for the video, there would always be at least two videocams circulating around the table like mosquitos around their target.

September 11. Internet goes down when everybody wants information about the terrorist attacks. Then people realise that the Digital Bauhaus lacks television connection. In this historical moment, the Digital Bauhaus stands isolated without any information channel to the outer world. Finally, somebody finds an old transistor radio in the electronics lab. As a re-enactment of a snapshot from World War II, people gathered around the radio in double rows, in order to capture at least something of the latest news.

– In retrospect, one should really be asking oneself why we have seen two computerized confession chairs over the years, remarkable machines, aiming at hypnotizing its confessors.

FLUID WALLS

»*Digital information and communication technology changes our understanding of time and space. A room is no longer only material and solid, but also virtual and fluid. We inhabit the same space, but not at the same time. The walls are there, but somewhere else. Someone is present, but still absent. Neither does time follow a solid pattern. It is not only cyclical as in a tradition-bound society, nor only linear as in modern society, but interactive and fluid as in a narrative where the reader, the observer, the consumer and the user participate in its creation.*

Virtual reality is perceived nearly as intensely with all senses as material reality. Material space is becoming permeated with virtual information. What happens to ourselves and our conditions for living and working when fact and fiction blend?

– It is not easy to make IT and computers disappear into the existing environment. It could take days creating a layout for a modular plexi-glass structure, gathering and tagging objects and stories of previous activities and designs, testing projections on different types of fabrics, etc. It wasn't particularly fluid: We would climb big ladders up underneath the ceiling to mount projection surfaces for showing image and video stories; we would crawl around the floor to connect »disappearing« computers to printers, tag readers or scanners.

Co-Wall: A physical/virtual repository of activities in the K3 building.
Creative Environments Studio, 2004.

– Hold the Virtualizer in front of you at the height of your eyes and at a distance of about 7–10 inches from the face. Adjust the focus of your eyes as to perceive sharply, not the Virtualizer itself but the objects that will appear on its translucent screen. You are represented by a personalized avatar inside the Virtualizer. Feel free to interact with other avatars that you may come across while exploring your Virtualizer. Normal rules of conduct apply within the world of the Virtualizer – use your common sense and contacts will prove both smooth and rewarding.

Concept project, Narrativity studio, 1999.

– The physical reality of virtuality in the Digital Bauhaus: No room for storage, no conceptual or physical space for junk. Piles of rubbish growing under the stairs to the mezzanines, in spite of all signs, interdictions and reminders from the janitor and the fire authorities.

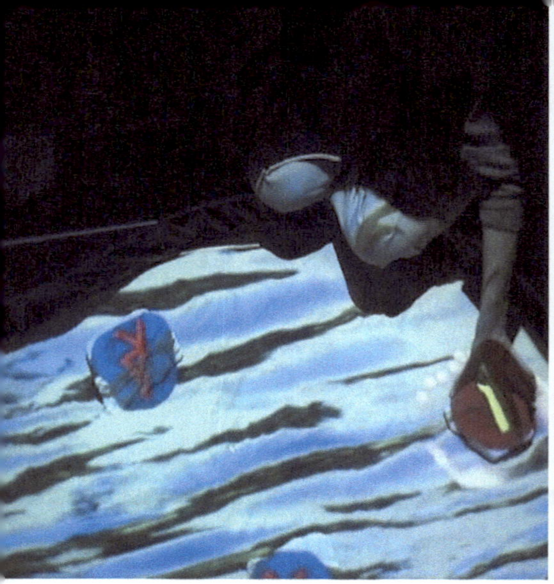

RuneCast: Runic prophecies delivered through ritual placing of stones on a surface of sand. The pictures to the right show the substructure of MDF board, coil springs and switches that made the magic work.

Narrativity studio, 1999.

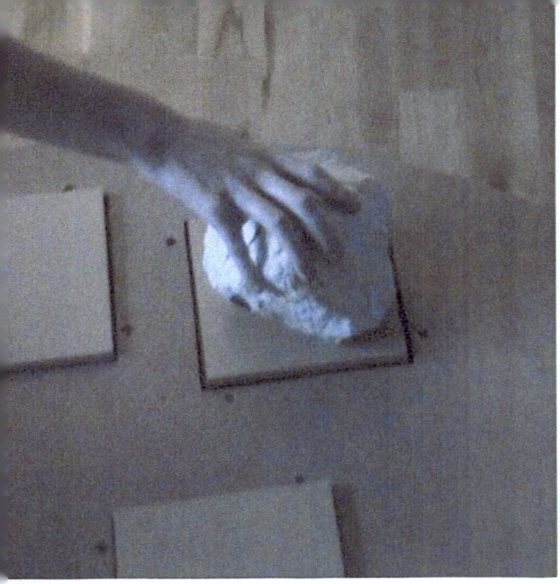

During a few weeks in 2000, K3 became the backdrop for *Jesus_c.odd_size*, a theatrical performance by the Danish theatre company Hotel Pro Forma.

The actors took over the open spaces, corridors, lecture halls and stairs of K3 exploring strange means of moving about, crawling along the walls, encapsulating themselves in plastic containers; moving around on wheels. Staff, students, audience and performers crossed paths in the same space at the same time, an interesting mix of the mundane and the mythical.

In the light of this (re-)search of the Digital Bauhaus, a discrepancy unfolds between, on the one hand, the Manifesto as optimized green-house and, on the other, the weedy grounds of its everyday manifestations.

Rather than a privileged *Gesamtkunstwerk*, the Digital Bauhaus turns out to be a sanctuary put at risk, an ideal endangered, a safe haven exposed. On its premises, an agitated spatial narrative opens out, an open-ended spatial plot with many ramifications.

What we have presented here is therefore by necessity only some samples, some fractions of the experiences of many students, guests and inhabitants of the Digital Bauhaus. And even though these samples might seem randomly selected and arranged, they hopefully mark out some directions, some fields of actions or some traces of tentative navigation, transforming the Digital Bauhaus into what it ought to be – an unpredictable, yet comprehensive, geography of research experience.

ABOUT THE AUTHORS

LIAM BANNON is Professor in the Department of Computer Science and Information Systems and Director of the Interaction Design Centre at the University of Limerick. His research interests include cognitive ergonomics, human-computer interaction, computer-supported cooperative work, computer-supported collaborative learning, new media and interaction design, and social dimensions of new technologies. He has served on the editorial boards of *CSCW; Cognition, Technology, and Work; Requirements Engineering; Universal Access in the Information Society; Web-Based Communities; CoDesign; Behaviour and Information Technology; Computer Assisted Learning.*

THOMAS BINDER is senior researcher at the Danish Center for Design Research. He has been involved with participatory design in the contexts of workplace learning, organizational change and product design. He is currently engaged with participatory approaches to workspace design. He was conference chair of the *Participatory Design Conference* 2002 and the *Nordic Design Research Conference* 2005. He holds a PH.D. from TU Copenhagen.

JEANETTE BLOMBERG manages the interdisciplinary Service Practices group at the IBM Almaden Research Center, where she helped establish the first services research group at IBM. Since joining IBM Research Jeanette has led projects focused on interactions among IT service providers and their clients, collaboration practices among globally distributed sales teams, standardization and localization of services in globally integrated enterprises, and new approaches to work-based learning. Prior to assuming her current position at IBM, Jeanette was Director of Experience Modeling Research at Sapient Corporation where she helped establish the Experience Modeling practice and managed Sapient's San Francisco Experience Modeling group. She also was an industry affiliated professor at the Blekinge Institute of Technology in Sweden where she taught graduate student seminars, helped develop the Work Practice Laboratory and guided and advised PH.D. students from throughout the Nordic countries. Jeanette was also a founding member of the pioneering Work Practice and Technology group at the Xerox Palo Alto Research Center (PARC).

Over the years her research has explored issues in social aspects of technology production and use; ethnographically-informed organizational interventions; participatory design; case-based prototyping; and service innovation. She has published on these topics, given numerous invited talks and offered workshops in the U.S. and Europe on aligning ethnography with product and service innovation and design. Jeanette is an active member of the Participatory Design community, serving as Program Co-Chair for the 2006 conference, and sits on a number of advisory boards including the Foresight panel of the IT University of Copenhagen; the Program in Design Anthropology at Wayne State University; and the Ethnographic Praxis in Industry Conference (EPIC). She also serves on the Editorial Advisory Board of the journal *Artifact* and is a member of the Whither Biometrics? committee of the National Academies Computer Science and Telecommunications Board. Jeanette received her PH.D. in Anthropology from the University of California, Davis and before embarking on her career in high tech she was a lecturer in cultural anthropology and sociolinguistics at the University of California at Davis.

MARGOT BRERETON'S primary interests are in participatory design, interaction design and studies of design practice. Her current work explores participatory design of community communications and participatory design of multimodal interfaces, particularly those using gesture. Her early work investigated the role played by objects in supporting the thinking processes of engineers.

Margot is a Professor of Engineering and Interaction Design at the Queensland University of Technology. She is a Research Leader in the Australasian Cooperative Research Centre for Interaction Design (ACID). She was one of the founding academics of the Information Environments Degree program, a design focussed, studio-based IT degree at the University of Queensland. She taught design, visual thinking, human-computer interaction and interaction design in this program. She has also taught Power Transfer Systems, Mechanical Design and Manufacturing. Margot holds a PH.D. in Mechanical Engineering (Design) from Stanford University, a Masters degree in Technology Policy from Massachusetts Institute of Technology and a B.SC. (Hons) in Mechanical Engineering from Bristol University. She apprenticed as an engineer for five years at Rolls Royce aircraft engines.

GIORGIO DE MICHELIS, professor, teaches Theoretical Computer Science and Information Systems at the University of Milano-Bicocca, where he has served as Director of the Department of Informatics, Systems and Communications from 2002 to 2007. His research focuses on models of concurrent systems (Petri Nets) and Computer Supported Cooperative Work, community-ware, knowledge management and interaction design, where his group has developed, and is developing, prototypes of support systems for cooperative processes and knowledge management systems (CHAOS, UTUCS, MILANO, CAMPIELLO, KLEE&CO, MILK, ATELIER). Among his current research interests are the emergence of augmented spaces and mixed objects within the practice of communities of people sharing an experience supported by ICT-based systems on the one hand, and the relationship between design artefacts and experience objects as the key issue for renovating the approaches to the design of interactive systems, understanding how designers manage complex interdependencies, on the other. He has authored four books and more than a hundred papers in the areas of his interest. Giorgio De Michelis is vice-president of Fondazione IRSO, a research institute devoted to the study of socio-technical systems, industrial innovation and government organzation.

WILLIAM GAVER is Professor of Design and leader of the Interaction Research Studio at Goldsmiths, University of London. He has pursued research on innovative technologies for over 15 years, working with and for companies such as Intel, France Telecom, Hewlett Packard, IBM and Xerox, gaining an international reputation for a range of work that spans auditory interfaces, theories of perception and action and interaction design. Currently Gaver's research focuses on design-led methodologies and ludic technologies for everyday life. A strong proponent of practice-based research, he leads projects that produce highly finished technical prototypes that are used by volunteers in their own surroundings for weeks or months. This results in methodological and conceptual contributions as well as a growing portfolio of unusual and evocative designs. Recent projects have included work on domestic ubiquitous computing as part of the Equator Interdisciplinary Research Collaboration; research with Intel on sensing well-being in the home; design for France Telecom on unusual forms of mobility; and a New Dynamics of Aging project with Sheffield Hallam and York Universities that explores how novel technologies can occasion conversations between the young and old. Gaver publishes and lectures extensively, serves on review committees for several international conferences, and on steering and review committees for national and international funding agencies.

YLVA GISLÉN has a background as a cultural journalist and critic. She received a PH.D. in interaction design in 2003, on the subject of collaborative narrative in digital media, and her later publications have focused on epistemological issues of practice-based research in art and design. She was associate professor in interaction design and Head of the Culture and Media Department at K3 in 2006–07 and is currently Head of Education at the Dramatic Institute, Stockholm.

JOAN GREENBAUM is professor emerita at City University of New York where she advises students in Environmental Psychology as well as in Interactive Technology and Pedagogy. Her background in programming and designing early computer systems dates back to IBM's mainframes in the 1960s, and she has dedicated her life to helping students and other researchers learn from the mistakes of non contextual design. Among her many published works are the 1991 book she co-edited with Morten Kyng entitled *Design at Work*. Her most recent book is *Windows on the Workplace* (2004).

KIM HALSKOV is professor of visualization and interaction design at the Department of information and Media Studies at Aarhus University, Denmark, where he is also director of the Centre for Advanced Visualization and Interaction. The Centre for Advanced Visualization and Interaction, CAVI, is a part of the University of Aarhus with activities within the fields of architecture, design, scientific visualization, art and culture. Kim has been an active researcher in the area of participatory design for almost 25 years. He has been member of the program committee of several Participatory Design Conferences (PDC) as well as member of the program committees of Designing Interactive Systems conferences (DIS).

ÅSA HARVARD is associate professor of Physical and virtual design at the School of Art and Design (K3), Malmö University. She is also a practising illustrator with a background from Ecole des Beaux-Arts, Paris. Åsa's research and teaching concerns design and cognition: drawing and sketching processes from a cognitive viewpoint, design of toys and play environments in relation to play and learning.

MARIA HELLSTRÖM REIMER, visual artist and researcher, received her PH.D. in Applied and Theoretical Aesthetics in Landscape Architecture at the Swedish University of Agricultural Sciences, Alnarp, Sweden. Currently she is a visiting researcher at Malmö University, School of Arts and Communication with a research grant from the Swedish Research Council for an artistic development project focusing on »intermediary urbanism and the filmic imaginary.«

SARA ILSTEDT HJELM is professor of product and service design at the Royal Institute of Technology (KTH) in Stockholm. She has a background as an industrial designer and a PH.D. in human-computer interaction. Sara has worked in design research at the Interactive Institute, with issues such as health, well-being and sustainable design. She was part of the team that developed the award winning relaxation game Brainball. Her team was also awarded »The coolest invention of the year« by *Time magazine* 2006 for Flower Lamp, a lamp that rewards energy saving. She has been published extensively in books, journals and conferences and was editor of the anthology *Under Ytan* about Swedish design research (Raster 2007).

KARI KUUTTI is a professor in HCI and Computer-Supported Cooperative Work in University of Oulu, Finland. Since the mid-1990s he has been working closely with representatives of other design professions – first with industrial designers in the context of designing smart products, and later with architects and urban designers in the context of studying and developing intelligent and ubiquitous environments. Currently he is the leader of the Finnish participation in the EU project IPCity – Interaction and Presence in Urban Environments.

BRENDA LAUREL is a researcher, teacher, writer and performer. She has worked in interactive media since 1976. She founded and chairs the Graduate Program in Design at California College of Art in San Francisco. She chaired the Graduate Media Design Program at the Art Center College of Design in Pasadena (2002–2006) and was also a Distinguished Engineer at Sun Microsystems Labs (2005–2006). Based on her research in gender and technology at Interval Research (1992–1996), she co-founded Purple Moon to create interactive media for girls (acquired by Mattel in 1999). Her books include *The Art of Human-Computer Interface Design* (1990), *Computers as Theatre* (1991), *Utopian Entrepreneur* (2001), and *Design Research: Methods and Perspectives* (2004). She earned her MFA (1975) and PH.D. in Theatre (1986) from the Ohio State University.

JONAS LÖWGREN is an interaction designer with 20 years of experience both in academia and industry. He is currently professor at Malmö University, where he teaches interaction design to students and professionals in the field. Jonas' research is focused on cross-media products, interactive visualizations and the design theory of digital materials. He has published three books and over 50 scientific papers, and his portfolio includes over 40 major pieces from research projects and external client work. Former affiliations include Linköping University, UI Design, Telub Teknik and Konstfack.

LONE MALMBORG is currently an Associate Professor of interaction design at IT University of Copenhagen, Denmark. She is a member of the Innovative Communication group. She has developed and headed a study program in interaction design at Malmö University, Arts and Communication, Sweden and has established and headed the research group Creative Environment at the same university. Her main research interests are in areas like kinaesthetic interaction; interaction design; mobile interaction; and design methodology. She has been a co-editor of the international journal *Digital Creativity* since 1998. She was conference chair of CADE 2004.

FRIEDER NAKE started as a mathematician but, already as a student, he had become an early algorithmic artist. A year after his doctoral degree (from Stuttgart) in probability theory, he went to Toronto. There he developed »Generative Aesthetics I«, a program to spit out lores of computer images. He proved that information aesthetics, so important for what he had done so far, did not work. He moved further West to Vancouver where he hit the wall of the Pacific without knowing. After returning, in 1972, to Germany (Bremen), he developed a theory of computer science as the discipline of the machinization of labor, of the computer as the semiotic machine and of software as algorithmic sign. He is a professor at the University of Bremen (in computer graphics) and the Hochschule für Künste Bremen (in digital media).

JOHAN REDSTRÖM is Design Director and Senior Researcher at the Interactive Institute, Sweden, and before that the Research Director of the RE:FORM studio in Göteborg. He has also been visiting as Associate Research Professor at the Center for Design Research at the Royal Academy of Fine Arts, School of Architecture, in Copenhagen, Denmark, and active as a lecturer and program manager of the Masters Program in Human-Computer Interaction and Interaction Design at the IT University in Göteborg, Sweden. His educational background is in philosophy, music and human-computer interaction, and he received a PH.D. in Informatics from Göteborg University. His research aims at combining philosophical and artistic approaches with a focus on experimental interaction design. Design research projects include »Slow Technology« on designing for reflection rather than efficiency in use, »IT+Textiles« on combining traditional design and new technologies, and »Static!« on increasing energy awareness through interaction design.

ERIK STOLTERMAN is Professor and Director of the Human Computer Interaction Design program at the School of Informatics, Indiana University. Stolterman's research is focused on interaction design; philosophy of design; information technology and society; information systems design; and philosophy of technology. Stolterman has published over thirty articles and five books, including *Thoughtful Interaction Design* (MIT Press 2004), *The Design Way* (ITP 2003) and *Methods-in-Action* (McGraw-Hill 2002).

YNGVE SUNDBLAD, born 1943, is professor in Computer science, especially Human-Computer Interaction, at KTH, the Royal Institute of Technology in Stockholm. His research and teaching interests include methods for user involvement in design; object-oriented methods for design and development of interactive programs; computer supported cooperation and workplace user certification of IT support. He has participated in, and coordinated, several research projects in these areas, notably about 15 projects in the user involvement tradition, including Utopia, with national and EU funding.

PETER ULLMARK was educated at KTH (the Royal Institute of Technology in Stockholm) and worked as researcher and senior lecturer at the department of Industrial Planning until 1996.

He has been professor in Work Space Design at the School of Architecture at Chalmers in Göteborg since 1998; from 2002 he is also part-time professor in Design at the School of Design and Crafts at Göteborg University and responsible for research education and research. He is member of the board of Faculty of Fine, Applied and Performing Arts at Göteborg University. He has been director of D&R (Swedish Design Research Network) since 2004. His thesis from 1982 dealt with methods and user participation in Work Space Design. Later projects have focused on problems in the interface between Work Science and Design Theory. He has been supervisor for five examined PH.D. students and two lic students and assistant supervisor for one PH.D. He is now main supervisor for seven PH.D. students.

From 1985–1999 he worked part-time as a consultant focusing on the early stages of complex design and development projects in industrial companies. From 1999–2000 he was project manager for the artistic creation and realization of *Tidsdokumentet*, the national Millennium Memorial in Göteborg. During 2005–2007 he has also designed three private houses.

ERIC ZIMMERMAN has been working in the game industry for 13 years. He is the co-founder and Chief Design Officer of Gamelab (www.gamelab.com), an independent game development company based in New York City. Gamelab creates and self-publishes innovative singleplayer and multiplayer games that are distributed online, on mobile phones and through retail, including the hit downloadable games *Diner Dash* and *Miss Management*. Pre-Gamelab titles include *SiSSYFiGHT 2000* and the PC title, *Gearheads*. Eric has taught courses at MIT, New York University, and Parsons School of Design. He has lectured and published extensively about game design and is the co-author with Katie Salen of *Rules of Play: Game Design Fundamentals* (MIT Press 2004), and *The Game Design Reader: A Rules of Play Anthology* (MIT Press 2006), as well as the co-editor of *RE:PLAY* (Peter Lang Press, 2004).

IMAGE CREDITS

pp. 15–35. Images published by permission of Yngve Sundblad.

pp. 36–37. Images published by permission of Erling Björgvinsson and Per-Anders Hillgren.

pp 84–85. Images published by permission of Mads Wahlberg.

p. 87, top. Image published by permission of ART+COM, Berlin.

p. 87, bottom. Image published by permission of Rafael Lozano-Hemmer.

p. 89. Image published by permission of Harald & Erhard Fotografie. All rights reserved.

p. 90, left. Image published by permission of Beta Tank.

p. 90, right; p. 91, top left. Image published by permission of Bitforms gallery NYC and ITP NYU. Photo by D. Plakke.

p. 91, top right. SpokePOV, by Limor Fried, ladyada.net/make/spokepov.

p. 91, bottom left. Image published by permission of Christopher Bauder, www.WHITEvoid.com.

p. 91, bottom right. Image published by permission of Martin Frey, www.freymartin.de.

p. 95. Image published by permission of The Alexandra Institute A/S.

pp. 111–113. Images published by permission of Margot Brereton.

pp. 167–175. Images published by permission of Bill Gaver.

p. 202. Images published by permission of Johan Redström.

p. 205. Shredder by Mark Napier, 1998. Screenshot by Johan Redström, 2007. Published by permission of Mark Napier.

p. 207. Social Cups by Kristina Niedderer, 1999. Photo by Kristina Niedderer, copyright 2004. Published by permission of Kristina Niedderer.

p. 209. The Information Deliverer by Staffan Björk, Lars Hallnäs, Rebecca Hansson, Peter Ljungstrand, Johan Redström and Linda Worbin, 2001. Photo by Johan Redström, 2001. Published by permission of Johan Redström.

p. 221. Absolut Wolgers published by permission of V&S Vin & Sprit AB. Absolut® vodka. Absolut contry of Sweden vodka and logo, Absolut, Absolut bottle design and Absolut calligraphy are trademarks owned by V&S Vin & Sprit AB (publ). Copyright 2007 V&S Vin & Sprit AB (publ).

p. 223. Photo by SVT. Published by agreement with SVT.

p. 224. Image published by permission of Sara Ilstedt Hjelm.

p. 225. Copyright Bruno Mathsson International. Published by permission.

p. 227. Copyright Philippe Migeat and Georges Méguerditchian, Centre Pompidou. Published by permission.

p. 228. Photo by Robaard/Theuwkens. Published by permission of Droog Design.

pp. 229–231. Images published by permission of Sara Ilstedt Hjelm.

pp. 255–259. Creative Commons Copyright Brenda Laurel. Published by permission.

p. 261. Creative Commons Copyright Rob Tow. Published by permission.

p. 262. Creative Commons Copyright Hilary Hulteen. Published by permission.

p. 263. Creative Commons Copyright Brenda Laurel. Published by permission.

p. 269. Photo by Theo Alexopoulos. Published by permission.

p. 271. Copyright Sean White. Published by permission.

pp. 272–273. Creative Commons Copyright Brenda Laurel. Published by permission.

pp. 335–349. Images published by permission of Ylva Gislén, Åsa Harvard and Maria Hellström Reimer.

pp. 350–351. Image by Hotel Pro Forma. Published by permission.

INDEX

MIX
Papier aus verantwortungsvollen Quellen
Paper from responsible sources
FSC® C105338

If you have any concerns about our products,
you can contact us on
ProductSafety@springernature.com

In case Publisher is established outside the EU,
the EU authorized representative is:
Springer Nature Customer Service Center GmbH
Europaplatz 3, 69115 Heidelberg, Germany

Printed by Libri Plureos GmbH
in Hamburg, Germany